Computer Science Education

Computer Science Education

Perspectives on Teaching and Learning in School

**Edited by Sue Sentance,
Erik Barendsen and Carsten Schulte**

BLOOMSBURY ACADEMIC
LONDON • NEW YORK • OXFORD • NEW DELHI • SYDNEY

BLOOMSBURY ACADEMIC
Bloomsbury Publishing Plc
50 Bedford Square, London, WC1B 3DP, UK

BLOOMSBURY, BLOOMSBURY ACADEMIC and the Diana logo
are trademarks of Bloomsbury Publishing Plc

First published in Great Britain 2018
Reprinted 2018 (twice), 2019

A catalogue record for this book is available from the British Library.

A catalog record for this book is available from the Library of Congress.

ISBN: HB: 978-1-3500-5711-1
       PB: 978-1-3500-5710-4
       ePDF: 978-3-3500-5713-5
       ePub: 978-1-3500-5712-8

Typeset by RefineCatch Limited, Bungay, Suffolk
Printed and bound in Great Britain

To find out more about our authors and books visit www.bloomsbury.com and sign up
for our newsletters.

Contents

Part 1 Why Teach Computer Science in School

Part 2 Aspects of Teaching and Learning

List of Figures and Tables

List of Figures

List of Tables

Contributors

Editors

Sue Sentance is Senior Lecturer in Computer Science Education at King's College London, UK. She has been involved with Computing at School in the curriculum changes surrounding computing in England and her research areas are teacher professional development in computer science, physical computing and pedagogical strategies for programming.

Erik Barendsen is Professor in Science Education at Radboud University, The Netherlands, and Professor in Computing Education at Open University, The Netherlands. His research interests include computational thinking, learning by design, context-based education, and pedagogical content knowledge. He chaired the national committee redesigning the computing curriculum in Dutch secondary education.

Carsten Schulte is Professor at the University of Paderborn, Germany, and Head of the computer science education research group. His main research interests include the conceptualization of Computing Education for the digital world; exploring computer biographies; CS teacher education with a focus on teacher students practicing inquiry and research and educational modelling of program comprehension.

Contributors

Tim Bell is Professor in the Department of Computer Science and Software Engineering at the University of Canterbury in Christchurch, New Zealand. His main current research interest is computer science education. His 'Computer Science Unplugged' project is widely used internationally and its books and videos have been translated into about twenty languages. Recently he has been actively involved in the design and deployment of new computer science curriculum in New Zealand schools.

Shannon Campe is Research Associate and Project Coordinator in the Research Department at Education, Training, Research (ETR), a non-profit organization. Her work focuses on bridging research and practice in K-12 education. In recent years, her work has focused on youth and technology – specifically game programming as a way to engage all students and increase interest in and confidence of underrepresented youth in the field of computer science.

Michael Caspersen is Associate Professor in Programming and Programming Didactics at the Department of Computer Science at Aarhus University, Denmark. His research interests are computing education, programming didactics, programming methodology and object-orientated programming. He is co-author of a two-volume textbook on programming and co-editor of *Reflections on the Teaching of Programming* (Springer, 2008).

Paul Curzon is Professor of Computer Science in the School of Electronic Engineering and Computer Science at Queen Mary University of London, UK. He created and edits the magazine and webzine *cs4fn*: an initiative to bring computer science research to schools and promote the fun side of the subject. He also leads on the Teaching London Computing project and CAS London, together with KCL. His research interests are in human-computer interaction.

Quintin Cutts is Professor of Computer Science Education within the School of Computing Science at the University of Glasgow, UK. His research centres on computer science education, with further interest in the use of technology to enhance face-to-face teaching and learning environments. He is involved in the development of school curricula for computer science, contributing to the new Curriculum for Excellence in Scotland, as well as initiatives further afield in England and internationally.

Jill Denner is Senior Research Scientist at ETR (Education, Training and Research), USA. She does applied research and evaluation with a focus on increasing the number of women, girls and Latino/a students in science, technology, engineering, and mathematics (STEM) fields. She has led the development of several after-school programmes designed to increase children's opportunities to become producers, not just users, of technology. She is nationally recognized as an expert in strategies to engage girls/women and Latino/a students in computer science, in both K-12 and community college.

Ira Diethelm is Professor of Computer Science Education at the University of Oldenburg, Germany, and there, preparing pre- and in-service teachers for teaching CS at secondary and vocational schools. She started her career as a teacher for CS, maths and chemistry at a secondary school in Braunschweig, Germany.

James Donohue works at Queen Mary University of London, UK, as a member of the Learning Development/Thinking Writing team, focusing on the role of writing in learning and teaching in engineering and computer science. He researches in the fields of academic and professional communication drawing on systemic functional linguistics, social semiotics, and Paulo Freirean learning theory.

Peter Donaldson is Lecturer of Computing Science and Education at the University of Glasgow, UK. His background is in secondary teaching, curriculum development and middle management.

Peter has organised several CAS Scotland conferences and co-developed a national programme of professional learning for Computing Science called PLAN C.

Caitlin Duncan is a PhD student from the University of Canterbury, New Zealand, working in the Computer Science Education Research group. Her research area is the integration of computational thinking, computer science and programming into primary school curriculum and the impacts of this on both teachers and students. She is a Google Anita Borg Scholar, active in supporting diversity in the computer science community.

Juliana Goschler is Professor of German as a Second/Foreign Language at the University of Oldenburg, Germany. She focuses on the use of language and terminology in different subjects at school to support learning.

Shuchi Grover is Principal Advisor (Learning Sciences) at ACTNext (a new R&D division at ACT, USA) while also consulting with Stanford University on issues of K-12 teacher preparation for teaching computational thinking (CT) and computer science (CS). Formerly a Senior Research Scientist at SRI International's Center for Technology in Learning, her research centres on studying pedagogies and assessments for CT and CS education mainly in K-12 settings. She has been awarded several grants from the National Science Foundation to conduct research on understanding the development of computational competencies in teens. Shuchi is a member of the ACM Education Council, CSTA Task Force on Computational Thinking, and an advisor to the national K-12 CS Education Framework effort in the US.

Peter Hubwieser is Professor in the Didactics of Computer Science at the Technical University of Munich (TUM), Germany. His research activities focus on the empirical investigation of learning processes in the subject area of computer science (definition, measurement and evaluation of competencies, skills and knowledge structures). His novel didactical approach triggered the introduction of computer science as a compulsory subject at Bavarian college preparatory high schools in 2004.

Maria Kallia is a PhD student at King's College London, UK. Her research interests focus on threshold concepts and the pedagogy of computer programming. Prior to her PhD, Maria worked as a computing teacher for six years in Greece where she taught Pascal and Java to high school students and informatics in vocational and second chance schools.

Timo Lampe is a master's graduate from the University of Oldenburg, Germany, and a prospective teacher for computer science and English, who focuses on the language that is being used in classroom settings.

William Marsh is Senior Lecturer in the School of Electronic Engineering and Computer Science in Queen Mary University of London, UK. He was a co-investigator on the Teaching London Computing Programme which has helped to equip London's teachers working with new school curricula. He has taught undergraduate courses on systems analysis, object-oriented programming, computer architecture and embedded systems, and his research interests are in decision support systems.

Peter McOwan is Professor of Computer Science in the School of Electronic Engineering and Computer Science at Queen Mary University of London, UK. He is also Vice Principal (Public Engagement and Student Enterprise). His research interests are in visual perception, mathematical models for visual processing, in particular motion, cognitive science and biologically inspired hardware and software.

Roy Pea is David Jacks Professor of Education and Learning Sciences at Stanford University, Graduate School of Education, and Computer Science (Courtesy), and H-STAR Institute Director, Wallenberg Hall, 450 Serra Mall, Bldg. 160, Stanford, CA 94305; roypea@stanford.edu. His work in the learning sciences focuses on advancing theories, findings, tools and practices of technology-enhanced learning of complex domains.

Cynthia Selby is a Senior Teaching Fellow in the Education School at the University of Southampton, UK. She has considerable experience in teaching computing and computer science at secondary and post-16 institutions. Her research interests include computational thinking, the pedagogy of programming, and assessment.

Juha Sorva is Senior University Lecturer at Aalto University, Finland. His research interests include the learning and teaching of introductory programming, learners' understandings of programming concepts, effective instructional design in ebooks, and program visualisation.

Matti Tedre is Professor in the School of Computing, University of Eastern Finland, Finland. His current research interests are methodology education in computer science, computer science/IT education, social studies of computer science, the philosophy of computer science, global netiquette, and ethnocomputing. He is the author of *The Science of Computing: Shaping a Discipline* (Chapman and Hall, 2014).

Seymour Wright works at Queen Mary University of London, UK, in Learning Development. His current focus is a series of collaborative projects with the school of Electrical Engineering and Computer Science. His current research interests are the relationship between spaces, language, and practical (situated) learning.

Foreword

In 2014, England introduced a new curriculum for computing: for the first time anywhere in the world, all children will learn computer science as a foundational discipline, from primary school onwards, just as they do mathematics and natural science. In the UK at least, this change reflects a seismic shift, away from regarding computing merely as a *technology* that we must all grapple with, and towards thinking of it as a *subject discipline* in its own right. The UK is not alone: every developed nation is engaged in a similar journey.

But once we say 'we should treat computer science as foundational, for every child, not only the software developers of the future', we must confront the deep questions: *what should we teach*, and *how should we teach it*? Other subject disciplines have had centuries to develop answers to these questions (and are still debating them) but computing has not. Yet the need is pressing, because educators across the world are hungry for an inspiring vision to frame their teaching, for pedagogies that provably work and for assessments that validly measure learning and progress.

So this book is extremely timely. It is written by many of *the* leading experts in computing education, across the world. It tackles both of the big questions (what? and how?), and does so from multiple perspectives. Because computer science education at school level is so new, it is hugely important that classroom practice is informed and guided by sound research rather than gut feelings; but it is equally important that research should, in turn, be focused on the realities of the classroom. So I'm delighted to see a whole section entitled 'Research-led teaching of computer science'.

But it's not an esoteric academic book. It is written in language that a classroom teacher or a student training to be a teacher can make sense of. Indeed, these teachers are the audience this book is intended to serve.

Nobody has a monopoly on truth. Really good education is *hard* and we are all feeling our way as we seek to inspire our young people with the joy and beauty of computer science. The authors of this book have spent their professional lives studying computing in the classroom, and I am absolutely delighted to see such a substantial contribution in such an under-served space. Enjoy!

Simon Peyton Jones

Preface

This book is the result of many, many conversations with teachers, researchers and teacher trainers in many different countries – all engaged in the broad field of computer science education. It is an attempt to bridge the gap between practical and country-specific 'how-to' books on teaching computer science/informatics/computing (different names for our subject exist!) and the growing body of computer science education research pertaining to schools. The goal of the book was to bring together key experts in the field to explain their areas of research and its relevance in the classroom, in an accessible way, whilst retaining enough depth to be useful and provide a basis for practitioners to follow and engage in research on CS education. We hope that in this volume we have managed to do this, and that our book will be useful to those training to teach computer science, as well as those already teaching computer science who wish to understand the issues in more depth.

This book specifically refers to school education (known as K-12 in USA and elsewhere), rather than computer science in higher education and will also be useful in identifying key areas of computer science education research relevant to bringing the subject into the school curriculum, as many countries are now doing.

The book is divided into three parts. Part 1 examines the rationale for teaching computer science in school, by looking at what the subject is, some fundamentals and attitudes towards it. Part 2 takes us into the nitty-gritty of the content, pedagogy and assessment of computer science within the school curriculum. In Part 3 we have presented some of the most important aspects of computer science education and some in-depth current research. However, the presentation of relevant research pervades the whole book, as we believe passionately in research-led teaching and engagement with research as a way of improving educational outcomes.

This book has been written by a number of authors from all over the world and is intended to be accessible to you wherever you live and work. Thus it does not relate to any particular country or curriculum, although some countries have been used as examples at times to illustrate key points. Although approaches to teaching computer science in school vary considerably in different countries, the key issues remain the same. We hope that drawing on a wide variety of perspectives has made this book even more valuable.

We hope you enjoy reading this book and find much to enhance your teaching!

Sue Sentance, Erik Barendsen and Carsten Schulte

Part 1

Why Teach Computer Science in School

1

Introduction to Part 1
Why Teach Computer Science in School

Sue Sentance

The last few years have seen a significant growth in interest in teaching computer science in school, from as early as primary school. Around the globe, curricular are being revised to either reform or introduce the subject of computing, computer science or informatics. Although media interest has focused on 'coding' as the main ingredient of this curriculum shift, in actual fact the new subject includes much more than this; it engages children in being creative with technology as well as understanding the fundamental principles of computer science that underlie all software development. The excitement around the teaching of computer science in school is wonderful to see; however, it reveals a need to examine what we know about how we can do this effectively.

There are terminological differences around how we name this subject that encompasses an understanding of the principles and practices within technology. Although the book uses, fairly consistently, the term 'computer science', others call this school subject 'Informatics'. In England, the change in curriculum was precipitated by the Royal Society's report 'Shut Down or Restart' (The Royal Society, 2012), which generated significant attention all around the world and has influenced both decision makers and curriculum designers.

In the Royal Society's analysis, the school subject is named 'Computing' and encompasses three different elements: computer science, information technology and digital literacy. In this book we are focusing on computer science, but hopefully in a way that references a range of aspects of the curriculum. However, we should not neglect the fact that we want all our children leaving school to be digitally literate and that information technology also encompasses a range of essential skills and knowledge that we need to incorporate into the school curriculum. Getting the balance right between these three elements of what we hope to teach in school may not be straightforward and may ultimately differ from country to country.

In this first part of the book, we consider what the subject of computer science really is, particularly so that we can focus on what it means to teach computing in school. This is the focus of Chapter 2 in which Matti Tedre invites us to consider whether computing is a mathematical, scientific or an engineering subject. It is important that all of us as professionals do reflect in this way about our subject as this will influence the way we present it to students.

In Chapter 3, Shuchi Grover and Roy Pea give a comprehensive account of what computational thinking is and how it can be seen to underpin the teaching of the computer science curriculum. Certainly, computational thinking has had a huge influence on recent developments, but as it has become part of the curriculum, it may be that what is really meant by this term has become confused; there has been both some over-promising and at the same time, narrowing, of the thinking that underlies work in computer science (Tedre and Denning, 2016). Grover and Pea describe computational thinking as a 'competency whose time has come' and their analysis, with examples, should help teachers to have a firmer grasp of the range of skills it encompasses.

To continue the journey towards an understanding of what computer science means and why it should be taught in schools, we move on to a discussion about attitudes to computer science, in particular, Mindset. Drawing on the influential work of Carol Dweck (2012) on the difference between a 'fixed Mindset' and a 'growth Mindset', in Chapter 4 Quintin Cutts and Peter Donaldson consider the Mindsets of both students and teachers when it comes to the teaching and learning of computer science. Our attitudes can act as restrictors on what we can achieve in the classroom, so it is important to reflect at this level on how we perceive our own abilities as well as those of our students. Cutts and Donaldson present some useful examples and activities that enable the reader to do this.

Chapter 5, the final chapter in this section, concerns interaction in terms of the way that humans, computers and society interact with technology, and the implications both for students and for the way we teach computer science. Computer science is not just computer programming, as recently explained by Michal Armoni in her regular column in the SIGCSE *Bulletin* (Armoni, 2016), although it is an important toolkit we use to explore the principles. Computer science is broader. Its applications impact all aspects of our lives: with the increasing importance of HCI (human-computer interaction), machine learning and artificial intelligence, it is crucial that children understand the implications of a technology-driven society, in which they may play a role in informed decision making, whatever their chosen career. This chapter complements the others and hopefully, together, the reader will find that they enable a consideration of what it means to teach computer science from a variety of perspectives.

References

Armoni, M (2016). 'Computing in Schools: Computer Science, Computational Thinking, Programming, Coding: The Anomalies Of Transitivity in K-12 Computer Science Education' 7(4) *ACM Inroads* 24–27.

Dweck, CS (2012). *Mindset: Changing the Way you Think to Fulfil your Potential* (London: Constable and Robinson).

Tedre, M, and PJ Denning (2016). 'The Long Quest for Computational Thinking' in *Proceedings of the 16th Koli Calling International Conference on Computing Education Research* New York, 120–29. ACM.

The Royal Society (2012). *Shut Down or Restart? The Way Forward for Computing in UK Schools.* (London, The Royal Society).

2

The Nature of Computing as a Discipline

Matti Tedre

Chapter outline

Chapter synopsis

What is computer science? What should we teach about computing and how? Which skills and knowledge are central to computing? Over the disciplinary history of computing, there has never been a consensus on the field's fundamental nature, aims, methods, essential skills and knowledge, its relations to other disciplines, or even the name of the field. In the course of their development, computing education initiatives, such as curriculum development (see Chapter 7 in this book), course design, and study programme design, often get to a point where the stakeholders start to question their consensus on how exactly people define their field of study. Debates on those questions have characterized computing education discussions ever since the birth of the field; many disagreements still remain. This chapter introduces the reader to what is at stake in debates of computing's disciplinary nature, what the central positions are and how those positions differ from each other.

2.1 Introduction: Computing as a discipline

Teachers of any subject have an explicit or implicit idea of the essence of their field. Each teacher has a view and opinion of, for instance, their discipline's subject matter, aims, fundamental questions, methods and most important achievements. Those ideas guide them when they teach their subject, develop courses, design curricula or engage in education in other ways. This is just the same in computing. We have our perceptions of computing as a discipline, as a profession and as a body of knowledge. Through our teaching, we impart some of our own ideas to students, affecting how they learn to perceive their field.

Over the years, pioneers have characterized the field of computing in a great number of ways. Some argue that computing is a branch of mathematical logic, others argue that it is a design and engineering field. Some emphasize computing's scientific nature while others its constructive character. All those arguments have been used to model computing education in different ways. Of the hundreds of characterizations of the field, some are more popular or influential than others, but there is no 'correct' interpretation of computing's disciplinary nature: different views are justified from different perspectives. The popularity of different views has also changed over the years with computing's evolving status in the university as well as its developing state-of-the-art technology and theoretical body of knowledge.

One characterization of computing's disciplinary nature is the report *Computing as a Discipline* (Denning et al., 1989), which was commissioned to support new joint curriculum recommendations by two major organizations in computing: the Association for Computing Machinery (ACM) and the IEEE Computer Society. The report describes computing as a combination of three intertwined traditions: theory, modelling and design. Those traditions derive from three intellectual traditions: analytical, scientific and engineering. The first is theoretically orientated and emphasizes formal methods of mathematics and logic. The second is empirically orientated and features data, simulation and abstraction. The third is technologically orientated and emphasizes design and engineering methods. The three traditions have their own aims and goals, and their differences have practical ramifications. They differ in terms of their methods, assumptions, views of knowledge, perceptions of the structure of reality, concepts of human nature and general world view.

Computing as a Discipline started to greatly affect how computing educators viewed their field. Most computing teachers indeed know some theory, do some design and engage in modelling or abstraction activities. Although those activities support each other, the three traditions of computing are also profoundly different; in many ways they are incompatible.

To be able to give students a balanced and rich view of computing as a discipline, it is important to understand these different traditions, their research agendas and their roots. Viewing computing from a variety of perspectives offers educators meaningful entry points to its topics and it offers students insight about the immense theoretical, practical, scientific and philosophical richness of computing.

This chapter introduces three dominant traditions of computing and characterizes their aims, questions, views of subject matter, methods and practices. Those traditions are surely not the only ones at play; one could easily argue that computing borrows many elements from social and human sciences or that it might best be described as an interdisciplinary field. However, as most computing's disciplinary debates boil down to its theoretical, scientific and engineering features, this chapter focuses on those three.

2.2 Computing is a field of engineering and design

Those who view computing as primarily a technological field or a field of engineering and design, have a strong case. Computing's development as an independent discipline started only after the birth of the modern computer. Computing's history reveals a rich collection of technical and technological breakthroughs, computing machinery and a union of theory and craftsmanship. Many pioneers of modern computing, such as Bush, Eckert and Atanasoff, were electrical engineers. The histories of automatic office machinery, scientific instruments, calculating instruments and military equipment are woven into the fabric of modern computing. Progress of computing has been driven by increasingly smarter designs as well as technological tendencies, such as the exponential growth rate of transistors in chips (Moore's Law), the even-faster growth of memory technology density (Kryder's Law) and the exponential growth of communication speed.

For decades, engineering and design were, however, downplayed in discussions about academic computing. Even though software technology and systems design were important drivers of progress – often developed in universities – they did not resonate well with computing's campaign to achieve an independent disciplinary identity in academia. The issue was not that computer systems and software design would not be important, but it was about the rigor and academic image of the aspiring discipline of computing. There was a widespread opinion among the more-established disciplines that design and engineering were not well suited for traditional research universities. So, in their quest to make computing an independent discipline, some pioneers proudly promoted a view of computing as an abstract field that downplayed everything to do with designing, building and developing computer systems, societally valuable applications and computing machinery. However intellectually justified, their views of computing as just a branch of mathematics and logic were far from what was really happening in computing practice and much of computing research.

The design and engineering aspects of computing were revived at the end of the 1960s, when a thought-provoking term *software engineering* was promoted as a solution to the sad state of software in the time of the so-called 'software crisis'. The software engineering movement quickly gained momentum, as many practitioners and software-orientated academics felt that their work was much better characterized by engineering and design than mathematics and logic. Over some three decades of development, software engineering matured into a progressive field and became a part of computing's core knowledge.

Proponents: We are designers and builders

Computing's engineering nature has been described and justified in many ways. Some proponents of computing's engineering character look at computing practice, and argue that instead of mathematics or science, the majority of computer scientists – both practitioners and researchers – actually do engineering, design and development. Others base their argument on methods and outcomes arguing that engineering approaches are required for reaching the solid reliability and safety record of rigorous engineering design in other fields. Yet others want designers to achieve the same sort of intellectual recognition and triumphant image that engineering did in the first half of the twentieth century. Those who argue that engineering describes best what people in computing actually do often justify their argument by looking at the aims and central questions, necessary skill set and methods and practices of computing.

Aims and questions

Frederick P. Brooks Jr, a computing pioneer and author of several classic works on software engineering, made a distinction between a scientist and an engineer: The scientist builds in order to study, and the engineer studies in order to build (Brooks, 1996). Similarly, while natural sciences focus on 'what' type of questions, some argue that computing's focus on 'how' type of questions reveals its engineering character (Hartmanis, 1993). Hartmanis (1993) wrote that whereas natural scientists ask 'What exists?' computer scientists ask 'What can exist?' The engineering view sees that many problems in contemporary computing are not *whether* a program, algorithm, technique or system can exist, but *how* to make one in practice.

Many people also argue that the aim of computing has, from the very beginning, been to design and construct useful things. Hence, similar to any other engineering field, research in computing is about the development of methods and tools that advance the state-of-the-art or enable new things to be done. Unlike natural scientists who deal with naturally occurring phenomena, engineers deal with artefacts, which are created by people; for many, that makes computing an engineering field. While knowledge in natural sciences progresses through experiments, in computing, demonstrations are key. In many computing fields the scientists' slogan 'publish or perish' has changed into the engineers' slogan 'demo or die' (Hartmanis, 1993).

Subject matter

Those who argue that computing is essentially an engineering field have a difficult question to answer: if it is engineering, what is it engineering *of*? If chemical engineering is the application of chemistry and mechanical engineering is the application of material science and physics, what is computing, as an engineering field, the application *of*? Attempts to address this issue include, for example, the engineering of mathematics (or mathematical processes), information engineering, cognitive technology, conceptual engineering, language of technology, and mechanization of abstraction (Tedre, 2014). None of those have received any widespread support.

From the subject matter viewpoint, the engineering view of computing boils down to two key issues: artifice and causality. Firstly, many engineering-orientated researchers and developers in computing pose problems and follow the design process to come up with a solution in form of an *artefact* (Denning et al., 1989; Simon, 1969). Different from the natural sciences, which deal with naturally occurring things, computing deals with artefacts, which have been designed for certain purposes in specific contexts. Different from mathematics, which deals with abstract objects, executable programs of computing are causal, physical things: they are swarms of electrons in the circuits of a computer. When run, they can cause changes in the world. Computer programs can make monitors blink and printers rattle; they can drive cars and guide missiles to their targets. Suggestions by the engineering camp for computing's subject matter include, for example, software, computer systems and computers.

Methods and practices

Some argue that the necessary skill set for computing reveals the field's engineering nature. Design, in particular, is essential to computing, and in line with that, programming has been described as an art, craft, trade or skill. Many pioneers of computing point out that, unlike research in many traditional theoretical and empirical sciences, development of working computer systems has to cater much more to material resources, social and human constraints, budgets, as well as laws of nature. Many people in computing design complex systems with limitations to resource consumption. Design involves studying users, groups of users, and communities, which requires methods from social sciences and humanities. Like engineers in other fields, programmers follow a systematic sequence of design decisions to exclude alternative options until a solution is ready (Wegner, 1976).

Examples of design view in schools

Countless initiatives have introduced computing in schools through designing and building artefacts – such as building and programming educational robots, designing and creating games without writing code, and creating apps for smartphones. At the university level, summative assessment is often based on students designing and implementing a solution to meet a concern, answer a threat or rise to an opportunity. They are design and engineering activities.

Opponents: Building things is not an academic aim

In addition to passionate supporters, the engineering view of computing has also strong opponents. In their attempt to improve computing's academic status, many pioneers of computing downplayed computing's constructive character and highlighted its theoretical aspects (Tedre, 2014). Early software engineering was accused of sloppy methodology and lack of rigorous theories. Some pointed out the short life-span of technical inventions: as a fundamental discipline, computing should focus on enduring fundamental principles instead of technological solutions that became obsolete quickly (Wegner, 1970). Many theoretically orientated pioneers of computing wanted to see computing focus on what is common to the use of any computer in any application instead of technical details or societal aspects of computing.

Accusations of lack of rigor in software construction and research undermined computing's engineering image. Those claims were first anecdotal and based on people's subjective perceptions of how software construction was done. Many people pointed out the undeveloped theoretical foundations of software engineering, its scarcity of theoretically and technically well-developed methods and that it seemed to be guided by rules of thumb, toying and tinkering. Later, in the 1990s, systematic reviews of publications in software engineering showed a lack of attention to methodology and theory.

However, some zealots aside, the argument against the engineering view was never about engineering and design being unimportant. Producing useful and reliable systems has always been a societally important aim that poses endless intellectual challenges. Instead, the critical voices regarding computing being a branch of engineering or technology are about the lasting value of engineering and design, its contribution to our common knowledge about the world and its centrality in the *academic* discipline of computing and in computing research.

Key concept: Computing as engineering

Many computing activities are centred around requirement analysis, design, implementation, evaluation and the production of useful artefacts. The questions that computing answers and the problems it solves are often of the engineering-type 'how' questions. Many problems in computing require design and engineering methods and a procedural knowledge base of rules, heuristics and processes. Design and engineering are an integral part of tertiary computing education, and their importance is acknowledged also at school levels.

2.3 Computing is a sort of mathematics

Ever since specialized disciplines started to form in the academia, there has been a tight connection between mathematics and sciences. Similarly, during the disciplinary formation of computing, many argued that mathematics and mathematical logic are central for the field. Many of computing's problems and their solutions are mathematical: the computer's basic operational principles can be reduced to mathematical logic, many pioneers of the field are mathematicians, even the word 'computing' refers to mathematical activity. Computing has appropriated parts of mathematics too. Many mathematical objects, like graphs, functions and matrices, can now be taught from a computing viewpoint instead of a mathematics viewpoint.

Computing's early emphasis on mathematics was based on ideals as well as practical needs. To obtain a foothold in traditional research universities, computing could not look like a toolmaker, so emphasizing theory created a desirable image of the discipline. Unlike technical inventions, many of which grew obsolete within a decade, theoretical research was considered to have lasting value. Until the late 1980s there was a strong narrative of computing being primarily a mathematical field. However, a gap was growing between that narrative and what went on in computing education, business and the industry. The software industry struggled with a multifaceted crisis in software production which theory-orientated research was unable to solve.

Since the 1990s, debates about the role of mathematics in computing have lost their zeal; today there is a broad consensus on the importance of different kinds of approaches to computing. In universities, the requirements in computing commonly include discrete mathematics, probability and statistics. Yet there is still debate about the relationship between computing and mathematics and how much mathematics a computing professional or a researcher shoud learn. As computing theory and practice are very closely connected, some pioneers emphasize their interplay. Knuth (1991), for example, advised those who spend their time mostly on the theory of computing to turn their attention to practice because 'it will improve your theories'. Similarly, he advised those who spend their time mostly on practice to turn their attention to theory as 'it will improve your practice'.

Proponents: Logic rules

Those who argue that much of the work in computing actually boils down to mathematics and logic have referred to the aims and central questions, necessary skill set, and methods and practices of computing as well as the computer's logical organization. Many aspects of computers and programs can be described using mathematical functions and symbol manipulation. Program states are often practically infinite – mathematics is the best tool for dealing with infinity. The theory of computing is very much a mathematical theory. Those who advocate for a stronger inclusion of mathematics in computing education point out that most areas of computing have a close relationship with specific areas of mathematics (Baldwin, Walker & Henderson, 2013).

Methods and practices

Many proponents of a mathematical view of computing argue that one can reason about algorithms, programs and procedures in the same way that mathematicians work with functions, theorems and proofs – in their minds or using a pen and paper (Smith, 1998). Hence, for reasoning about programs, skills and knowledge of methods and practices in mathematics and logic are absolutely essential. Even more, formal methods provide a variety of ways for greatly increasing reliability and robustness of programs.

Even when computing professionals do not use mathematics and logic explicitly, they are a part of our 'computational thinking' habits (Aho, 2011). Although most software engineers, programmers and other computing professionals cope well in their professions without explicitly applying mathematics, mathematics and logic are implicit in very large parts of their work. Consequently, many share the opinion that computing education should include more mathematics, especially more applicable and relevant mathematics (Baldwin, Walker and Henderson, 2013).

Subjects and questions

From the mathematical point of view, computer programs and other objects of computing are essentially abstract objects or can be modeled as such. For example, every executable program can be expressed as an algorithm, which is an abstract object one can reason about in terms of mathematics and logic. Mathematical knowledge is of lasting nature because it consists of necessary truths – truths that cannot be otherwise in the set of axioms and rules where they are stated.

Favorite descriptions of computing's subject matter on the theoretical side are algorithms, classes of computations, models of computing, procedures, and abstraction. Yet, there are differences between computing and traditional mathematics: Knuth (1974) wrote that unlike mathematics, computing often deals with finitary constructions and dynamic relationships. While mathematics is more declarative, computing is more imperative, which can clearly be seen in computing's problems, aims and methods. Still, mathematics is the best tool for answering questions about the theoretical limits of different models of computing – 'What can be automated?' – as well as the practical limits set by how much computing is needed – 'What can be efficiently automated?'

Examples of mathematics and logic in school computing education

In school curricula, mathematical principles include activities such as learning how to count from zero to 1023 using ten fingers for binary digits, learning to use logic to solve mystery problems and learning binary data error detection through card flip magic tricks. In the school curriculum recommendations, children learn simple concepts like binary representation in Year 3 and continue to explore connections between mathematics, logic and computing in Years 6–9.

Opponents: It's not what we do most of the time

No serious argument has ever claimed that mathematics plays no role in computing. Instead, the critics argue that mathematical methods do not play a dominant role in computing, that mathematical knowledge and skills are not central to most work in computing and that what matters the most in computing is the computer and its effects on science, society and our lives. Many researchers as well as professional practitioners of computing usually engage in activities that are not mathematical by nature: they elicit requirements (e.g. they design interfaces, build models, debug programs, test systems and write manuals).

Even those who acknowledge computing's mathematical nature are often opposed to strong conclusions about the relationship between computing and mathematics. Although both might be dealing with symbols on some level, their aims and objectives differ: mathematics is interested in the relationships between symbols as well as semantics of symbols, while most of computing is about applications of mathematics to solve problems. While mathematics is supposed to be independent of any social or human concerns, computing is very much about social and human concerns. One can argue that if computing were only a theoretical discipline, it would have never revolutionized both science and society. It is the machine that counts.

Key concept: Computing as mathematics and logic

Computers are logic machines. Some of the most impressive achievements in computing are proven and presented using the language of mathematics and many mathematical structures like matrices, vectors and graphs have become standard computing concepts. Large parts of computing studies formal objects, such as algorithms and models of computing. Many questions of computing are best solved using mathematics and logic as tools. School curriculum recommendations have acknowledged the tight connection between computational, mathematical and logical thinking.

2.4 Computing is a science

Computing and science have always been deeply intertwined: the relationship goes both ways. From Newton's prolific numerical calculations to large-scale tabulation operations, computing or numerical analysis has served as a tool for science. Secondly, many pioneers of computing aimed to found computer science on similar scientific principles as natural sciences. Thirdly, many people argue that modern computing started a whole new era of science. Natural sciences gradually developed computational branches – such as bioinformatics, computational physics and computational chemistry – and computer simulation became a central element of progress in science.

The science discussions manifest in many ways, one of which is the debate about whether computer *science* is the correct name. The terms informatics, algorithmics and datalogy are used in different countries. Another discussion is concerned with the subject matter of the field: if astronomy is the study of celestial objects and zoology the study of animals, what is computing a study of? Yet another branch of the discussion is concerned with methodology: research fields are characterized by their methods, but what *is* the method of computing – if there is one? Finally, some debates are concerned not with whether computing is a science but whether it might be the most important science today, given the amazing success of computational approaches in a broad variety of fields.

One striking feature of the debate is that the debaters do not share a common view of what science is. By science, some mean natural science while others mean any empirical science; some refer to methods, others to theories; and some talk about a body of knowledge or laws and others a world view. In the absence of any common ground, debaters are often talking over each other and have great difficulty achieving consensus.

Proponents: It's a new kind of science

Those who argue that computing is a scientific discipline often refer to the aims of science – exploration, description, prediction and explanation of phenomena. They argue that computing shares those aims. Some research also follows the experiment cycle of observation, description, prediction and testing; this is sometimes called the scientific method. Many debaters see computing as an interdisciplinary field that combines theories from a variety of domains and contributes to an even-broader variety of fields. Computing's unique scientific nature has been described as an unnatural science, artificial science, synthetic science and even a completely new domain of science that follows its own paradigm (Rosenbloom, 2013).

Subjects

Many arguments about computing's scientific nature rely on its subject matter. There are a dizzying number of arguments about what computing is a science *of*, ranging from data, information and symbols to algorithms, processes, procedures and information flows as well as complexity, representation, users and designs (Tedre, 2014). All those can be studied using scientific principles. While earlier it was widely agreed that computing's subject matter is artificial – making computing a science of the artificial (Simon, 1969) – more recent studies argue that computing examines phenomena both artificial and natural, stating that computing has become a 'fourth great domain of science' (Rosenbloom, 2013).

Methods and practices

Computing's large range of subjects makes it a methodologically rich field. Its scope and aims are so broad that it excludes few methodological strategies. Due to its broad variety of subjects of study, such as computability, usability, reliability and efficiency, it flexibly adopts methods from natural sciences and formal fields to social sciences and humanities. More importantly, computing's amazing success in triggering methodological changes in other fields of science and creating new fields – such as bioinformatics, computational physics and computational chemistry – has led many people to argue that computing has become the most important of all the sciences.

The 1980s saw a rapid increase in the use of computers to simulate a growing number of phenomena. One by one, research fields spawned 'computational' branches; computer simulation quickly became a central tool for sciences. Today, it has been characterized as a third pillar of science, alongside the two traditional pillars of theory and experiment. The changes in how research is done using simulations are so radical that they have been described as the most disruptive shift since quantum mechanics and the computing era of science as the age of computer simulation (Tedre, 2014).

Examples of science in school computing education

In many countries computing is integrated in the teaching of other subjects. For instance, in grades 9–10, computer simulation is used in both physics and biology to represent and experiment on natural phenomena. In the CSTA school curriculum, computational modelling is used to understand how interactions between individual elements in complex systems (e.g. people, animals or cars) give rise to emergent patterns that can be fundamentally unpredictable.

Opponents: If computing is science, it is bad science

Opposition towards computing's status as a science comes in many forms, of which two are particularly common. Firstly, some people argue that computing is not really a science, based on a variety of arguments. If by 'science' one means 'natural science' then computing surely is not similar to, for instance, physics and chemistry, because many of its subjects are artificial and because it is not methodologically united. Some also argue that while in the natural sciences theories compete with each other in explaining the fundamental nature of their subject matters, computing does not have a track record of competing theories of the fundamental nature of, for example, data or information. Neither are theories in computing developed to reconcile theory with anomalies revealed by experiments, which is common in other sciences (Hartmanis, 1993).

Secondly, some people argue that computing is bad science. Large surveys of computing research have revealed that experimental validation of results is not as common in computing as it is in most other sciences. Even further, similar surveys show that research reports in computing often exclude important details of methodology, making it impossible for others to replicate or even properly evaluate the merits of those reports. The role of experiments in computing is another common targets of criticism: while natural sciences are driven by crucial experiments, many parts of computing are driven by crucial demonstrations.

Computing's inclusive pick-and-mix attitude towards methodology has been interpreted in two ways. While the proponents of computing's scientific nature see computing's methodological multiperspectivism in a positive light, those who criticize computing's scientific nature quote the same characteristic as methodological eclecticism and lack of shared principles. For many people 'everything goes' is a sign of methodological anarchism and not a desirable feature of science.

Key concept: Computing as a science

Computers have become the most common tool of science, and simulation has become a standard feature of modern natural science. Many people argue that computing has become a third pillar of science, aside the traditional theory and experiment. Computing helps theoretically oriented scientists to solve their equations and experimenters to analyse massive amounts of data, and it has given rise to a new way of doing science in form of simulation.

2.5 Summary: Understanding intellectual traditions is important in computing education

The above sections present various windows to computing as a discipline, rooted in the traditions of engineering, mathematics and empirical sciences. They all have their advantages and disadvantages and are all justified in different ways. As integral parts of computing's practice and theory, the traditions are deeply intertwined and support each other. Some of the greatest achievements of computing happen at the intersections of different intellectual traditions and others purely within one.

However, combining theory, design and empirical research in one educational programme is not always easy. One has to be aware of the limitations of each tradition. For example, one cannot formally prove that a design has the intended qualities or that a computer system will not fail. Showing that something can be built does not demonstrate any of its qualities, such as usefulness, usability, or reliability. Empirical research is not a tool for proving things. Explanations of human behaviour are very different from those of electromagnetic phenomena. When working at the intersection of computing's traditions, one should know each of them well or risk results that are flawed from the point of view of each of the traditions.

Working at the intersection of many intellectual traditions has posed problems for educators throughout computing's disciplinary history. Teaching design and engineering requires different educational strategies than teaching the theory of computing. The aims and goals of engineering are different from those of theoretical or empirical fields. In theses and degrees on systems and software, engineering ingenuity or programming virtuosity are often not enough, but questions are raised about scientific validation. These issues and many others, may be alleviated by understanding computing's unique disciplinary ways of thinking and practicing and the intellectual traditions behind them. Throughout the development of modern computing, the focus of computing research and education has also frequently shifted between different traditions.

Understanding computing's traditions is also important for locating oneself within the landscape of computing fields (see also Chapter 7). Those who have strong preferences and opinions about computing's essential features will benefit from understanding the strengths, and weaknesses of alternative viewpoints. Those who are more ambivalent will benefit from contemplating different intellectual traditions with regard to courses, curricula and aims of education. A rich and balanced view of computing is also important for students who are still building their identities as computing professionals. By being aware of the pros and cons, promises and challenges as well as the landmark achievements of each of the major traditions in computing, we can give students a fascinating tour of computing in its full richness.

Key points

- Throughout the disciplinary history of computing, there has been a lively debate on the field's fundamental nature, aims, methods, essential skills and knowledge, its relations to other disciplines, or even the name of the field.
- This chapter introduces three dominant traditions of computing and characterizes their aims, questions, views of subject matter, methods and practices. The traditions are deeply intertwined and support each other.
- Computing as engineering: Many computing activities are centred around requirement analysis, design, implementation and the evaluation and production of useful artefacts.

- Computing as mathematics and logic: Computers are logic machines, some of the most impressive achievements in computing are proven and presented in the language of mathematics. Large parts of computing studies use formal objects such as algorithms and models of computing.
- Computing as a science: Computers have become the most common tool of science and simulation has become a standard feature of modern natural science. Many people argue that computing has become a third pillar of science.

Further reflection

1 Which of computing's design, logico-mathematical and scientific aspects are you most familiar with? What are the most motivating assignments for students in each tradition? Which school subjects do students consider to be closest to computing?
2 What kinds of skills and knowledge seem to be important for learning computing principles? How can computing be integrated in other subjects? How do we measure students' abilities in computing?

References

Aho, AV (2011). Ubiquity Symposium: Computation and Computational Thinking, *Ubiquity* (January).

Baldwin, D, HM Walker and PB Henderson (2013). 'The Roles of Mathematics in Computer Science' 4(4) *ACM Inroads* 74–80.

Brooks, Jr, FP (1996). 'The Computer Scientist as Toolsmith II' 39(3) *Communications of the ACM* 61–68.

Denning, PJ, DE Comer, D Gries, C Mulder, A Tucker, AJ Turner and PR Young (1989). 'Computing as a Discipline' 32(1) *Communications of the ACM* 9–23.

Fetzer, JH (1988). 'Program Verification: The Very Idea' 31(9) *Communications of the ACM* 1048–1063.

Hartmanis, J (1993). Turing Award Lecture on Computational Complexity and the Nature of Computer Science 37(10) *Communications of the ACM* 37–43.

Knuth, DE (1974). 'Computer Science and its Relation to Mathematics' 81 *American Mathematical Monthly* 323–343.

Knuth, DE (1991). 'Theory and Practice' 90 *Theoretical Computer Science* 1–15.

Rosenbloon, PS (2013). *On Computing: The Fourth Great Scientific Domain* (Cambridge, MA, MIT Press).

Simon, HA (1969). *The Sciences of the Artificial* (Cambridge, MA, MIT Press).

Smith, BC (1998). *On the Origin of Objects* (Cambridge, MA, MIT Press).

Tedre, M (2014). *The Science of Computing: Shaping a Discipline* (New York, NY, Taylor & Francis/CRC Press).

Wegner, P (1970). 'Three Computer Cultures: Computer Technology, Computer Mathematics, and Computer Science' in FL Alt and M Rubino (eds), 10 *Advances in Computers* 7–78.

Wegner, P (1976). 'Research Paradigms in Computer Science' in *ICSE '76: Proceedings of the 2nd International Conference on Software Engineering* (Los Alamitos, CA, IEEE Computer Society Press) 322–330.

3

Computational Thinking:
A Competency Whose Time Has Come

Shuchi Grover and Roy Pea

Chapter outline

Chapter synopsis

Computational thinking encompasses a range of specific thinking skills for problem solving including abstraction, decomposition, evaluation, pattern recognition, logic and algorithm design. While what exactly is included in computational thinking has been the topic of some debate, this chapter will consider each of the elements of CT, how the learning of these concepts and practices can be facilitated within the school curriculum, and the role of CT skills in other domains.

3.1 Introduction

The United States presidential election of 2016 was one for the ages. Beyond the theatrics and intrigues, it also spotlighted the undeniably growing role computing is playing in momentous geopolitical events. Whether it was AI's coming of age in the form of chatbots to influence (for better or worse) critical news and information or the e-mail server issue that dogged one major political party, the election underscored the need for the citizenry to be better equipped to understand the fundamentals of computing and engage in computational thinking. When a federal agency announced the examination of 650,000 e-mails over nine days, individuals across mainstream and social media and on the election stump, pondered:

> A couple of questions are probably running through many Americans' minds right now: Is it possible to 'review' 650,000 emails in just eight days? Does the FBI recruit superhuman speed readers to process and internalize vast amounts of information? Is the FBI lying?
>
> Yasmeh, 2016

In contrast, observers familiar with computing and automation understood this as a problem readily solvable by computing. The minimal press that attempted to explain 'de-duping' and how enormous quantities of data, such as e-mails could, in fact, be examined efficiently and effectively using programs searching for specific strings and patterns, did little to alleviate the suspicions of sceptics unfamiliar with how computation works.

The twenty-first century is arguably the century of computing. Artificial intelligence has finally come of age as it becomes embedded in the transformation of work, commerce and everyday life. Big data, speech and facial recognition, robotics, internet of things, cloud computing, autonomous vehicles and 24×7 access to anyone, anywhere in the world via social media is changing how and where people work, collaborate, communicate, shop, eat, travel, get news and entertainment, and quite simply, live. Computing is also transforming industry and innovation in every discipline, becoming an integral tool that is spurring new ways of doing and thinking. In such a world saturated by computing, 'Computational Thinking' or CT (Wing, 2006, 2011) is now recognized as a foundational competency for being an informed citizen and being successful in STEM work, one that also bears the potential as a means for creative problem solving and innovating in all other disciplines. In this decade, systematic endeavours have gained momentum to take computer science (CS) education and CT to scale in K-12 classrooms in states across the US and internationally. In 2012, the UK National Curriculum programme began introducing CS to all students at all class levels. US efforts found heightened legitimacy with the 2016 Presidential mandate of 'Computer Science For All' initiated in collaboration with federal funding agencies, academic research institutions, professional associations, prominent industry partners and non-profit organizations. In his call supporting CS education, President Obama echoed the beliefs of many in the education community with his assertion that all children from kindergarten to high school need to learn CS and be equipped with computational thinking skills they need to participate in our technology-driven world (Smith, 2016).

3.2 What is computational thinking?

We have witnessed over the last two decades a concerted paradigm shift (Kuhn, 1970) in our beliefs of what is important to learn not only in STEM subjects but also in the humanities. This shift privileges teaching higher-order critical thinking abilities fundamental in each and every domain beyond rote learning and procedural skills, in what has been designated as 'deeper learning' (Pellegrino and Hilton, 2013). Nationwide US efforts around the Common Core standards for subjects such as mathematics and English language, and the Next Generation Science Standards (NRC, 2013) mirror similar shifts in other countries which emphasize disciplinary thinking and ways of knowing and being beyond rote learning. So, teaching mathematics has moved towards thinking like a mathematician; science learning now involves developing competencies for thinking like and enacting the authentic practices of, a scientist.

It seems only logical, then, that educators and policy makers keen to teach computer science are attempting to privilege computational thinking or thinking like a computer scientist, over other aspects of computing (such as learning binary arithmetic). What is 'computational thinking' anyway? How is it defined and understood?

Jeannette Wing's definition

Though somewhat opaque, Jeanette Wing's definition of computational thinking first articulated in a 2006 *Communications of the ACM* article (Wing, 2006, 2011) deserves mention for capturing the collective imagination of educators and researchers worldwide and spurring global efforts to create a generation of computational thinkers. She uses *'computational thinking' as shorthand for 'thinking like a computer scientist'*.

Key concept: Computational thinking

Computational thinking is the thought processes involved in formulating a problem and expressing its solution(s) in such a way that a computer – human or machine – can effectively carry out.

Informally, computational thinking describes the mental activity in formulating a problem to admit a computational solution. The solution can be carried out by a human or machine. This latter point is important. First, humans compute. Second, people can learn computational thinking without a machine. Also, computational thinking is not just about problem solving, but also about problem formulation (Wing, 2014).

Computational thinking is fundamentally about problem solving using concepts and strategies most closely related to computer science (hence its name). Problem formulation should be considered a key part of this problem-solving process. Since formulating the solution for the problem using CT need not involve the computer, even though the execution of the solution usually does, CT can be taught without the use of the computer. K-12 educators now aspire to teach these skills, with and without the computer, in ways that equip students to apply them in various contexts and domains, and more often than not, where a computer or computing device must carry out the solution. This is somewhat of a shift from early views of CT promulgated by Papert (1980), whose pioneering work in children and programming continues to inspire student-centred, constructionist CS curricula and pedagogies even today.

Given the computing-saturated direction in which the world is moving, CT is thus especially relevant as a widely applicable thinking competency along with other critical thinking needed to solve the challenges posed in this century throughout various domains. CT played a key role in changing the course of World War II when computing pioneer Alan Turing used it to break the code of The Enigma Machine underlying the Nazi war efforts (Hodges, 2012). More recently, CT made its most compelling case for deserving serious attention when, at the dawn of this century, it was credited with cracking the human genome, touted to be among the thorniest problems that the biomedical community had struggled with for decades. Futurists believe that CT will similarly play a role in tackling thorny issues with which current and coming generations will have to contend, such as climate change, shortages of critical resources such as water and social inequities that continue to plague societies around the world.

Key concept: What CT is not!

It is easy to fall into the trap that CT is thinking like a computer. Yet it is a trap conveniently avoided if one keeps in mind our framing of *'thinking like a <domain expert>'* for <domain-specific> thinking competencies. Thinking is an inherently human trait that involves reasoning. Computers do not think, so CT is NOT 'thinking like a computer', rather it is about *thinking like a computer scientist*. It's the problem-solving approaches commonly used by computer scientists that constitute computational thinking.

What are these problem-solving approaches and ideas that CS embraces? Let's look at these next.

3.3 Elements of computational thinking (Breaking it down)

What does CT mean? What thought processes does it involve? Obtaining answers to these queries will help teachers and designers to develop curricula to prepare children's computational thinking competencies. Jeanette Wing's article and subsequent efforts to define CT – especially for K-12 education – spawned a large body of articles breaking CT down into several elements that aimed to clarify and outline what 'thinking like a computer scientist' means, including our CT 'state-of-the-field' review in AERA's *Educational Researcher* (Grover and Pea, 2013).[1] All these elements comprise some combination of a list of competencies most will agree are facets of the thinking processes that computer scientists engage in when they solve problems. Keeping in mind that there is not yet an unassailable list, the elements that we find to be most comprehensive and useful to describe CT to teachers, with a few of our own tweaks, is that outlined by the British Computing At School initiative.

By observing what kinds of thinking computer scientists activate when they engage in problem solving, we find that CT encompasses the following *concepts* and *practices*. The inclusion of the practices view of CT in addition to CT concepts, is in keeping with the *'thinking like a <domain expert>'* notion and describes the behaviours that domain experts engage in in the field.

Key concept: CT concepts and practices

CT concepts include:

1 Logic and logical thinking
2 Algorithms and algorithmic thinking
3 Patterns and pattern recognition
4 Abstraction and generalization
5 Evaluation
6 Automation

CT practices include:

1 Problem decomposition
2 Creating computational artefacts
3 Testing and debugging
4 Iterative refinement (incremental development)
5 Collaboration & Creativity (part of broader twenty-first century skills)

We now describe each of these along with examples set in everyday non-computing contexts as well as computing and programming contexts. Where possible, we also provide a simple example or two of how teachers might teach these concepts and practices in the classroom.

3.4 CT concepts

Logic and logical thinking

Logical thinking involves analysing situations to make a decision or reach a conclusion about a situation. An everyday example of logical and analytical thinking might involve analysing whether

---

[1]Among the other more influential articles breaking down CT include the 'working definition' by ISTE, Google's 'Exploring Computational Thinking' (available at: https://goo.gl/eUBk7v); the UK's 'Computing at School' initiative and the APCS Principles' six CT Practices and seven Big Ideas of Computing.

it is worthwhile going to *Shop A* to buy a dress for $30 or *Shop B* where it's available for $20, taking into account factors such as distance to the shops, the time of day and weather. It may not make logical sense to go to *Shop B* if it is farther away than *Shop A* and the cost of travelling to *Shop B* is greater than the $10 difference in price of the dress.

Computer scientists also often use more of a formal logic framework in their work. *Boolean logic* is at the heart of all computing from computational circuitry to its use in software and programming to make decisions in flow of algorithmic control. As part of CT competency development, students must build analytical thinking skills by working on logical puzzles and problem-solving scenarios as well as learning formal Boolean logic through an understanding of AND, OR, NOT (and other variants of Boolean operators) and how to construct Boolean expressions using combinations of these primitive logic elements.

Example activity: Boolean expressions set in real-world settings

A simple example of logic thinking might involve constructing a Boolean expression for an alarm that would ring for soccer practice on Mondays at 4pm and Wednesdays at 5pm, like so:

SoccerAlarm rings **IF** ((WeekDay is Monday **AND** Time is 4pm) **OR** (WeekDay is Wednesday **AND** Time is 5pm))

Being able to reason thus with Boolean logic also translates well to game programming when games require the use of control statements involving Boolean expressions, such as, *'Game over if the player has collected all the gold coins or has no more lives left'*.[2] Of course, the program will require an additional logical check to determine whether to announce *'You won!'* or *'You lost!'* before it ends.

Algorithms and algorithmic thinking

Algorithms are precise step-by-step plans or procedures to meet an end goal or to solve a problem; algorithmic thinking is the skill involved in developing an algorithm. Cooking recipes are a common everyday example of algorithms (albeit less precise than what would be considered algorithms in computer science). Other common examples are route maps suggested by applications such as Google Maps or instructions for assembling a piece of furniture, instructions for knitting or crocheting a scarf, and so on. In fact, the precise set of actions to get ready for school every morning could be construed as an algorithm.

Most of the algorithms that students encounter in the context of K-12 CT learning involve three basic building blocks – *sequence, selection* and *repetition*. The steps in all algorithms follow a sequence; however, there could be conditional checks that make the algorithm select either one of another, or set(s) of actions that are repeated. In the context of programming, conditional checks

---

[2] Several examples drawn from Grover, Pea and Cooper (2015), Grover (2017), and Grover and Basu (2017).

involve the *if-then-else* constructs, and looping involves constructs such as *do-while*, *for*, *repeat*, or *repeat-until* to perform repetitive actions. Recursion is a related idea to repetition that is a technique unique to computer science although it is a more advanced idea and relevant mostly to curricula in high school and beyond. Grover, Pea and Cooper (2015) describe a structured middle school curriculum aimed at teaching algorithmic thinking skills.

Computer scientists use this concept of algorithms to devise precise solutions to problems. These solutions could be described in the form of flowcharts, pseudo-code or a bulleted list written in an abstract everyday language that could then be coded or programmed (by the same computer scientist who creates the algorithm or by other programmers) using a programming language to be interpreted and carried out (or 'executed') by a computer. As with logic, disciplinary learning in computer science at the undergraduate level also involves a more formal study of algorithms that students may not encounter in their K-12 CS learning, involving examining aspects of efficiency, resource optimization and complexity of algorithms.

Patterns and pattern recognition

We are all familiar with the concept of patterns and pattern recognition from our early learning of shapes or math topics such as multiplication and number series completion. Computational thinking includes these ideas of pattern recognition and extends the idea to problem-solving settings. Pattern recognition in CT could lead to the definition of a generalizable solution (which also has overlaps in maths) that can leverage automation in computing for dealing with a generic situation, for example any *Step n* of a series no matter how large *n* gets. Recognizing a repeating pattern also informs how to incorporate iteration or recursion in an algorithmic solution or a functional breakdown of a problem (that also serves the cause of creating manageable and modular solutions). CT also leverages pattern recognition by examining what parts of a problem are similar to something one has already solved (or programmed) before. This is the bedrock of the powerful idea of design patterns or programming paradigms in software development.

In addition to these basic ideas of pattern recognition, computer scientists have advanced more formal use and understandings of the idea of pattern recognition in topics such as machine learning and artificial intelligence that focus on recognizing patterns in data. Pattern recognition is used in computer vision algorithms for recognizing images and faces (recall how Facebook is able to automatically 'recognize' and tag a face?) or for recommending products on Amazon, your next article on a news site or your next song using iTunes 'Genius'.

Abstraction and generalization

There is broad consensus that abstraction is the keystone of computer science (and consequently, computational thinking). Abstraction, however, is a general property of symbolic systems that has been leveraged in arithmetic, algebra and other mathematical sub-domains for centuries.

Jeanette Wing refers to abstraction as the most important and high-level thought process in CT. It is related to several elements of CT described above. Simply put, abstraction is 'information hiding'. The act of 'black-box'-ing details allows one to focus only on the input and output. In this sense, then, abstraction provides a way of simplifying and managing complexity. It is also the ability to generalize based on similarities and differences. CT involves knowing the right types of abstractions to create and use in a computation solution.

K-12 education should strive to provide children with a sense of how computers and programming languages are also abstractions. Though the computer is a complex, physical machine made up of circuits and wires, as users of computers we interact with it through sophisticated operating systems and applications. Even computer application software developers don't need to think in terms of the physical circuitry. Programming languages used by software developers represent an abstraction of the computer that understands the constructs and keywords used in that language. These higher-level languages hide the complexity of performing operations in the more primitive instructions that are used in lower-level programming languages and ultimately the lowest level 'machine language'. A developer or engineer at any stage typically needs to know only how to interact with one level below and what is to be seen by the next higher level. Every algorithm is also an abstraction as is every model or simulation that represents some real-world phenomenon. Every procedure defined within a program that stands for a set of instructions is also an abstraction. Data, stored in variables and data structures in programs, is the abstract 'stuff' procedures or programs act on and manipulate. They are abstract because they encapsulate and hide the details of the physical things they represent. In this important respect, computer programs are akin to more familiar algebraic equations, which also hide the details of the physical things represented in algebra equations by their variables and values.

Abstraction, admittedly, is among the more abstract ideas to teach and assess as part of a CS/CT curriculum. It is *so* pervasive, however, that it pops up nearly everywhere. As Wing puts it:

> Abstraction is used in defining patterns, generalizing from specific instances, and parameterization. It is used to let one object stand for many. It is used to capture essential properties common to a set of objects while hiding irrelevant distinctions among them. For example, an algorithm is an abstraction of a process that takes inputs, executes a sequence of steps, and produces outputs to satisfy a desired goal. An abstract data type defines an abstract set of values and operations for manipulating those values, hiding the actual representation of the values from the user of the abstract data type. Designing efficient algorithms inherently involves designing abstract data types.
>
> Wing, 2014

Evaluation

Evaluation goes hand-in-hand with several of the elements of CT described above. Solutions to problems in the form of algorithms or abstractions in the form of programs, models or simulations must be evaluated for correctness and appropriateness based on the goal as well as constraints. While it involves analysis and analytical thinking, the idea of evaluation is grander. Solutions to problems are *evaluated* for accuracy and correctness with respect to the desired result or goal. There are often other grounds for evaluation. Think of the algorithm that provides directions. It could be evaluated based on any of several criteria – shortest, fastest, most scenic or other constraint such as: *Does it take you past a grocery store or gas station where you may need to make a stop?* Computer scientists dealing with complex problems and algorithms often evaluate their solutions based on efficiency constraints such as time to completion, resource usage and human factors or user experience considerations.

Automation

'Computing is the automation of our abstractions' (Wing, 2008, p. 3718). A key part of computational thinking, for computer science as well as computing in other domains, is working towards a solution that will be executed by a machine. Automation as a rationale to address a need that cannot be solved otherwise is often the motivation for using CT for problem solving in the real world. In such instances, recognizing when automation is needed and what abstractions and data representations will best help develop an automated solution is a key part of CT.

At the K-12 level, even though the end goal of applying CT is not always a computational solution implemented on a machine, it is important for learners to develop an understanding of when automation is the answer to the problem – what aspects of problems are better solved by humans and which are better solved by the machines.

3.5 CT practices

The CT practices described below outline *approaches* that computer scientists often use when they engage in computational problem solving.

Problem decomposition

This approach is not unique to computer scientists. It is suggested in Polya's (1957) seminal work on problem solving in the context of mathematics. Such a method for problem solving was enumerated as one of the rules for right thinking by Rene Descartes (1637) in his Discourse on Method: 'divide each of the difficulties under examination into as many parts as possible, and as might be necessary for its adequate solution'. It is, however, a key approach in computational problem solving. Breaking a problem down into smaller sub-problems makes the problem more tractable and the problem-solving process more manageable. Examples abound in everyday life. Getting ready for school or work usually involves getting cleaned up, getting dressed, having breakfast, packing lunch or a snack, and ensuring you have the right contents in your bag as you leave. Each of these sub-tasks contains its own set of actions, is independent of the other and often happens in the same sequence every day. Going back to the algorithmic process of cooking and the recipe as an algorithm, one can easily see problem decomposition at play when the recipe separates the pre-preparation process of marinating or getting the ingredients together, from preparing some portion of the dish (e.g. the dressing or gravy) and the preparation of the main dish and *then* combining it with some post-processing steps (cooling, garnishing and such) to get the dish ready for serving.

In the context of programming, the task of breaking down a problem often leads to pieces of code being written separately. These component parts of the program need to 'come together' when the whole solution is composed. This process is simple when the different sub-problems are independent of each other. Take, for example, the task of calculating the average score of an exam. The first sub-problem could involve asking for user input and creating a list or array of scores; the second could address traversing the list and adding up all the scores in some aggregator variable; and the final step could simply involve calculating the average by dividing the total of all scores by the number of student scores (after appropriately performing a divide-by-0 check!).

But the process of composing a solution or 'plan composition' is not always as straightforward for novice programmers when the sub-problems are intertwined or connected in some way. This was famously demonstrated by Elliot Soloway's 'Rainfall problem' (Soloway et al., 1983) where students were tasked with the following problem: 'Write a program that repeatedly reads in positive integers, until it reads the integer 99999. After seeing 99999, it should print out the average.' Here, the tasks of reading an input value, checking the input for the sentinel value and whether it is negative are intertwined with aggregating the values. This problem has repeatedly been shown to trip up novice programmers.

This example suggests that computational thinking requires not only the skill to decompose a problem but also to compose the solution after the sub-problems have been addressed.

Creating computational artefacts

Wing's definition suggests that the goal of computational thinking is to solve problems that can be executed by humans or computational devices. While several examples of computational thinking described above are situated in the real world and do not involve a computer, creating solutions to be executed by a computer is often a natural end goal of computational thinking and problem solving. Sometimes, the computational artefact is merely a simulation or model or interactive prototype of something that will eventually be a physical artefact; at other times the computational artefact is itself the end goal – a game or story or artefact of creativity and personal expression or software that could be used by others.

Programming is therefore seen as an especially useful platform for teaching CT since it brings together several of the elements – both concepts and practices – that are central to CT. In Grover and Pea (2013), we asserted, 'Programming is not only a fundamental skill of CS and a key tool for supporting the cognitive tasks involved in CT but a demonstration of computational competencies as well.'

Even so, it is important to observe that CT involves problem solving and thinking competencies that can be invoked in settings outside of programming. Programming, although important, cool, interesting and fun, is but one of the possible vehicles for developing CT competencies. The current rush to focus on coding often attracts attention towards the features of the programming environment and away from the important aspects of computational thinking that must be involved. Often these 'low-floor' programming environments allow for tinkering without the mindfulness and meta-cognition called for by deeper learning. This is akin to learning the syntax of *a specific programming* language (what the constructs mean and accomplish) without a deeper appreciation for the deeper CT concepts and practices that equip learners with the competencies to be used in *any programming* context, whatever its specific features.

Testing and debugging

Testing and debugging are integral to any kind of problem solving (Miller, Galanter and Pribram, 1960). Evaluating one's solution for accuracy, detecting flaws in a faulty solution and fixing them, is part and parcel of any problem-solving process, such as hammering in a nail to be flush with the surface of the wood. We're all constantly 'debugging' all kinds of problems at hand, from tasting the amount of salt and spice in a dish (some problems are harder to fix even if you've identified the bug!) to proofreading our essays and e-mails to fix typos and grammar errors.

Like other CT concepts and practices, testing and debugging are related to many of the other elements described here. They are part of the process of evaluating a computational solution – whether it satisfies relevant rules and assumptions, whether the solution works for boundary conditions and all relevant inputs and situations, and whether it acts as expected for illogical or erroneous inputs. This also involves logical and 'if-then' analytical thinking to isolate the problem and zero in on the error. It is also integral to the incremental development and problem decomposition strategies described above.

Rigorous, systematic testing and debugging is an art and science in computing, and especially in software development. Developing test cases and taking the software through its paces is a significant part of the software development process, and it is a process that itself can become automated. In the context of programming, systematic testing the solution for correctness for the range of valid and invalid inputs is an integral competency in learning to program. It is worth noting that, despite the surface similarity with the scientific process, testing and debugging is far more pronounced in CT than, say, scientific thinking where one is evaluating the results and evidence from an experiment and revising the hypothesis as necessary.

Incremental development (or iterative refinement)

This is a very common strategy used in the context of programming. Though similar to the process of problem decomposition, it focuses not so much on the idea of decomposing the problem into sub-problems, as it does on 'growing the solution or program' iteratively with frequent testing and debugging in between to develop improvements. This is contrasted with – and preferable to – writing large chunks of code that make it difficult to isolate the bug(s) if the solution does not work as intended. The most frequently used avatar of this approach in professional software development circles goes by the moniker 'agile development' (Martin, 2003).

Consider a simple example from robotics. Imagine a roving bot that needs to turn around when it hits an obstacle. The student could first simply code and test the movement – have the robot go forward in a straight line. Then s/he adds the obstacle collision test by making the motors stop when the touch sensor indicates a collision. Once this is tested and found to be working, the student would then add the reverse-and-turn-upon-collision code instead of simply stopping. This kind of incremental growth of the solution can be contrasted to coding all the pieces all at once and then testing. Imagine how unmanageable it can all become if the problem is more complex!

Collaboration and creativity

A couple of other elements, though not considered part of CT in earlier definitions of CT, are often described as common practices in computational problem solving. These include collaboration and creativity. Both are acknowledged as critical competencies for a new century, but they do also have a special meaning as CT practices and in the world of computer science. Collaboration is often fostered in K-12 computing classrooms through 'pair programming' (Williams and Kesseler, 2002) a practice that is increasingly popular in industry. The norms of collaboration in pair programming require programmers to alternate between taking the lead on typing or reviewing code and have been shown to be beneficial to problem-solving processes. There are other forms of collaboration that are unique to CS. The division of development tasks in software engineering is necessitated by CT practices such as problem decomposition and modularization. Parallel computing has also led to the division of computing tasks and is at the heart of globally important programming paradigms such as MapReduce used for many years at Google. Other interesting forms of collaboration in the world of CS include the use of Github to build on one another's work in projects, crowdsourcing computer games to advance a scientific agenda (as in FoldIt and Xylem) and collaborative software development as part of the free and open source movement that led to the creation of Linux and other systems.

Creativity as a CT practice acts on two levels – it aims to encourage out-of-the-box thinking and alternative approaches to solving problems; and it aims to encourage the creation of computational artefacts as a form of creative expression. Block-based 'open-ended' introductory programming environments such as Scratch, Alice and App Inventor have been developed with the goal of teaching creative coding and motivating learners as a conduit for teaching CT, especially in K-12 settings.

Fostering CT in the classroom and CT across subjects

Key concept: Programming and CT

Is programming the only way to foster CT? The answer to that question is a resounding 'No!' While we have many articles and discussions about the relationship between programming and computational thinking, there is little debate that computational thinking is about more than codifying a solution for execution by a computer through programming and that it is the loftier, more worthy goal of CT that we must strive to achieve through appropriate pedagogies even when students are engaging in programming. In fact, some believe that the typical design challenges and design tools of modern computing involve little coding (Tedre and Denning, 2016). At the same time, few would challenge the proclamation that programming is an important – and engaging – vehicle for learning and applying (and hence teaching and assessing) CT. Few other activities involve as many concepts and practices of CT as does programming.

Nonetheless, it is abundantly clear from the description of CT concepts and practices that there *are* other ways of fostering CT. Analytical and logical thinking can be fostered through puzzles and word problems that require learners to engage in this crucial aspect of CT.

Problems involving such logical argumentation and thinking can be tackled in language arts, mathematics classrooms or CS classrooms.

Example activity: Logical thinking in the language arts classroom

Here is a simple problem involving logical thinking described in Grover (2009) an early ISTE article on CT ideas for teachers –

- If the Giants beat the Dodgers, then the Giants win the pennant.
- If PlayerX is out, then the Giants beat the Dodgers.
- PlayerX is out.

What is the conclusion?

Example activity: Logical thinking in the maths classroom

In a game, exactly six inverted cups stand side-by-side in a straight line. Each has exactly one ball hidden under it. The cups are numbered consecutively 1 to 6. Each of the balls is painted a single solid colour. The colours of the balls are green, magenta, orange, purple, red and yellow. The balls have been hidden under the cups in a manner that conforms to the following conditions:

The purple ball must be hidden under a lower-numbered cup than the orange ball.

The red ball must be hidden under a cup immediately adjacent to the cup under which the magenta ball is hidden.

The green ball must be hidden under cup 5.

Which of the following could be the colours of the balls under the cups, in order from 1 to 6?

(A) Green, yellow, magenta, red, purple, orange
(B) Magenta, green, purple, red, orange, yellow
(C) Magenta, red, purple, yellow, green, orange
(D) Orange, yellow, red, magenta, green, purple
(E) Red, purple, magenta, yellow, green, orange.

Currently, computational and algorithmic thinking problems such as these are found mostly in competitions such the Enigma Computational and Algorithmic Thinking contest run by Edfinity along with the Australian Math Trust[3] and Bebras,[4] but there is no doubt that students would be well-served by tackling such non-programming puzzles and problems as part of CT competency building.

There are several ways of encouraging algorithmic thinking practices in learners that involve articulating precise step-by-step procedures – storyboards, an ordered set of sentences, pseudo-code, flowcharts and the like. Even in the context of programming, expressing an algorithm in such ways *before* coding it into a programming language to be executed by a computer, is a well-established and recommended practice. One fun exercise used in the context of robotics involves writing a set of detailed steps in plain English to verbally guide a blindfolded student partner to perform a certain task. Ideas of exception handling, iterations and conditional actions could be woven into this fun exercise.

To learners, practicing these computational thinking concepts and approaches in contexts outside programming signals the importance of the CT and problem-solving process rather than simply codifying the solution in the syntax of a programming language. Grover, Pea and Cooper (2015) describe an example of a curriculum focusing on deeper, transferable learning of algorithmic thinking skills using a pedagogy that incorporates various pedagogical ideas from the learning sciences, in addition to assessments that cover cognitive as well as affective dimensions of deeper learning.

3.6 CT within and across subjects

It is reasonable to argue that it is in all the contexts outside of CS classrooms that CT truly shines with its generativity. From music, maths, social studies, history, language arts and throughout the sciences and engineering, curricular ideas can come alive with CT. Just as in disciplinary research in each of these fields, where computational thinking advances both everyday practice and its innovations, there is a role for creativity in curriculum design and teaching of other subjects through the integration of CT in those classrooms, while also providing rich and varied contexts for developing CT competencies.

---

[3] See https://edfinity.com/competitions
[4] See www.bebraschallenge.org/

Key concept

Computing and STEM share a deeply symbiotic relationship, and as such, mathematics and science classrooms provide perhaps the most intuitive and easy non-CS contexts for CT learning and use. The use of computational tools to enable deeper STEM learning has been shown in numerous prior research studies, and the reverse has also been shown to be true. STEM can enrich computational learning while also providing valuable opportunities to embed CT in established and accessible (as well as required) STEM courses. This latter point is especially relevant as many states and countries worldwide still struggle with providing adequate computing experiences to all students as part of K-12 education. Based on successful investigations in prior research, computational modelling and simulation are concrete mechanisms for integrating computing and STEM, and can benefit the learning of both the STEM content as well as the development of CT skills in such an emphasis (e.g. Honey and Hilton, 2011).

CT through STEM can also address the issue of teacher shortages, as preparing STEM teachers to use CT within the context of the disciplinary content areas with which they are familiar already may be more practical and amenable to scaling implementation of CT in school education.

Bringing CT into STEM classrooms will also better prepare students for the modern landscape of the STEM disciplines. This view is endorsed by the Next Generation Science Standards, calling for the use of mathematics and CT in science. We can call this the 'CT-in-STEM-Learning' research agenda, and it would need to seek answers to several key questions, including, 'What CT competencies are most important for various STEM disciplines?', 'How can learners best develop these competencies through their learning experiences with STEM coursework curricular units?' and 'How can we collaborate with STEM teachers towards their effective appropriation and uses of computational thinking methods and approaches in their curriculum?' Efforts to bridge CT and STEM in K-12 science, have centred mostly on building computational models and simulations to understand and study phenomena in science (e.g. Hansen et al., 2015; Sengupta et al., 2013; Sherin, 2001; Wilensky, Brady and Horn, 2014) and have shown much promise. These efforts can also be informed by substantial work from the mathematics education research community in their curricular studies of the functional mathematical thinking involved in real-world problem-solving processes and mathematical modelling by students and teachers (e.g. Burkhardt, 2006; Lesh and Lehrer, 2003; Lesh and Zawojewski, 2007). Growing the knowledge base on how best to effect the integration of CT and STEM has been called out as one of the imperatives for computing education research (Cooper et al., 2014).

The role of CT in non-STEM subjects such as music, social sciences, visual arts, language arts, history, is manifold. Barr and Stephenson (2011) and Barr, Harrison and Conery (2011) outline examples of what this integration might look like, as does Google's Exploring Computational Thinking. Examples of documented efforts for meaningfully integrating CT and non-STEM subjects can be seen in Repenning, Webb and Ioannidou (2010), Settle et al. (2012), and Wolz et al. (2010), among others.

Fablabs, making and computational crafts also open a whole world of possibilities of CT development in the context of art and craft that involves creating tangible computational artefacts. Michael Eisenberg's Craft Tech lab[5] and Leah Buechley's [6] innovative tool designs including the Lilypad Arduino[7] for e-textiles and 'sketch' electronics using microcontrollers and conductive ink have been found to reach audiences beyond those that robotics clubs and competitions typically attract.

3.7 Summary

In a world infused with computing, computational thinking is now being recognized as a foundational competency for being an informed citizen and being successful in all STEM work, and one that also bears the potential as a means for creative problem solving and innovating in all other disciplines. The roots of CT in education date back to Papert's work in the 1980s that centred on children developing thinking skills through programming computers. Recent efforts on bringing CT to school education, while still inspired by that early work, is informed by Wing's 2006 definition and call to action. Definitions and elements of CT have been broadened in this last decade to include aspects of collaboration and creativity.

Computational thinking is defined as the set of the thinking skills used by computer scientists to address a broad range of problems in computing and other domains. Learning CT, much like learning scientific and mathematical thinking, is more about developing a set of problem-solving heuristics, approaches and 'habits of mind' than simply learning how to use a programming tool to create computational artefacts. That said, programming is a key vehicle for teaching, learning, expressing and assessing CT that is unarguably also deeply engaging for students in K-12 classrooms.

Much like recent movements in science and maths that have adopted a practices-view to STEM learning, the key elements of CT are broken down into concepts and practices. CT concepts are commonly believed to include logic and logical thinking; algorithms and algorithmic thinking; patterns and pattern recognition; abstraction and generalization, evaluation and automation; whereas CT practices include problem decomposition, creating computational artefacts, testing and debugging, iterative refinement (or incremental development). Collaboration and creativity, now seen as cross-cutting skills for the twenty-first-century learner, are also viewed as CT practices that often acquire a unique flavour in the context of CT.

It is reasonable to argue that it is in contexts outside of CS classrooms that CT truly shines with its generativity. As Denning (2017a) points out, CT emerged from within the scientific fields – it was not imported from computer science. Computing and STEM share a deeply symbiotic relationship, and as such, mathematics, science and engineering classrooms provide perhaps the most intuitive contexts for CT learning and use. Computational modelling and simulation are

---

[5] See http://l3d.cs.colorado.edu/~ctg/Craft_Tech.html
[6] See http://leahbuechley.com
[7] See www.arduino.cc/en/Main/arduinoBoardLilyPad

concrete mechanisms for integrating computing and STEM, and can benefit the learning of both the STEM content as well as the development of CT skills in such an emphasis (e.g. Honey & Hilton, 2011). The role of CT in non-STEM subjects such as music, social sciences, visual arts, language arts and history, is promising but as yet underdeveloped.

The thoughts and ideas reflected in this chapter present the current dominant framing of CT in the K-12 school education context. We adopt the disciplinary view of thinking lens that is driving new ways of teaching and learning across all subjects. However, it is by no means the last word on this evolving topic in education and fertile field of inquiry in education research.

Key points

- Computational Thinking (CT) is a key twenty-first century skill that helps students both to understand and take advantage of computing in various domains.
- Learning CT is about learning to think like a computer scientist – developing a specific set of problem-solving skills that can be applied in any domain to creating solutions that can be executed by a 'computer' (machine or human).
- Elements of CT include concepts such as logic, algorithms, abstraction, pattern recognition, evaluation and automation. It also includes practices such as problem decomposition, creating computational artefacts (usually through programming), testing and debugging, and iterative refinement. Collaboration and creativity are broader twenty-first century competencies that take on a special flavour in the context of CT.
- Although programming is a key vehicle to teach and learn CT, it can be taught in the classroom with or without a computer or programming.
- Bringing CT into STEM classrooms will also better prepare students for the modern landscape of the STEM disciplines; computational modelling and creating simulations are concrete mechanisms for integrating computing and STEM.
- The role of CT in non-STEM subjects such as music, social sciences, visual arts, language arts and history, is promising but still underdeveloped.

Further reflection

- Critics of the current movement to introduce CT warn against falling into the trap of assuming that CT will help learners build thinking skills that can be transferred to other domains. Both, the critics as well as the those who make the claim against and in support of transfer, ignore something we learning scientists know well. *Transfer of learning across contexts does not happen automatically.*

Pea's own research in the 1980s showed that students who were programming in LOGO did not automatically do well in problem-solving situations in maths or in planning route scheduling. The learning sciences advocate that transfer needs to be mediated through empirically established techniques that call for, among others things, making explicit connections between the original and transfer learning contexts. For example, in past work our classroom intervention included explicit mechanisms to mediate for, and assessing transfer from block-based to text based programming (Grover, Pea and Cooper, 2014).

- Denning (2017a, 2017b) urges the CS/CT movement in K-12 education not to lose sight of the fact that CT emerged from within the scientific fields – it was not imported from computer science. Indeed, computer scientists were slow to join the movement. He goes on to argue that to use CT productively in science domains one also needs the ability to design computations. *Computational design* is a better term to design the skill set than computational thinking. This view closely aligns CT to the domain of computational science. Does CT have much of a role besides computational science? We tend to believe so, however it is hard to ignore that evidence for good examples outside science are less abundant.

- Lastly, there are some who believe that CT, if broken down into elements as described and taught through unplugged or non-programming means, will be reduced to learning thinking skills that will not necessarily translate into the abilities necessary to create computational solutions and apply CT, in various domains as per the promise. In order to learn and apply CT, students need to be working with abstractions and thinking about general solutions along with other concepts such as patterns, logical and algorithmic thinking. Writing a cooking recipe alone, although an example of algorithmic thinking is not going to translate into providing learners the ability to develop computational solutions at the level of rigour that K-12 educators of CT and CS aim for their students.

References

Barr, V and C Stephenson (2011). 'Bringing Computational Thinking to K-12: What is Involved and what is the Role of the Computer Science Education Community?' 2(1) *ACM Inroads* 48–54.

Barr, D, J Harrison and L Conery (2011). 'Computational Thinking: A Digital Age Skill for Everyone' 38(6) *Learning & Leading with Technology* 20–23.

Burkhardt, H (2006). 'Modelling in Mathematics Classrooms' 38(2) *Zentralblatt für Didaktik der Mathematik* 178–195.

Cooper, S, S Grover, M Guzdial and B Simon (2014). 'A Future for Computing Education Research' 57(11) *Communications of the ACM* 34–36.

Denning, PJ (2017a). 'Remaining Trouble Spots with Computational Thinking' 60(6) *Communications of the ACM* 33–39.

Denning, PJ (2017b). 'Computational Thinking in Science' 105(1) *American Scientist* 13.

Descartes, R (2006). *A Discourse on Method: 1637*. Pomona Books.

Grover, S (2009). 'Computer Science: Not Just For Big Kids' 37(3) *Learning and Leading with Technology* 27–29. International Society for Technology in Education.

Grover, S (2017). 'Assessing Algorithmic and Computational Thinking in K-12: Lessons from a Middle School Classroom' in P Rich and CB Hodges (eds), *Emerging Research, Practice, and Policy on Computational Thinking* (Boston, Springer International Publishing) 269–288.

Grover, S and S Basu. (2017). 'Measuring Student Learning in Introductory Block-Based Programming: Examining Misconceptions of Loops, Variables, and Boolean Logic' in *Proceedings of the 48th ACM Technical Symposium on Computer Science Education (SIGCSE '17)* Seattle, WA. ACM.

Grover, S and RD Pea (2013). 'Computational Thinking in K-12: A Review of the State of the Field' 42(1) *Educational Researcher* 38–43.

Grover, S, R Pea and S Cooper (2014). 'Expansive Framing and Preparation for Future Learning in Middle-School Computer Science' in *Proceedings of the 11th International Conference of the Learning Sciences*, Boulder, Colorado. ACM.

Grover, S, R Pea and S Cooper (2015). 'Designing for Deeper Learning in a Blended Computer Science Course for Middle School Students' 25(2) *Computer Science Education* 199–237.

Hansen, AK, A Iveland, H Dwyer, DB Harlow and D Franklin (2015). 'Programming Science Digital Stories: Computer Science and Engineering Design in the Science Classroom' 53(3) *Science and Children* 60–64.

Honey, MA and M Hilton (eds), (2011). *Learning Science through Computer Games and Simulations* (Washington DC, National Academies Press).

Lesh, R and R Lehrer (2003). 'Models and Modeling Perspectives on the Development of Students and Teachers' 5(2–3) *Mathematical Thinking and Learning* 109–129.

Lesh, R and J Zawojewski (2007). 'Problem Solving and Modeling' in FK Lester Jr (ed), *Second Handbook of Research on Mathematics Teaching and Learning* (Charlotte NC, Information Age Publishing) 763–804.

Martin, RC (2003). *Agile Software Development: Principles, Patterns, and Practices* (Harlow, Pearson).

Miller, G, E Galanter and K Pribram (1960). *Plans and the Structure of Behavior* (New York, Holt, Rinehart and Winston).

National Research Council (2013). Next generation science standards: For states, by states. Washington, DC: National Academy Press.

Pellegrino, JW and ML Hilton (eds), (2013). *Education for Life and Work: Developing Transferable Knowledge and Skills in the 21st century* (Washington DC, National Academies Press).

Papert, S (1980). *Mindstorms: Children, Computers, and Powerful Ideas.* (New York, NY, Basic Books).

Polya, G. (1957). *How to Solve It: A New Aspect of Mathematical Method* 2nd edn (Garden City, NJ, Doubleday).

Repenning, A, D Webb and A Ioannidou (2010). 'Scalable Game Design and the Development of a Checklist for Getting Computational Thinking into Public Schools'. In *Proceedings of the 41st ACM Technical Symposium on Computer Science Education* 265–269. ACM.

Sengupta, P, JS Kinnebrew, S Basu, G Biswas and D Clark (2013). 'Integrating Computational Thinking with K-12 Science Education using Agent-based Computation: A Theoretical Framework' 18(2) *Education and Information Technologies* 351–380.

Sherin, BL (2001). 'How Students Understand Physics Equations' 19(4) *Cognition and Instruction* 479–541.

Smith, M (2016). *Computer Science for All*. Online blog post. Available at: www.whitehouse.gov/blog/2016/01/30/computer-science-all

Soloway, E, J Bonar and K Ehrlich (1983). 'Cognitive Strategies and Looping Constructs: An Empirical Study' 26(11) *Communications of the ACM* 853–860.

Tedre, M and PJ Denning (2016). 'The Long Quest for Computational Thinking' in Proceedings of the 16th *Koli Calling* Conference on Computing Education Research, 24–27 November 2016, Finland, 120–129. ACM.

Wilensky, U, CE Brady and MS Horn (2014). 'Fostering Computational Literacy in Science Classrooms' 57(8) *Communications of the ACM* 24–28.

Williams, L and R Kessler (2002). *Pair Programming Illuminated* (Harlow, Addison-Wesley).

Wing, J (2014). 'Computational Thinking Benefits Society'. *Social Issues in Computing.* Available at: http://socialissues.cs.toronto.edu/2014/01/computational-thinking/

Wing, JM (2006). 'Computational Thinking' 49(3) *Communications of the ACM* 33–35.

Wing, JM (2008). Computational thinking and thinking about computing. Philosophical transactions of the royal society of London A: mathematical, physical and engineering sciences, 366(1881), 3717–3725.

Wolz, U, M Stone, SM Pulimood and K Pearson (2010). 'Computational Thinking via Interactive Journalism in Middle School' in *Proceedings of the 41st ACM Technical Symposium on Computer Science Education* 239–243. ACM.

Yasmeh, J. (2016). 'Is The FBI Lying About Reading 650,000 Emails In 8 Days?' Available at: www.dailywire.com/news/10561/fbi-lying-about-reading–650000-emails–8-days-joshua-yasmeh

4

Investigating Attitudes Towards Learning Computer Science

Quintin Cutts and Peter Donaldson

Chapter outline

Chapter synopsis

This chapter explores the attitudes of computer science learners towards learning, as well as those of their teachers and how teaching practices may affect these attitudes. The exploration is set in the context of Carol Dweck's *Mindset*, a concept with which many readers will be familiar or will have at least read about (Dweck, 2008). Mindset concerns how learners' beliefs about their ability to learn directly affect their learning outcomes, and Mindset-based interventions have been successfully applied in computing contexts, for example in our own study (Cutts et al., 2010). However, Mindset has subtle consequences for teachers, which are often lost. For, as we shall show, teachers' own Mindsets and the practices they adopt are instrumental in the formation of their learners' Mindsets. Teachers must explore their own attitudes and practices carefully and examine why their students may be getting blocked in their studies. As we move from being an optional or self-selected subject at late secondary or tertiary education to a mainstream school subject starting in primary level and taken *by all*, this exploration is ever more important if we are to expect success for our learners. An exercise is provided in the chapter to help the exploration, which tends to lead to a re-evaluation of our underlying understanding of how learning and skill development work, encouraging us to raise important questions about our own practices.

4.1 Introduction to Mindset

Carol Dweck's thirty-year research programme broadly captured under the title 'Mindset', aims to foster more appropriate attitudes and practices among learners and teachers so that learning outcomes can be improved. It centres not on the identification of some natural ability as the predictor of learning success, but instead on the learner's attitude to whether they *think* they can get better. In summary, those who do believe they can improve have a so-called *growth* Mindset, whereas those who think ability levels are traits one is born with have a *fixed* Mindset.

It is important to note that Dweck is not disputing the observation that some people find some types of activities or learning easier than others. What she disputes is that others can't learn (Dweck, 2008):

> Just because some people can do something with little or no training, doesn't mean that others can't do it (and sometimes do it better), with training. This is so important, because many, many people with the fixed mindset think that someone's early performance tells you all you need to know about their talent and their future.

Some key aspects deriving from the Mindset work are as follows:

- A person's Mindset can vary depending on which skill or ability is considered. In everyday life, we hear this all the time, for example: *'Oh I just can't do maths at all!'* or *'I haven't got an ear for music'*. The people who uttered this aren't saying they believe they can't do *anything* at all, just not maths or music. In our discipline, Scott and Ghinea (2014) provide evidence that students' Mindsets relating to computer science ability are distinct from general views about intelligence.
- Mindset can be measured and is malleable. Although the word might imply something *set* and unchangeable, Mindset is, in fact, highly malleable. Experiences that learners go through can influence their Mindset towards certain fields of study. For example, how many blame their inability in, say, maths, on a particular teacher? The experience of learning created by that teacher has encouraged the learner to believe they can't do maths. Conversely, numerous experiments have now shown that simple interventions can switch learners from a fixed to a growth Mindset (Mueller and Dweck, 1998).
- Educationally, *performance* and *mastery* goals are associated with fixed and growth Mindsets (Dweck and Legget, 1988). Fixed Mindset learners tend to value performance (i.e. some

measure the outcome of a learning exercise, whereas those with a growth Mindset value gaining mastery of the subject matter). In computing, for example, a performance measure may be a running program as the outcome of a programming exercise – for a fixed Mindset learner, as long as the program is working, all is good; a more mastery-orientated valuation of the exercise would be that the learner fully understands how the program works or that they had learned enough from the exercise that they could solve a related problem. Zingaro and Porter (2016) showed that mastery goals evidenced in computer science students were a predictor of continued interest and success in the subject.

- Directly related to the performance and mastery goals, learners with different Mindsets adopt different *responses to feedback*. Growth Mindset learners are likely to largely ignore a mark on a piece of work (a performance measure) and concentrate on feedback that will help them to improve next time. They understand this as a fundamental learning cycle – learn about something, try it out, receive feedback on how to do better next time, try again. By comparison, studies show that fixed Mindsetters focus only on the mark and do not cognitively engage with formative feedback that could help them improve; instead they are stuck in the emotional centres of the brain (Mangels et al., 2006). In the face of failure to achieve a goal, which is in itself a kind of feedback, those with a growth Mindset will try again using one of a number of alternative strategies to reach their goal; fixed Mindsetters tend to either give up or hopelessly retry using the same strategy over and over. Dempsey, Snodgrass, Kishi, and Titcomb (2015) demonstrated that improving students' self-efficacy is an important goal for success in computer science; having multiple strategies in the face of difficulty will clearly enhance self-efficacy.

Summarising, a growth Mindset learner is able to continue learning even in the face of difficulties and challenges whereas a fixed Mindset learner may do okay while they are succeeding, but their attitudes and strategies can prevent them from progressing when the going gets tough.

Key concept: Mindset

Our *Mindset* or our attitude towards whether we can learn something is at least as important as any natural ability we may have. We can have different Mindsets towards different subjects to be learned. Our Mindset towards learning a subject can change from growth to fixed and vice-versa. A growth Mindset person has the learning goal to master a subject; a fixed Mindset person will attempt to perform well only. Growth Mindset learners make use of feedback; fixed Mindset learners favour a rating or mark, ignoring formative feedback.

The early advice and experiments around Mindset encouraged a focus on the *messages* that learners were receiving. Most prevalent was the notion that praising young children for their *achievements* is harmful for their intrinsic motivation to learn. The message received is that achieving is highly valued by teachers and parents, so a major motivation picked up by the learner is not to be seen to fail and so they avoid taking on harder tasks.

4.2 Should Mindset concern only the learners?

Much of the Mindset work appears to focus principally on the learner. In the description of Mindset in the previous section, it is the learners' beliefs that influence their ability to succeed; it is the learners' response to feedback that will keep them stuck or enable them to progress; it is the learners' willingness to try a new strategy in the face of failure that will ultimately get them to the goal. In studies, the learners' Mindsets are measured and interventions are designed to directly influence the learners' beliefs, via, for example, the messages mentioned above.

In computer science Mindset studies, the focus has also been on the learners. In Simon et al. (2008), students took part in a so-called 'saying is believing' intervention, in line with earlier successful studies (Aronson, Fried and Good, 2002): having learned about Mindset in a short lecture segment, the students wrote about applying Mindset ideas in the context of solving difficult problems. This intervention was relatively separate from their actual computer science work and ultimately, changes in their computer science Mindset were not significant. If anything, they became more fixed as they went through the course, a result also found by Scott and Ghinea (2014). In our own study (Cutts et al., 2010), more intensive Mindset training did produce significant changes, but again, the focus of the training was the learners.

Should the focus be broader? A simple model of a learning context includes learner, teacher and the instructional design adopted by the teacher. Both learner and teacher have Mindsets towards the ability to learn computer science. The teacher, with whatever Mindset he or she holds, creates the instructional design experienced by the learner. Some questions come to mind:

- What is the influence of *teachers'* Mindsets on the learning of those in their care?
- Does influencing the learners' Mindsets directly, via some form of instruction about Mindset concepts, lead to increased learning? What is the influence of the instructional design itself on the learners' Mindsets and consequently their learning?

4.3 Considering teachers' Mindsets

We will address the second issue raised above later in the chapter. On the first question, studies of managers were the first to show that the Mindset of those in a mentoring/training role was related to their actions towards their charges (Heslin, Vanderwalle and Latham, 2006). Where the manager had a growth Mindset, he or she was more likely to coach an employee in difficulty and was able to come up with more suggestions for going forward. This makes absolute sense: if we believe that a person can improve, then it is a logical decision to put effort in to help them make that improvement; if, however, we believe that a person's difficulties with a task demonstrate their fixed level of competence, then there is no point in attempting any intervention to help them.

Similar effects have been observed in studies of teachers. For example, in Schmidt, Shumow and Kackar-Cam (2015), the students had better outcomes when their teacher placed emphasis on growth Mindset concepts such as mastery learning and multiple learning strategies, compared to a teacher who did not. Leroy et al. (2007) studied 336 fifth-grade teachers and found that those with a more fixed Mindset created learning environments in their classrooms that were less likely to promote intrinsic motivation in their pupils.

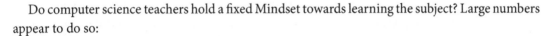

Key concept: Teachers' Mindset

The Mindset that teachers and managers hold towards learning can affect the Mindset of those in their charge, because it will influence every aspect of their learning design. For example, if a teacher believes that being able to program is an innate ability, then they may give a struggling learner too much help, believing they won't cope otherwise – yet this is counter-productive to learning because the learner picks up the idea that they can't do this on their own – fixed Mindset. Alternatively, the teacher may not provide a genuine developmental pathway to success in the subject, because they don't believe it can be learned – it's something someone just has. Learners will get stuck through no fault of their own and develop a fixed Mindset.

Do computer science teachers hold a fixed Mindset towards learning the subject? Large numbers appear to do so:

- Lewis (2007) polled junior and senior students and also academic staff asking them to rate their agreement to the statement 'Nearly everyone is capable of succeeding in the computer science curriculum if they work at it.' Of the staff, 77 per cent disagreed with the statement. In Kinnunen et al.'s (2007) study, the majority of the sixteen CS educators interviewed talked about students on their courses who just 'get it' and about those who never will.

- The fact that there is heated ongoing debate around whether computer science/programming ability is innate or learned speaks to the lack of consensus on this issue. One of this chapter's author's own twenty-year computer science education research career started with this question (Cutts, 2001); Ahadi and Lister (2013) introduce the term 'geek gene', while arguing that innate ability is only part of the picture; Guzdial (2014) argues against the findings by Macnamara, Moreau and Hambrick (2016) that deliberate practice only minimally explains expert performance; Patitsas et al. (2016) demonstrate that bimodal distributions in computer science don't exist and are folk-lore based on instructors' prejudices about innate ability. Most recently, McCartney et al. (2017) have proposed a malleable 'Geekiness Quotient' which balances the concepts of innate ability and acquired skill.

- In our own work with teachers over the years, we have come across those who undoubtedly pigeonhole their pupils into ability levels, demonstrating a fixed Mindset attitude. During the CS Inside project (Cutts et al., 2007) which was an early adopter of the *Unplugged* style of computer science education, teachers often expressed surprise when particular pupils, obviously generally viewed to be low-achieving, made more valuable contributions than their more highly-rated peers during sessions using this alternative pedagogical approach. Surprisingly, most teachers we've encountered tell us that they are aware of Dweck's Mindset work, yet their comments and actions belie a fixed Mindset attitude.

It seems essential that we should be considering *teachers'* Mindsets at least as enthusiastically as those of the *learners*: from the former, directly or indirectly, are created the latter. The takeaway message here is that *we, the teachers, are actually at the heart of the Mindset issue, not the learners.*

4.4 Exploring our own Mindset and practices as teachers

In our experience, it seems easy to hear about the Mindset work but not necessarily fully absorb it. The teachers we refer to above are in this category. Dweck herself, on the basis of numerous studies (e.g. Sun, 2015), identifies the notion of a *false growth* Mindset, where teachers state they have a growth Mindset but aren't acting as though they do (Dweck, 2015). Their teaching practices, considered as a whole, do not embody a deep understanding of the Mindset principle. In Dweck's words (2015), 'the path to a growth mindset is a journey, not a proclamation'.

Having read this far, where do you think you stand? What is your own view of the potential for any learner to develop their computer science ability? This is a fundamentally important question as computer science is globally transformed from its erstwhile position as optional subject taken only by those who chose it in upper secondary or tertiary education into a mandatory part of all pupils' education starting in early primary. Even as an optional subject, when one might sensibly conjecture that those taking it would have some expectation of success, computer science has had a notoriously high failure rate (Watson and Li, 2014). If one holds a view of computer science ability as innate (fixed Mindset), how can one then subject young people everywhere to a computer science education programme, knowing that large numbers must fail?

Key concept

Question: Is our stated expectation of what learners can achieve (i.e. our Mindset or belief about what can be learned and by whom) at odds with our own teaching practices or those we have experienced?

Here is a question to facilitate an exploration of our position. *Is our stated expectation of what learners can achieve* (i.e. our Mindset) *at odds with our own teaching practices, or those we have experienced?* A teacher who believes that computer science ability is innate (fixed Mindset) most likely has adopted, consciously or unconsciously, a set of teaching practices that mirror his or her belief. For example, the programme may move too fast, provide little feedback, offer no opportunity for catching up and so on.

More importantly, however, even if a teacher says that he or she has a growth Mindset attitude towards the learning of computer science, we conjecture that very often the learning and teaching approaches used are still not sufficiently supportive – they are still likely to foster a fixed Mindset attitude in learners.

Do you disagree with our conjecture? Are you outraged that we might suggest this disconnection between growth Mindset belief and fixed Mindset practices? If so, then consider the following exercise, which we have used with large numbers of teachers to shed light on this disconnect.

The exercise starts with a familiar pseudo-code example – making a cup of tea – as is often used as a first example of creating a plan. Don't be side-tracked though: this is nothing to do with program planning and any example algorithm written in plain English would be fine. Take your time answering the questions and don't read ahead! So, the example is:

1 Fill the kettle.
2 Flick the switch on.
3 While the kettle is boiling, get a cup and put a teabag into it.
4 Once boiled, pour water into cup.
5 Wait a few minutes.
6 Remove teabag.
7 Add milk to taste.

The first question we have posed to numerous teachers about this is as follows: *What do you need to know to understand these instructions in plain English as a solution to the task of making a cup of tea?* We do this at a whiteboard, and ask the group to shout out the answers – take a moment yourself now to consider your own answer. You should range right from issues to do with tea making down to elements of syntax.

This takes a while and there's usually a lot on the board by the time we've finished. The following categories at least usually emerge from the discussion:

• Appreciating the gross structure of a set of steps within the body of text.
• Being able to parse sentences, seeing the structure, picking out verbs as actions or operations, nouns as things and all the necessary grammatical connecting tissue.
• A hierarchy of concepts, from those specific to this problem to more general concepts – from tea-making specifically, such as what teabags are, the steeping time necessary for tea to brew, to liquids more generally, such as milk, water, boiling, kettle, cups, to primitive process concepts such as sequence, parallel activity, time and pauses.
• Contextual connections, some implicit such as in line 6 – remove the teabag *from where?* – some explicit words such as kettle, cup and teabag being referred to in many places and across many lines (e.g. switch on/once boiled).

We then ask: *How long does it take for the typical human being to learn about all of this?* There's a bit of thinking, before answers of *around five to six years* emerge.

We then transition to a program fragment of 10–15 lines in a language that the teachers are familiar with, using constructs that they'd use with their pupils. It could be any simple program, but this one reads in a mark that should be out of 30, checks it is in range and repeatedly reads a new number in if it is not, and finally converts the validated mark to a percentage, and writes it out:

```
Dim Mark as Integer
Dim Percentage as Single
Dim OutOfRange as Boolean
Percentage = 0
OutOfRange = True
Do
        Mark = InputBox("What mark did you get?")
```

```
      OutOfRange = Mark < 0 Or Mark > 30
      If OutOfRange Then
        MsgBox("Error! Mark not in range 0-30")
      Endif
   While OutOfRange
   MsgBox("You got" & (Mark/30)*100 & "%")
```

We ask the same question again: *What do you need to know to be able to read and understand this?* An even longer list of categories tends to emerge, including:

- Being able to see the gross structure of the program, including variable declarations and initializations, the loop to validate the input, the calculation and the output of the result.
- Being able to remember all the syntactic elements, as well as all their meanings.
- Understanding that a formal language is different from a natural language (related to Pea's *superbug* (Pea, 1986) and further explained in Tenenberg and Kolikant (2014) and Cutts et al., (2014).
- Variables, including what they are as a concept, what the types associated with them mean, what an assignment is.
- Expressions, including literal values in the program text such as True, 0, 30, 'You got', simple binary operations and then complex expressions combining a number of operators, either numeric or logical. Also concatenation and type coercion.
- What input and output library functions do and how to use them.
- Control flow constructs of sequence and conditional loop.
- Understanding the context – exam marks and how they can be out of range and arithmetic conversion to percentages.

When asked the related question *How much time do you give your pupils before expecting them to be able to understand a program like this?* the typical answer is *about three weeks.*

The comparison of six years to three weeks is obviously not entirely fair, but unpicking in this way how much there is to be learned, deeply, by comparing natural and programming language texts is often a radical eye-opener for teachers. In any introductory course, these concepts would be expected to be understood in three to five weeks and the introduction of new concepts will build on these. Studies and learning models now indicate that missing the early building blocks is a key signal for failure in a course, including Robins' Learning Edge Momentum (2010), Ahadi and Lister's stumbling points (2013), and Porter, Zingaro and Lister's prediction of student success on the basis of analysing fine-grained clicker data (2014).

Key concept: Fixed Mindset

A fixed Mindset can cause us to move too fast as teachers, overlooking the need to develop foundational knowledge and skills before moving on. The inability of some learners to keep up reinforces the fixed Mindset.

Is the conjecture that we presented earlier now more reasonable – that a teacher stating they have a growth Mindset could accidentally be using an instructional design that fosters a fixed Mindset? As just one example, is it reasonable to expect a learner to be able to pick up all of this in just a few weeks and fluently enough that they can analyse such a program precisely enough to be able to identify and fix errors – something that we expect them to be able to do? We think not. Do you agree? Do you recognize this high expectation either in your own learning design or the designs that you were part of in your own learning process?

In the next section we use the literature to strengthen the argument that the typical instructional design in introductory computer science courses is likely also to foster a fixed Mindset in learners.

4.5 Do typical computer science learning designs foster a fixed Mindset?

When reviewing the available evidence from both the Mindset-specific studies and more general research that examines how students' attitudes and beliefs change over the course of their CS education, there is evidence that our courses are fostering a fixed Mindset. For example, Scott and Ghinea (2014) found that nearly a third (30.2 per cent) of students' beliefs about programming aptitude became more fixed with nearly a fifth (18 per cent) of these changing completely from a growth Mindset to a fixed Mindset. Even where an introductory course has been specifically designed to provide extra support, there is evidence of a modest reduction in growth Mindset. For example, in our own Mindset study (Cutts et al., 2010) those who did not receive Mindset training experienced a 5 per cent reduction in growth Mindset score over just a short six-week period. More broadly, studies like those of Settle, Lalor and Steinbach (2015) indicate decreases in student confidence and engagement during their initial CS1 experience.

To begin to understand the reasons why, let us consider the typical instructional design of an introductory computer science course. This involves covering a range of programming concepts, one at a time; each concept is introduced using example code fragments and the output they produce, leaving learners to individually come up with an internalized model for how the fragment actually works; a small number of worked examples may be explored and learners are then given programming problems to work on, where they are expected to develop working programs using a development environment. This is a generally accepted format whether using an educational programming environment such as Scratch, or an industry language such as Java.

Examining this design against the key Mindset aspects introduced at the start of the chapter, we can explore how the fixed Mindset may be being developed:

- Performance vs Mastery goals. The predominant measure of success in a programming course is whether the learner is able to get a working solution to a problem. The running program is taken as a proxy for successful learning, but in truth, how much do we know about what the learner has learned? Has the learner been asked to explain the program in detail or the process followed to arrive at the solution? Usually not. Do we evaluate how much help was received from tutors, peers, the internet and so on, to get the program working? Usually not. The concept of running a program as king is further underlined by the increasing use of automated acceptance tests for marking and recording progress. It doesn't matter how the student gets the program, as long as it passes the test. This whole approach will clearly foster a performance goal in learners – learning to program is presented as an exercise in getting programs to run, not in understanding why they do or don't work. This is backed up by Buffardi and Edwards (2015) who found that automatic grading systems were discouraging reflective testing, an indicator of deep thinking about programs.

- Response to feedback. What kind of feedback do learners typically receive? In a typical context where learners are attempting to solve problems by getting a working program, the programming environment is providing feedback every time the learner tries to run their program. The ratio of failure to success is high in favour of failure, which in itself is disheartening to someone not used to it. Furthermore, the error messages of the programming environment are usually quite opaque and many learners take no useful information from them that might help them identify the cause of the problem. Given these factors, alongside the limited focus in most courses on developing code reading skills that would otherwise be useful in diagnosing problems, it is hardly surprising that the typical learner response to all this negative feedback is to put their hand up and ask for help or to get help from peers or the web. Students with this response were characterized by Perkins et al. (1986) as *Stoppers*. On top of this, large class sizes reduce the amount of personalized feedback that any one learner can receive; this often comes back some time after the exercise was completed; and automated acceptance tests can provide as little as a pass/fail result. In both cases, it is hard to proactively learn anything from the feedback.

- Alternative strategies. We rarely explicitly teach debugging strategies, which would provide learners with options when faced with challenges. Anecdotally, more experienced students have often commented on how essential the web is as a tool to be used to find the cause of problems they're facing, but teaching students about appropriate search techniques for solving problems is not common practice. For students who are struggling, the predominant behaviour observed by tutors and teachers is of students making almost random changes to their program, over and over again, in the hope that it will magically start working. This is a clear sign of the adoption of a fixed Mindset: the repeated application of a hopeless strategy that is not working. Such students were characterised by Perkins et al. (1986) as *extreme movers*.

You may well ask at this point why *all* learners don't fail, given the apparent weakness in typical learning designs that we are describing. Furthermore, given that some succeed, it is easy to attribute their success to some innate ability, the exact explanation the general Mindset philosophy is arguing against! The next section explores an alternative explanation for why some succeed while others fail.

4.6 The influence of prior experience on novices' success

Key concept: Prior experience

A learner's prior experiences will influence their current learning endeavours. This is obvious in sport, for example where a learner who can catch a ball will be better at catching a flying disc than someone who can't, or in maths, where factoring numbers will be easier if elementary multiplication is firmly in place. The same is most likely in play in computer science learning, but we are less familiar with the appropriate early experiences.

At the core of this explanation are the *prior experiences* that contribute to the learners' performance. Those who have succeeded at some form of programming before are very likely to succeed in an introductory course (Ramalingam, LaBelle and Wiedenbeck, 2004). How do we explain those who have never programmed before? Considering aspects of the computer science concepts outlined in the example above that a novice must master:

- Experience with languages of a more formal nature, including mathematical algebras and, anecdotally, Latin and Greek, will have given the learner skills to both appreciate the nature of a formal language as one with strict definitions, as well as an experience of reading texts out of order (e.g. precedence rules in maths, verbs at the end of the sentence in Latin and German and so on). The experience of working with mathematical language and processes may explain why studies have shown a correlation between prior high school maths performance and success in computer science course (Bennedsen and Caspersen, 2005; Bergin and Reilly, 2005). This may be a better explanation than mathematics' contribution to the development of general abstraction ability, which has been shown by Bennedssen and Caspersen (2005) not to correlate with learners' overall performance in a wide range of topics in computer science.

- It is well known that a single construct, such as variable assignment, may have multiple valid interpretations (Bornat, Dehnadi and Barton, 2012). Teaching styles that introduce concepts by example enable the learner to adopt any one of these so-called *alternative conceptions*, which will work for some exercises they complete, but not all (Ma et al., 2011). The fortunate learner picks the correct conception first time; the unfortunate may labour for a significant time under an alternative conception – long enough to seriously and often fatally hinder their progress. Misconceptions are covered in detail in Chapter 13.

Example: Alternative conceptions (misconceptions) of simple assignment

Below is a short sequence of assignment statements and two alternative ways simple variable assignment, in an imperative language, may be interpreted by novices.

1	SET A TO 3	**Association Model-** A and B are linked to whatever is on the right-hand side of the assignment.
2	SET B TO 5	
3	SET A TO B	9 is displayed both times because A was linked with B and the value of B changed
4	SET B TO 9	**Everything is a Value Model-** Anything on the right-hand side of the assignment is a value to be stored.
5	SEND A TO DISPLAY	
6	SEND B TO DISPLAY	B is displayed and then 9 is displayed because B is a value to be stored in variable A not a variable to be looked up.

Code Fragment in Haggis Reference Language

- Studies are showing that those with visualisation skills tend to achieve better in STEM subjects, including computer science (Cooper et al., 2015; Sorby, 2013). More importantly, the same studies have shown that visualisation skills can be acquired with training. Being able to visualize the working of the virtual mechanism that a program describes lies at the heart of du Boulay's *notional machine* concept (1986), increasingly seen as a crucial stepping stone to success in learning to program (e.g. Sorva, 2013). There is some emerging evidence that learners who have engaged in mechanistic reasoning, whether from the toys they played with, from watching older siblings or parents working with mechanical devices or via some other route, will have an advantage in terms of appreciating the concept of a deterministic mechanism (e.g. such as the notional machine) that can be inspected, adjusted, tested and so on (Bolger et al., 2012; Ching and Lin, 2015).

In summary, there is sufficient evidence to propose that the spread of outcomes in our classes is at least partly based on prior experiences.

4.7 Summary: Teacher and learner attitudes and learning designs

We have now laid sufficient groundwork to come back to the questions posed but not answered earlier in the chapter:

- Does influencing the learners' Mindsets directly, via some form of instruction about Mindset concepts, lead to increased learning?
- What is the influence of the instructional design itself on the learners' Mindsets and consequently their learning?

With respect to the second question, we have shown that typical instructional designs are highly likely to foster a fixed Mindset towards computer science learning in learners with limited relevant prior experiences. Hence we may now expect the answer to the first question to be no. To back up this expectation, the minimal Mindset training intervention of Simon et al. (2008) didn't influence the students' Mindsets, let alone increase their learning. The more in-depth Mindset training of our study (Cutts et al., 2010) did influence students towards more growth Mindsets but, crucially, the Mindset training alone was not enough to increase learning. In the study, three interventions were used: one was the Mindset training; a second explicitly encouraged the students to try new strategies in the face of failure; and the third emphasized the importance of making good use of available high quality feedback to their learning. Only when students had both the Mindset training and one of the other interventions were improvements in learning noted.

The importance of this result is that the additional growth Mindset-based interventions changed the instructional design of the course and as a result of the teacher fully taking on board the ramifications of Mindset as laid out in Dweck's work and the many related studies.

As Dweck said, teaching with a growth Mindset is not a statement, it's a journey. The journey requires a deep reevaluation of our own understanding of how learning computer science skills can take place, from an understanding of both general education theory and also the increasing understanding we have about computer science education in particular. It requires a continual investigation of our own practices and how they are affecting students' success. It must inevitably lead to a major rethink of the typical instructional design for an introductory computer science course. As we move to the *teach-all* era for computer science education, it is an essential path for all computer science educators. This book can represent the start of that journey or, if you are already on the journey, it can sustain you heartily as you travel.

Key points

- Mindset is the belief that people hold about whether ability is mostly innate (fixed) or can be improved through deliberate practice in a specific area of learning (growth).
- Educationally, performance and mastery goals are associated with fixed and growth Mindsets respectively – Mindset has a huge influence on outcomes.
- Mindset towards a particular skill or ability can be measured; it can, and does, change with learners able to move between growth and fixed Mindsets depending on their learning experience.
- A teacher's Mindset is easily transferred to their learners. It's crucial therefore that teachers develop a growth Mindset to create instructional designs that can foster a fixed Mindset in learners.
- Teachers of computer science have been shown to have a fixed Mindset. Exercises such as the one in this chapter help to shift them towards a growth Mindset.
- Typical learning and teaching techniques in computer science foster a fixed Mindset.

- Just saying 'I believe in growth Mindsets' isn't enough – a teacher needs to re-evaluate their teaching practices to determine how they could be influencing learners' Mindsets.

Further reflection

Examining the design of your own course or programme of learning:

- Do you get learners to carry out a survey or exercise at the start of the course to help you judge the beliefs they start with and again towards the end of the course to see how they've changed?
- Have you provided a range of suitable strategies that learners can use when they get stuck on known areas of difficulty?
- Can you reorganize tasks so that learners have an opportunity to directly apply the feedback they receive soon afterwards?
- Do you have mechanisms in place for learners to move at different speeds?
- For programming in particular, do you explain that repeated failure in to be expected? – programs don't work correctly for most of the development period, and then finally do!

References

Ahadi, A and R Lister (2013). 'Geek Genes, Prior Knowledge, Stumbling Points And Learning Edge Momentum: Parts Of The One Elephant?' in *Proceedings of the Ninth ACM International Computing Education Research Conference* (ICER '13), San Diego, CA.

Aronson, J, CB Fried and C Good (2002). 'Reducing Stereotype Threat and Boosting Academic Achievement of African-American Students: The Role of Conceptions of Intelligence' 38 *Journal of Experimental Social Psychology* 113–125.

Bennedsen, J and ME Caspersen (2005). 'An Investigation of Potential Success Factors for an Introductory Model-Driven Programming Course' in *Proceedings of the First ACM International Computing Education Research Conference* (ICER 05), Seattle, WA.

Bergin, S and R Reilly (2005). 'Programming: Factors that Influence Success' in *Proceedings of the 36th SIGCSE Technical Symposium on Computer Science Education*, St Louis, Missouri, USA.

Bolger, MS, M Kobiela, PJ Weinberg and R Lehrer (2012). 'Children's Mechanistic Reasoning' 30(2) *Cognition and Instruction* 170–206.

Bornat, R, S Dehnadi and D Barton (2012). 'Observing Mental Models in Novice Programmers' in *Proceedings of the 24th Annual Workshop of the Psychology of Programming Interest Group*, London, UK. Available at: www.ppig.org/library/paper/observing-mental-models-novice-programmers/

Buffardi, K and S Edwards (2015). 'Reconsidering Automated Feedback: A Test-driven Approach' in *Proceedings of the 46th ACM Technical Symposium on Computer Science Education* (SIGCSE '15), Kansas City, KA.

Ching, MF and JL Lin (2015). 'Investigating the Relationship between Students' Views of Scientific Models and their Development of Models' 37(15) *International Journal of Science Education* 2453–2475.

Cooper, S, K Wang, M Israni and S Sorby (2015). 'Spatial Skills Training in Introductory Computing' in *Proceedings of the Eleventh ACM International Computing Education Research Conference* (ICER '15), Omaha, NA.

Cutts, Q (2001). 'Engaging a Large First Year Class' in M Walker (ed), *Reconstructing Professionalism in University Teaching* (Buckingham, UK, Open University Press) 105–128.

Cutts, QI, MI Brown, L Kemp and C Matheson (2007). 'Enthusing and Informing Potential Computer Science Students and their Teachers' 39(3) *ACM SIGCSE Bulletin* 196–200.

Cutts, QI, RCH Connor, P Donaldson and G Michaelson (2014). 'Code or (not Code) – Separating Formal and Natural Language in CS Education' in *Proceedings of the Workshop in Primary and Secondary Computing Education* (WiPSCE '14), Berlin, Germany.

Cutts, QI, E Cutts, S Draper, P O'Donnell and P Saffrey (2010). 'Manipulating Mindset to Positively Influence Introductory Programming Performance' in *Proceedings of the 41st ACM Technical Symposium on Computer Science Education*, Milwaukee, Wisconsin.

Dempsey, J, RT Snodgrass, I Kishi and A Titcomb (2015). 'The Emerging Role of Self-Perception In Student Intentions' in *Proceedings of the 46th ACM Technical Symposium on Computer Science Education* (SIGCSE '15).

du Boulay, B (1986). 'Some Difficulties of Learning to Program' 2(1) *Educational Computing Research* 57–73.

Dweck, C (2008). *Mindset: The New Psychology of Success* (New York, NY, Ballantine).

Dweck, C (2015). 'Growth Mindset, Revisited' 35(5) *Education Week* 20–24.

Dweck, CS and EL Legget (1988). 'A Social-cognitive Approach to Motivation and Personality' 95(2) *Psychological Review* 256–273.

Guzdial, M (2014). 'The 10K Hour Rule: Deliberate Practice Leads to Expertise, and Teaching can Trump Genetics'. Available at: https://computinged.wordpress.com/2014/10/13/the–10k-rule-stands-deliberate-practice-leads-to-expertise-and-teaching-can-trump-genetics/

Heslin, P, D Vanderwalle and G Latham (2006). 'Keen to Help? Managers' Implicit Person Theories and their Subsequent Employee Coaching' 58 *Personnel Psychology* 871–902.

Kinnunen, P, R McCartney, L Murphy and L Thomas (2007). 'Through the Eyes of Instructors: A Phenomenographic Investigation of Student Success' in *Proceedings of the Third ACM International Computing Education Research Conference* (ICER '07), Atlanta, GA.

Leroy, N, P Bressoux, P Sarrazin and D Trouilloud (2007). 'Impact of Teachers' Implicit Theories and Perceived Pressures on the Establishment of an Autonomy Supportive Classroom' 22(4) *European Journal of Psychology of Education* 529–545.

Lewis, C (2007). 'Attitudes and Beliefs about Computer Science among Students and Faculty' 39(2) *SIGCSE Bulletin* 37–41.

Ma, L, J Ferguson, M Roper and M Wood (2011). 'Investigating and Improving the Models of Programming Concepts held by Novice Programmers' 21(1) *Computer Science Education* 57–80.

Macnamara, B, D Moreau and D Hambrick (2016). 'The Relationship between Deliberate Practice and Performance in Sports: A Meta-analysis' 11(3) *Perspectives on Psychological Science* 333–350.

Mangels, JA, B Butterfield, J Lamb, C Good and CS Dweck (2006). 'Why do Beliefs about Intelligence Influence Learning Success? A Social Cognitive Neuroscience Model' 1(2) *Social Cognitive and Affective Neuroscience* 75–86.

McCartney, R, J Boustedt, A Eckerdal, K Sanders and C Zander (2017). 'Folk Pedagogy and the Geek Gene: Geekiness Quotient' in *Proceedings of the 48th ACM Technical Symposium on Computing Science Education* (SIGCSE '17), Seattle, WA.

Mueller, CM and CS Dweck (1998). 'Intelligence Praise can Undermine Motivation and Performance' 75 *Journal of Personality and Social Psychology* 33–52.

Patitsas, E, J Berlin, M Craig and S Easterbrook (2016). 'Evidence that Computer Science Grades are not Bimodal' in *Proceedings of the Twelfth ACM International Computing Education Research Conference* (ICER '16), Melbourne, Australia.

Pea, RD (1986). 'Language-independent Conceptual "Bugs" in Novice Programming' *Educational Computing Research, 2*(1), 25–36.

Perkins, DN, C Hancock, R Hobbs, F Martin and R Simmons (1986). 'Conditions of Learning in Novice Programmers' 2(1) *Journal of Educational Computing Research* 37–55.

Porter, L, D Zingaro and R Lister (2014). 'Predicting Student Success using Fine Grain Clicker Data' in *Proceedings of the Tenth ACM International Computing Education Research Conference* (ICER '14), Glasgow, Scotland.

Ramalingam, V, D LaBelle and S Wiedenbeck (2004). 'Self-efficacy and Mental Models in Learning to Program' in *Proceedings of the Ninth ACM Innovation and Technology in Computer Science Education Conference* (ITiCSE '04), Leeds, UK.

Robins, A (2010). 'Learning Edge Momentum: A New Account of Outcomes in CS1' 20(1) *Computer Science Education* 37–71.

Schmidt, JA, L Shumow and H Kackar-Cam (2015). 'Exploring Teacher Effects for Mindset Intervention Outcomes in Seventh-grade Science Classes' 10(2) *Middle Grades Research Journal* 17–32.

Scott, MJ and G Ghinea (2014). 'On the Domain-specificity of Mindsets: The Relationship Between Aptitude Beliefs and Programming Practice' 57(3) *IEEE Transactions on Education* 169–174.

Settle, A, J Lalor and T Steinbach (2015). 'Reconsidering the Impact of CS1 on Novice Attitudes' in *Proceedings of the 46th ACM Technical Symposium on Computer Science Education* (SIGCSE '15), Kansas City, KA.

Simon, B, B Hanks, L Murphy, S Fitzgerald, R McCauley, L Thomas and C Zander (2008). 'Saying Isn't Necessarily Believing: Influencing Self-Theories' in Computing' in *Proceedings of the Fourth International Workshop on Computing Education Research* (ICER '08), Sydney, Australia.

Sorby, S (2013). 'The Case for Spatial Skills Instruction in Computer Science' *Future Directions In Computing Education Summit White Papers (SC1186)*. Available at: http://pdf.oac.cdlib.org/pdf/stanford/uarc/sc1186.pdf

Sorva, J (2013). Notional Machines and Introductory Programming Education 13(2) *ACM Transactions on Computing Education*, Article 8.

Sun, KL (2015) 'There's no Limit: Mathematics Teaching for a Growth Mindset' (PhD), Stanford University.

Tenenberg, J and Y B-D Kolikant (2014). 'Computer Programs, Dialogicality, and Intentionality' in *Proceedings of the Tenth ACM International Computing Education Research Conference* (ICER '14), Glasgow.

Watson, C and FWB Li (2014). 'Failure Rates in Introductory Programming Revisited' in Proceedings of the 2014 Conference on Innovation and Technology in Computer Science Education, Uppsala, Sweden.

Zingaro, D and L Porter (2016). 'Impact of Student Achievement Goals on CS1 Outcomes' in *Proceedings of the Proceedings of the 47th ACM Technical Symposium on Computing Science Education (SIGCSE '16)*, Memphis, Tennessee.

5

Computer Science, Interaction and the World

Carsten Schulte, Sue Sentance and Erik Barendsen

Chapter outline

Chapter synopsis

This chapter addresses the implications of digital technology for everyday life and society for teaching computer science at school. The reader will get an overview on how to address these issues as an integral part of teaching computing. Using the opportunity to address the interaction of computing and the world when discussing computing is preferred, instead of addressing it only in separate teaching units which are then presented as a separated perspective on computing.

5.1 Introduction

Interaction might be a strange term to read in a book about computer science education at school. Given the history of the subject at school in most countries you may think that what we mean by interaction is how to use a computer. That is indeed one aspect of interaction, but here we intend to focus on the implications for the interaction between computing and the world.

While it may seem that the idea of interaction being a key aspect of the teaching of computer science in school is new – particularly as there have been questions recently about future jobs (Frey and Osborne, 2013), the future of education and required skills (Sefton-Green, Nixon and Erstad, 2009) and even the future of humanity (Harari, 2017) – the integration of these aspects of computing education date back to the first approaches to computing education in schools in the 1960s, when computers and robots were first used in industry – although at that time there was only sparse computing power.

Teachers (of computer science) generally want to have an understanding of the broad nature of the discipline (see Chapter 2) and their own attitudes towards it (see Chapter 4). This shapes our whole experience of teaching and our perspectives on effective learning. As well as facilitating a secure understanding of the many different aspects of computer science, we also need to prepare students for an ever-changing world where computers affect the way they and others communicate live and work. We have a responsibility to ensure that students are aware of the ethical, moral and societal implications of advances in computer science as part of their core education: this is why these topics appear on school curricula.

In previous approaches to computing education at school, we have seen a gap between core computing topics and what is seen as the 'softer' side of computer science: the general role of computing in individual lives and in society as a whole. This can make the subject rather distorted, if it is chunked in such a way that its application and impact are regarded as being either somewhat separate or not as an essential part of the discipline. In this chapter, we warn against that view, by considering the importance of a broad view of computer science and its implications for our lives, focusing on how this is a key aspect of the learning of computer science in school. We hope we can help teachers to put the pieces together, which in turn will help learners to understand the relationship between computing ideas, technology, individual use and the general effects on society.

Interaction is not a single event, but a sequence of events, including actions and reactions. Consider a user inputting data into a digital artefact, for example a computer: the input is processed by the digital artefact; this produces output, which in turn leads to the next input. This leads us to ask who is the driver in this interaction and who is merely reacting to the input from the other side? Will technology be shaped so that humans are the drivers or will they be programmed and thus told what to do? By simply using the individual pattern or type of interaction as an example of 'how it works in general' we can very quickly debate the future of society as it is changed by ubiquitous computing. Following on from this, we immediately ask the question 'Is society really being shaped by technology or is it the other way around?' This brings us to interaction on a large scale: the interaction between technology and society.

In the age of ubiquitous computing (Weiser and Brown, 1996) almost all areas and aspects of life are penetrated by computing – even taking a shower triggers some computing systems, measuring and controlling data (e.g. for the landlord, the water supply company or municipal bureaucracy). As Kitchin and Doge put it: 'Turning the tap therefore indirectly but ineluctably engages with software, though the infrastructure appears dumb to the consumer who simply sees flowing water.

In other cases, the elevator arrives, the car drives, the mail is delivered, the plane lands, the supermarket shelves are replenished, and so on' (Kitchin and Dodge, 2014). In the past, it was easy to distinguish between computing systems and the world and capture the interplay between computing and society by the automation of processes in socio-technical informatics systems, in which technological systems had a clear border and interacted by clear interfaces with some surrounding social systems. Nowadays, even mundane activities are permeated by numerous technological systems and aspects; it makes more sense to conceptualize the role of technology with the notion of hybrid systems. Understanding health care, production, distribution, household activities and so on, where computational systems are being used, cannot rely on automation alone, but must take into account interaction processes and the ability to perceive the overall situation as a hybrid system. A hybrid system consists of human and digital actors interacting. From an engineering perspective, the goal is to design such systems so that the potential (skills, abilities) of human and digital actors are combined for the best outcome. For example, humans are often better in pattern recognition, whereas algorithms outperform humans in accuracy and speed of computation. From a general or societal perspective, the goals are more unclear, but questions concerning the future development for individuals and humankind are evolving.

In the next sections, this argument will be deepened and discussed within the following framework of interaction levels:

- **Human and computer interaction** refers to forms of interaction within a 'simple' configuration of a person and a computational artefact.
- **Hybrid network interaction** is a term used to capture various forms of interaction in a networked setting consisting of humans and computational artefacts.
- **Computing and society interaction** widens the perspective to the interdependence of technology and society as a whole.

5.2 Level 1: Human and computer interaction

Who is in control?

In this section, we look at the ways in which we interact with computers. We are used to a traditional Input-Process-Output (IPO) model as the way in which we use/interact with computational artefacts, but this is changing. The original IPO model implicitly assumed the core activity of a computer process was to process data: it stems from batch processing and client-server structures of the 1970s, where terminal input was transferred to the server, processed and awaited some checking of the output by the user. In this model, it is important to think clearly about the structure of the input and how data is processed.

However, this has changed profoundly. Based on much shorter response times and advances in user interfaces, the so-called 'What You See Is What You Get' (WYSIWYG) paradigm allows immediate feedback on user input, so it seems as if a user can directly change an item presented on the output. This concept underlies direct manipulation interfaces. Interaction with a computer thus changes from a batch-processing orientated style to a more interactive style with many short input-processing-output cycles which are perceived as direct manipulation (e.g. of text to be written on a screen).

It has been claimed that in future there will only be two types of interaction: program, or be programmed (Rushkoff, 2010). In *Human and computer interaction,* this is conceived as a technological challenge: the problem is to design useful interactions where the individual is 'in control'. In other words, interactions where the human is the programmer, not being programmed.

These changes can be seen not only as a change in usability or comfort level in using a computer, but also a change in computing itself. From the perspective of theoretical computer science Peter Wegner (1997) argues that this new paradigm allows computing beyond the quality level of Turing machines, which describe the quality or power of computing in terms of the IPO model.

The two perspectives on human control (to be programmed or to program) can be illustrated as follows. Let us consider a flight booking system.

Human as user view

This implies that in an everyday end-user scenario the user is guided or prompted by a system which tells her what to do. A customer can search for a flight and then choose and book a specific flight; however, she can do so only in a very restricted way. The system ensures that no missing input is allowed, checks the input thoroughly and only then confirms the booking. The user can choose only between pre-given choices (e.g. choose from a list of flights to book). The system guides this booking process in a predefined order: search, select, add additional input about the customer, and finalize the booking. If, for example, one airline is not in the system, the user cannot book it. Thus, the computer defines what the user can do and the order in which it is done.

Human as designer view

The opposing view would be that the optimization of the system contains some hard problems, including the optimal distribution of customers to flights, additional cargo to be transported if there is space available or a system that allows airlines to charge the highest price possible without losing customers. There may be no optimal solution. However, where designers exist who have experience and intuition they will be able to choose optimal parameters so the system produces the best results. Thus, the human is still in charge of the process.

In summary, one view conceives the user as passive object – the other as a designer who can influence and manipulate the system: system control vs user control.

We can see that the role of end-users is shifting: this role is less and less restricted to a human-as-user perspective. For example, the new intelligent systems that are based on self-learning algorithms usually start outperforming humans in such tasks.

We now have machines that are more powerful than Turing machines because these systems are ultimately based on huge amounts of input data from external sources. Do these systems only get as good as they are because they are trained on human experts? The additional computing power is not only based in the idea of the training or learning algorithm but also in the quality of the training data, and little tweaks and tricks during the training phase. In the human designer view, in the end this quality stems from human cognition, from human input into the system.

Design and meta-design

From a human and computer perspective, Fischer and Giaccardi argue beyond the dichotomist view of design vs use for a spectrum of design activities for users – and programmers as meta-designers, allowing users to re-design the software at use time (Fischer and Giaccardi, 2004) which no doubt would mean that end-user programming and end-user development is a more relevant skill. Another argument for a range of design possibilities beyond use vs design comes from research in artificial intelligence: traditional views on problem solving and computational thinking in computer science conceptualize the problem-solving process as analysis and understanding the problem, followed by design as an analysis and understanding of the algorithmic solution – no problem could be solved without designing an algorithmic solution. With techniques like deep learning, this changes: the problem needs to be understood, and data or examples of problem solutions collected. The machine can then learn from these examples (learn a model of the problem solution) generalize on its own and use this generalization to solve new instances of the problem (see Figure 5.1).

Figure 5.1 can be described as follows. In the top row is shown the classic view on problem solving as programming and finding an algorithmic solution. This requires (a) an understanding of the problem space, and (b) an understanding of the generalized algorithmic solution. The bottom row demonstrates problem solving via model learning. It requires an understanding of the problem

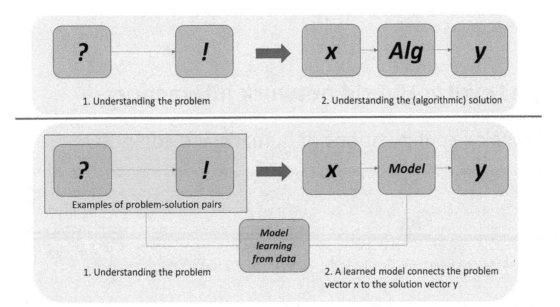

Figure 5.1 Views of problem solving

and getting data through many examples of concrete problem instances and their solutions. By using that data the machine learns the underlying general solution and can solve future problem instances based on the learned model.

These different views (human as designer vs human as user) seem to imply a normative difference (e.g. booking flights is probably optimized so that the airline makes the most profit, not so that the customer gets the cheapest flights). The algorithm uses data from previous users of similar systems, but the humans may not have agreed to this. However, the human as user is not always a negative thing: some people happily use smartphone apps that track their daily routines – the benefit to the person is that the system can present alerts and notifications that get better and better at predicting what they want or need in a certain situation (e.g. they may be prompted to take an earlier train home to ensure they make an appointment).

In summary, the discussed examples should show that human computer interaction cannot solely be evaluated on the basis of the technical features of the system alone. In some situations, it might be very useful if the digital artefact tells the human what to do, in other situations it might be best if the human can adapt or change the system so that it behaves differently in the future.

Key concept: Interaction

Interaction with a computer usually relies on immediate feedback. In Graphical User Interfaces (GUIs) this is also known as WYSIWYG paradigm: What You See Is What You Get. While interaction is based on the IPO-model of Input–Processing–Output, current systems employ quick and short IPO-cycles so that interaction is better defined as *cyclic process of action and reaction between two agents* (e.g. a human and a computer). Interaction is a relationship between structure and function of digital artefacts and the design and use contexts in which the content occurs.

Interaction can be seen on different levels: Human and computer, hybrid network, computing and society.

5.3 Level 2: Hybrid network interaction

Complex configurations of humans and computers

In the beginning, digital devices were perceived as replacement for human computers.[1] From the 1930s on, humans used machines to compute; these machines were called computers. Interaction was carried out by primitive interfaces, which we could call programming. After designing the input, probably consisting of data and an algorithmic description of how to process that data, it was processed within the machine; afterwards – after some time – the output was done. The idea of IPO and the term 'computer' stems from those days. Nowadays, computers are a part of sociotechnical systems.

---

[1] See: www.nasa.gov/feature/jpl/when-computers-were-human

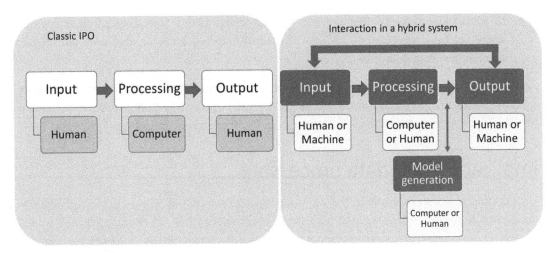

Figure 5.2 Adaptations of the Input-Process-Output model

A hybrid network consists of both human and digital agents participating in data transformation processes, where each partner takes turns and can change its role. Both are important to consider in the different steps of (a) data generation, (b) data transportation and transformation and (c) data consumption.

In such hybrid systems various forms of interactions can be observed (see Figure 5.2). In this figure we see that the old linear model of Input-Processing-Output is transformed by direct manipulation interfaces into cyclic interactions which make the internal computation invisible and make it hard to distinguish who starts the interaction and who is just responding.

The hybrid nature of networks provides possibilities, but also raises the need to protect against unintended interactions. Many webpages containing forms for human use are protected against (presumably malicious) computer-computer interactions by so-called *Captchas* with the purpose of detecting whether or not the interaction partner is human.

Human vs computer traits in interaction

The computer science researcher Keil is interested in designing computational artefacts so that humans and machines in interaction processes can contribute their particular strengths (e.g. Hampel & Keil-Slawik, 2001; Keil-Slawik, 1992) as introduction to his work).

Keil argues that describing technological and human actors as (in principle) the same or as equal partners in interaction unavoidably leads to misunderstandings due to unjustified transfer features of technology to humans, or vice versa. For example:

- A human forgets details; in a machine data can only be deleted.
- A machine can be instructed to exclude some aspects; a human cannot be instructed to (e.g. 'not think about the next break!').
- A human can learn from mistakes; a machine (at least not in the foreseeable future) cannot learn from mistakes, or only in a frame foreseen by the developers.

- How machines process data is based on precisely defined steps (algorithms), human cognition is not yet fully understood, but relies in contrast to machines on the body and physical experiences (Barsalou, 2008).

Keil therefore suggests that we should clearly distinguish between technical *structures* and technical *effects* and social/cognitive *structures* and social/cognitive *effects*. Key to this understanding is the idea that social/cognitive processes to some part entail or are based on technical processes.

Implications for data processing

For example, this idea is visible in the way data is processed in a hybrid network: such data will need to be digitized. Indeed, human perception and memory rely on external stimuli; humans can use media as external memory. By representing data in some media we don't need to memorize all the details (e.g. written language is storing what was oral data beforehand in a new medium). By using external storage mechanisms to store the process of a calculus (e.g. summing up the value of several items), a human can then reperceive and thus trace the calculation process to check for errors. In analogous media, this storing of data is done by inscription. The visual inscription and the visual layout of the data *is* the data. Thus, computers as digital media have brought a fundamental change in that for the first time the data itself and its visual layout are separated. A computer can produce different visual layouts without destroying the original data! Perceiving different representations of the same data can help humans to understand them better. Keil labels this process 'the experience of difference' – the potential for producing all kinds of different representations makes the algorithmic processing of data such a powerful technology in terms of 'mind tools' or thinking tools, which Keil labels as digital media.

Key concept: Hybrid network interaction

A hybrid network consists of human and digital agents participating in data transformation processes, where each partner takes turns and can change its role. Both human and digital agents are important to consider in the different steps of (a) data generation, (b) data transportation and transformation, and (c) data consumption. In such hybrid systems, various forms of interaction can be observed. The hybrid nature of networks provides possibilities, but also raises the need to protect against unintended interactions.

5.4 Level 3: Computing and society interaction

Objectivation

One approach introduced in the German literature on the philosophy of technology and computing education (Frank and Meyer, 1972) proposed a basic or philosophical account of digital technologies, to account for the anticipated tremendous growth and development of that technology. The core idea is that the advent of technology in our lives brings with it the final evolutionary step of the development of humankind. Frank and Meyer suggest three evolutionary phases, each associated with substantial changes in the self-view of people and the overall abilities of humankind:

1 Phase: The so-called objectivation of organs and limbs (e.g. teeth, hands by tools like stones or hand axes).
2 Phase: Objectivation of physical work by machines.
3 Phase: Objectivation of intellectual work by computing devices.

To make sense of this view, we would interpret *objectivation* in Phase 1 as automation. In Phase 2 we can see that formerly essential human skills are becoming obsolete due to new technological developments: machines now do the work of humans. Phase 3 adds even more; it is on a larger scale, and concerns the very nature of what it means to be a human. What is it that distinguishes us from animals? It is not the physical strength nor the ability to socialize, but our intellect: the ability to think, and deductive and logical reasoning. We could regard this as a development that shatters the last resort of humans' uniqueness: our intellectual capabilities. Humans become ever-more marginalized in this view. We should, however, embrace this development, because humans are weak, laden with emotions, prejudices and with a tendency to rush decisions. Humans have individualistic and subjective approaches to any task. Technology, however, can now lead humankind to an era where all decisions can be objectivated (hence the term) and thus become fair, just, devoid from subjective emotions, prejudices and values. For this to happen, the task at hand just needs to be transformed into an algorithmic problem and the input variables transformed into digital data.

The goals of education in the context of moving from the subjective to the objective era are pretty straightforward: instead of objectivation the terms now in use are problem-solving skills, algorithmic thinking or computational thinking (Tedre & Denning, 2016) – but all of them still aim at marginalizing subjective humanity by processes of automation. This is the reason the topic under discussion is *interaction* and not *automation* – hybrid and socio-technical systems have interaction as the dominant-use behaviour instead of conceptualizing automation as Input-Processing-Output where the problem solving is entirely done by and delegated to the machine.

Socio-technical perspective

Another way of viewing change in technology and its impact is through the lens of socio-technical approaches (Magenheim and Schulte, 2006). The aim is to uncover the interplay between technology and society (and the individual actors or agents). In these approaches, the interaction between human and technology is a central notion for understanding how technology is constructed and shaped, in its turn shaping society as well as the human being. In traditional approaches, agency is defined as the purposeful acting (e.g. planning, foresight and making decisions) and is a term used solely for human actors. With the increased responsiveness and autonomy of digital interactive technologies we can give them the label 'secondary agency' (Mackenzie, 2006). This can be seen as a substitute or imitation of human agency. The dichotomy of product and process mirrors the fact that during design time, a solution is built with a world in mind that ceases to exist when the product is in use – thereby changing the situation so that most likely another or different ideas and solutions emerge. This leads to the next generation of products, thus forming a development path.

Structure and function

Kroes and Meijers (2006) argue that artefacts (things made by humans) cannot be fully understood by what we could call the science perspective ('how does it work?'). Physics, for example, could deliver a physical description of a hammer such as weight, material, etc. However, this would not explain why humans call it a hammer, and perceive it as a tool for hammering. Therefore, two perspectives are needed to fully grasp a technological or digital artefact: *structure* and *function*. That gives us another reason why computer science *cannot* exclude the function perspective to teach both concepts relating to computer science and also the interaction between computing and society, and the individual experiences. The concept of duality reconstruction uses this as a basis for an approach that supports developing teaching units for computer science education that relate to interaction (Schulte, 2008).

Key concept: Computing and society interaction

The societal, as well as the ethical and value-laden, implications of the use of computer science can be captured using varying models, giving both sides different roles. Here we suggest capturing the process as interaction between two sides – human and digital – or technological actors glued together by interaction processes. Both can essentially play the same roles – especially influencing the other side – but do so based on different perspectives and skill sets.

5.5 Implications for pedagogy

Interaction is a relationship between structure and function of digital artefacts and the design and use contexts in which the content occurs. What does this imply for teaching computer science?

Teaching interaction is not a new idea. However, we suggest perceiving interaction not as additional content to be taught and also not as a recipe for teaching, but a perspective for thinking and designing teaching. It requires a mindset useful for thinking and reflecting that shapes how content, teaching methods and goals are chosen and integrated. This approach is not claiming to change content, but to think about a wider perspective and the underlying educational goal when teaching computer science content (see chapter 10.5 on page 140 for an example).

In this way, we might avoid the pitfall of teaching computer science by teaching children absolute facts about technology (i.e. by teaching them 'how it really works' before – or even without – focusing on interaction aspects ('what it is good for'). In light of the discussion above, we hope it is clear that by such separation of concerns, the role of digital technology and of the underlying ideas and concepts from computer science for everyday life, together with their impact on the changes and development of contemporary societies in all their aspects, cannot be captured. In order to achieve this when teaching computing, letting students discover the dual nature of digital artefacts is crucial (Schulte, 2008). The same holds for the intertwined relationship between product and process (Magenheim and Schulte, 2006).

When planning teaching, one can analyse and reflect on possibilities for the different levels and the different viewpoints within each level. In Figure 5.3 we can see that interaction within a nd between the three levels can be analysed by looking at structure, function and contexts. Using this scheme it is possible to reflect on societal issues based on knowledge and experiences gained from levels 1 and 2, so that the societal issues are closer linked to concrete examples and experiences. Teaching level 3 in isolation could result in teaching sociology, but by grounding it in level 1 examples, the abstract implications and reflections can be integrated. It therefore seems useful to switch between levels in a teaching unit, to demonstrate the interaction between levels.

This can also be described as a pars-pro-toto principle; students should be enabled to make inferences from a small example to the whole – to transfer and generalize. For planning teaching this means to ask which example can be chosen that allows such generalization.

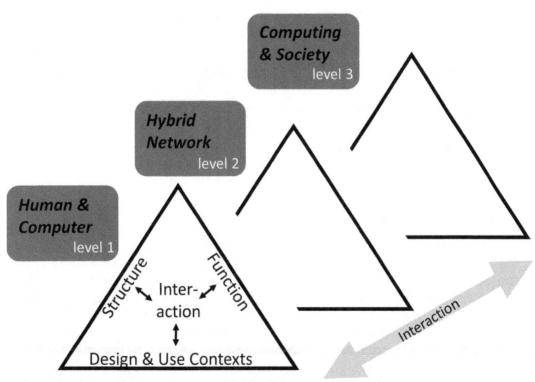

a) Product – Process   b) Aligning structure to function
c) Use – Design Continuum   d) Development Path

Figure 5.3 Interaction within and between the three levels

Example activity

Interaction can be explored based on analysing a digital artefact.

Your task is to pick a digital artefact of your choice and to describe it with regard to the three levels.

Take a word processor for instance – presumably you are familiar with using one, so the function aspect is easy to describe – but what about the underlying structure? For example, how is digital text represented and saved on a hard drive? How is it rendered – what algorithm is used for text alignment? The interaction between algorithmic layout procedures and user functions can be explored. Such aspects demonstrate interaction level 1. Can you find similar examples at level 2? (E.g. if you are text processing in the cloud, is there any algorithmically generated text? What hybrid interactions (human–computer, computer–computer, human–human) can you recognize?) Finally, at level 3, what are more general implications of the digitalization of text processing (e.g. change in job description, change in text-based media, . . .)?

Extension activity: Can you see interactions between the levels?

With respect to level 1, students should become aware of the different views of the human-as-user vs the human-as-designer; that there is a continuum of interaction pattern between the two extremes (Fischer and Giaccardi, 2004).

As to level 2, it is important to discuss how the hybrid nature of human-computer networks affects the interfacing and the way data is processed, as well as the nature of problem solving (see Figure 5.3).

Regarding level 3, the role of objectivation in society in light of the dichotomy of product and process and how this triggers the intertwined development path of society and technology should become clear.

We illustrate our approach with an example in the area of robotics.

Example: Robotics

Robotics might be a common topic to discuss with students. The starting point for thinking about how to introduce this topic might be to analyse robots on level 1 and the IPO-model. A robot can be seen as a hybrid system where sensors provide input values (measuring distance, colour of underground, etc) and process this to adapt the driving behaviour (e.g. follow a line or avoid bumping into obstacles). This can be observed in small educational robots, but also in everyday households using robot vacuum cleaners and most likely in the future in robot cars – which provides a use context, where we could analyse the role of the human in the interaction. Who is in control when driving the robot car? After specifying the destination, who is in control of choosing a route? Will the human be perceived as a passenger (*Human-as-user view*) or can they still be the driver (*Human-as-designer view*) (i.e. configure and adapt how the robot car operates)?

With regard to the idea of design and meta-design, questions can be asked such as how such cars can be built to allow for design at use time; and where are technical, legal and ethical issues to prevent the user from re-designing the robot car system. This can be discussed largely on the basis of the classical IPO model by experimenting or so-called 'Exploring' (Schulte et al., 2017) how sensor data are processed and control actuators.

This then quickly widens to the perspective of hybrid networked systems, because many features of robot cars will depend on them communicating both with each other and the cloud. In this network view, again the question arises of how best to acknowledge human vs computer traits in this interaction and the implications for data processing (e.g. changing the traffic environment to be more machine readable).

This quite naturally engages a debate on the level of computing and society. Most likely, the behaviour of humans with regard to driving cars will change. Such experiences affect the difference between product and process (Magenheim & Schulte, 2006) and will most likely lead to changes in product as well as in the environment (development path (Schulte, 2008)). One can debate about how robot cars will change transport systems, jobs, ownership, legislation and transform urban space and traffic patterns.

5.6 Summary

It sometimes seems there is a dichotomy between ideas and technology. With interaction as a central notion we aim to lay the foundations for a relational understanding. This provides the depth which is sometimes lacking in the teaching of computer science and prevents us from teaching digital artefacts from a use – or indeed from a structural – perspective only.

Teaching in an integrative way would mean that for each computer science topic, an activity or reflection is added to draw out the implications of this topic for human–computer interaction, human–human interaction and human–computer–society interaction. By also addressing the interaction *between* the different levels it is possible to address societal issues of computing without either overwhelming student on the one hand, and also without detaching the discussion of societal issues from the domain of computing. This approach might be very useful in providing a context for computer science theory and some motivation for studying it.

Key points

- While it sometimes makes sense to teach topics from the field of computing and the world in isolation, we aim for an integrated approach, where the interaction between technology and society becomes more visible.
- Interaction can be analysed on three levels: human and computer, hybrid networks and computing and society. A conceptual analysis gives rise to key properties within each of these levels.

- These key points can be addressed in computing education by analysing interaction in concrete systems. It is crucial to connect these, so examples should allow for an analysis on all three levels.
- The interplay between *structure* and *function* of digital artefacts implies that interaction should not be taught as a separate notion, but rather in conjunction with the question how digital artefacts work.

Further reflection

- Ask students to consider systems that they have used for their own entertainment (e.g. to play, download or store music). Let them reflect on the balance between the system affecting control over the user's use of the system ('listen to this') and the benefits of using the system.
- Ask the students to discuss a system they know and outline some feature or problem of the system that plays a role on each of the levels of interaction.
- Review the local formal curriculum. Look for explicit and implicit occurrences of interaction aspects. Classify them in terms of the interaction levels. Suggest how to integrate the aspects you found with the more 'functional topics' in the curriculum.

References

Barsalou, LW (2008). 'Grounded Cognition' 59 *Annu Rev Psychol* 617–645.

Fischer, G and E Giaccardi (2004). 'Meta-design: A Framework for the Future of End-User Development' (Online-Version) in H Lieberman, F Paternò and V Wulf (eds), *End User Development* (Vol 9) (Dordrecht, The Netherlands, Kluwer Academic Publishers,) 1–26.

Frey, CB and MA Osborne (2013). 'The Future of Employment: How Susceptible are Jobs to Computerisation?' 17 September 2013. Available at: http://archedepotoire/autoblogs/wwwinternetactu net_8a3fe3331e0ad7327e18d9fe6ec3f0ad04dcea58/media/3722fa7dThe_Future_of_Employmentpdf

Hampel, T and R Keil-Slawik (2001). 'sTeam: Structuring Information in Team-distributed Knowledge Management in Cooperative Learning Environments' 1(2es) *J Educ Resour Comput* 3.

Harari, YN (2017). *Homo Deus: A Brief History of Tomorrow* (London, Vintage).

Keil-Slawik, R (1992). 'Artifacts in Software Design' in C Floyd, H Züllighoven, R Budde and R Keil-Slawik (eds), *Software Development and Reality Construction* (Berlin Heidelberg, Springer) 168–188.

Kitchin, R and M Dodge (2014). *Code/Space* (Cambridge, MA, MIT Press).

Kroes, P and A Meijers (2006). 'The Dual Nature of Technical Artefacts' 37(1) *Studies in History and Philosophy of Science Part A*, 1–4.

Magenheim, J and C Schulte (2006). 'Social, Ethical and Technical Issues in Informatics—An Integrated Approach' 11 (3–4) *Education and Information Technologies* 319–339. Available at: wwwspringerlinkcom/content/658435n54601048x/

Rushkoff, D (2010). *Program or Be Programmed: Ten Commands for a Digital Age* (New York, NY, Or Books).

Schulte, C (2008). 'Duality Reconstruction – Teaching Digital Artifacts from a Socio-technical Perspective' in RT Mittermeir and MM Syslo (eds), *Informatics Education – Supporting Computational Thinking: Third International Conference on Informatics in Secondary Schools – Evolution and Perspectives, ISSEP 2008, Torun Poland, 1–4 July 2008 Proceedings* (Berlin, Heidelberg, Springer-Verlag) 110–121.

Schulte, C, J Magenheim, K Müller and L Budde (2017). 'The Design and Exploration Cycle as Research and Development Framework in Computing Education' in *Global Engineering Education Conference (EDUCON), 2017 IEEE* 867–876. Available at: http://ieeexploreieeeorg/abstract/document/7942950/

Sefton-Green, J, H Nixon and O Erstad (2009). 'Reviewing Approaches and Perspectives on "Digital Literacy"' 4(2) *Pedagogies: An International Journal* 107–125.

Tedre, M, and PJ Denning (2016). 'The Long Quest for Computational Thinking' in *Proceedings of the 16th Koli Calling International Conference on Computing Education Research* New York, 120–129. ACM.

Wegner, P (1997). 'Why Interaction is more Powerful than Algorithms' 40(5) *Communications of the ACM* 80–91.

Weiser, M and JS Brown (1996). 'The Coming Age of Calm Technology' 8 *Xerox Parc* 17. Available at: wwwjohnseelybrowncom/calmtechpdf

Part 2

Aspects of Teaching and Learning

6

Introduction to Part 2
Aspects of Teaching and Learning Computer Science

Sue Sentance

In this part of the book we consider the teaching and learning of different aspects of computer science in the classroom, drawing on relevant research in the field. Teachers do learn to teach by practically trying things out in the classroom and by reflecting on their experiences, and these chapters offer a range of strategies and perspectives that will both enhance your understanding of how to teach the subject and give you some concrete ideas that have emerged from research in the field. Research in computer science education has existed for several decades now in higher education, although less so relating to school. Thus the evidence available is partly drawn from the way we teach slightly older 'novices' with new, emerging ideas relating directly to school. There is no doubt that we need more research around pedagogy and assessment of computer science education in school; these chapters should enable you to consider where future research will be focused going forward.

The first chapter in this part considers how we design and implement curricula in computer science in school. This can be at a national level or at a very local level, in a particular school. The chapter draws on the distinction between the intended, implemented and attained curriculum (Van den Akker, 2004) and discusses the goals, content and skills identified in different curricula. Most importantly, we need to consider why we include particular content from computer science in our curriculum – this is informed by the context in which we teach and overall goals.

The next three chapters look at pedagogy. In an area of the school curriculum where we find that teachers are still adapting to the new subject, professional development initiatives have been largely focused on subject knowledge development and particularly around programming. However, through experience and reflection, teachers develop what Shulman describes as pedagogical content knowledge (PCK) (Shulman, 1986) which describes the interaction between the core content knowledge in a subject and strategies that can be used to teach it. We look here at pedagogy as it relates to teaching computing concepts, then programming, and finally consider primary education. The chapter by Curzon and colleagues introduces a wide variety of strategies for teaching computing concepts which should give inspiration to many teachers. These strategies include computing unplugged, and using art, games, dance and writing in the teaching of computing; they are informed by a constructivist view of learning and provide some inspirational ideas for teaching. Chapter 9 moves us on into programming. There is a long history in computing education research around the teaching of programming, from the 1970s or even earlier. Michael Caspersen demonstrates the depth of this research and how it can be structured: particularly in this chapter we learn about the value of worked examples and stepwise improvement as key strategies for developing a secure understanding of programming concepts and skills. Reflecting on programming at this level may give you some surprising insights into your understanding of programming. In Chapter 10, Tim Bell and Caitlin Duncan consider some of the reasons for introducing computer science in primary schools and consider how computational thinking skills and areas of data representation can be introduced to younger children. Finally, this part concludes with a focus on assessment, often neglected in the discussion of computing education. Chapter 11 looks at research that has been carried out in this area in terms of different ways of assessing computing, including rubrics, multiple-choice questions, self and peer assessment, amongst other strategies. There is, in addition, an increasing focus on automated tools to aid the teacher in assessment. but it needs to be remembered that formative assessment should help learners to understand their own learning, in such a way that they can make progress. Thus the focus in the chapter is primarily on assessment for learning.

References

Shulman, LS (1986). 'Those who Understand: Knowledge Growth in Teaching'. 15(2) *Educational Researcher* 4–14.

Van den Akker, J (2004). 'Curriculum Perspectives: An Introduction' in *Curriculum Landscapes and Trends* 1–10. Available at: http://link.springer.com/chapter/10.1007/978-94-017-1205-7_1

7

Perspectives on Computing Curricula

Erik Barendsen and Carsten Schulte

Chapter outline

Chapter synopsis

In this chapter we explore computer science curricula from various perspectives, ranging from the underlying rationale to the intended learning outcomes. We present the theories behind these perspectives as well as characteristic examples taken from actual curriculum documents and practices. The perspectives presented in this chapter can be used as lenses for analysing and understanding existing curricula, as well as for developing new curricula and for translating them into classroom practice. Finally, we discuss personal factors influencing teachers' interpretation and implementation of curricula. Awareness of the perspectives and personal factors is crucial for teachers' professional development.

7.1 Introduction

Due to rapid growth and changes in our field, computer science standards cannot be static. These standards must be reviewed and updated on a regular basis, and not considered complete and finalized. CSTA[1] is committed to an inclusive, iterative process that allows multiple drafts and revisions of the CSTA K–12 CS Standards. (. . .)

CSTA 2016, p 8

There are many stakeholders involved in using and refining a curriculum, not least the teachers, who are often also are members of curriculum development teams. This chapter intends to provide background and tools to critically review curriculum documents and practices, and to participate in discussions about computer science education.

Overall, a curriculum gives information on various aspects of teaching and learning. Thijs and Van den Akker (2009) call them *components* (see Table 7.1). The rationale is the most fundamental component, influencing many others.

The *curricular spider web* (see Figure 7.1) outlines the different aspects described in a curriculum – if one changes one aspect, the others will be affected by this change. The centre of the curricular spider web is the rationale, answering the core question why students should learn. The interconnectedness of the components stress that the components should be coherent ('aligned') to be effective.

Thijs and Van den Akker describe the curricular spider web as a fragile thing:

Although a spider web is relatively flexible, it will most certainly rip if certain threads are pulled at more strongly or more frequently than others. The spider web thus illustrates a familiar expression: every chain is as strong as its weakest link. It may not be surprising, therefore, that sustainable curriculum innovation is often extremely difficult to realize.

Thijs and Van den Akker, 2009:12

As a consequence, the underlying rationale that holds together the parts and provides coherence to the curriculum can be identified (see Table 7.1).

Table 7.1 Curriculum components (Thijs and Van den Akker (2009:12))

Component	Core Question
Rationale	Why are they learning?
Aims and objectives	Towards which goals are they learning?
Content	What are they learning?
Learning activities	How are they learning?
Teacher role	How is the teacher facilitating their learning?
Materials and resources	With what are they learning?
Grouping	With whom are they learning?
Location	Where are they learning?
Time	When are they learning?
Assessment	How is their learning assessed?

[1] CSTA: The computer science teacher association. See www.csteachers.org/

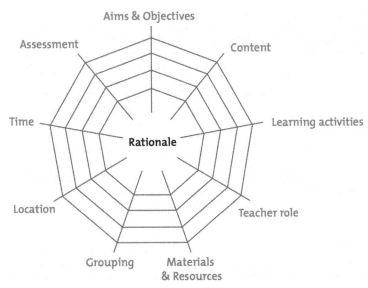

Figure 7.1 The curricular spider web (Thijs and Van den Akker (2009:11))

Moreover, in order to use a curriculum document to review and refine standards and plan teaching, it is crucial to be aware of the central component of the curricular spider web, the underlying rationale. By so doing, the wording, choices and gaps in a curriculum can be understood and explained.

In addition, to understand the effects of a curriculum, it is useful to distinguish between the curriculum as it was conceived and the teaching practice. Van den Akker (2004: 3) has developed a framework describing the different types of curriculum representations:

- Intended curriculum:

  - *Ideal*: The vision of the society underlying the curriculum
  - *Formal/Written*: Documents describing a national curriculum. Specifies intentions

- Implemented curriculum:

  - *Perceived*: How teachers perceive and interpret the curriculum
  - *Operational*: The so-called 'curriculum-in-action': What is taught and learned in the classroom

- Attained curriculum:

  - *Experiential*: How learners experience their learning
  - *Learned*: The learning outcomes of the learners.

The intended curriculum is described often as a document on a national level or is presented as a suggestion from a teacher association, aiming to influence what is taught in schools. They usually (or hopefully) rely on a rationale that is shared by the community. On a more local level, such a curricular framework is then implemented at schools and in individual classrooms – this may be

Table 7.2 Curricular levels and influence factors

Curriculum model (Van den Akker, 2004: 3)			Influenced by . . .
Intended	Ideal	Vision (rationale or basic philosophy underlying the curriculum)	Perspectives on higher level: policies, standards (*Actors*: policymakers, standards, government, experts, professional organizations such as ACM, CAS, GI)
	Formal/Written	Intentions	. . . Shared/collective perspectives
Implemented	Perceived	Interpretation by users	Influenced by teachers' perspectives on Computing (Tedre, Chapter 2); Influenced by curriculum emphasis (van Driel et al., 2007, 2008)
	Operational	Actual process of teaching/learning	Influenced by teachers' orientations, knowledge (PCK, CK), beliefs Actors: teachers . . . individual perspectives
Attained	Experiential	As experienced by learner	Learners' beliefs, interests, motivation
	Learned	Learning outcome	. . . individual perspectives

done by a group of teachers for a local school or by an individual teacher outlining a curriculum (lesson plan) for the next school year. How this is done depends on individual perceptions and interpretations. One final aspect is the level of the attained curriculum, capturing the learners' view on the implemented curriculum – it describes the results.

Table 7.2 presents some influence factors and the curricular levels they influence. It summarizes some concepts and theories, some of which we will present and discuss in the following sections.

7.2 Curriculum perspectives: Rationale

The underlying rationale of a curriculum is crucial for alignment of content and internal coherence. In essence, the rationale asks: Why teach this? The answer therefore needs to reflect on a general account of the roles and aims of education.

In an analysis of the role of programming, Schulte (2013) identifies the following general goals:

- *Cope with affordances*: developing competencies and skills to be able to cope with affordances of life in a variety of different situations.
- *Participation in society/democracy*: being able to act in terms of participation. It refers to what is called 'education for democratic citizenship'. This is the ability to engage with and responsibly participate in the democratic sustainment and development of society.
- *Development of identity*: developing a sense of identity; getting to know what interests me, what resonates with me or what repels me, etc.

These goals reflect the relative consensus on the general rationale of education, articulated by Tyler (1949): to provide *knowledge, social preparation* and *personal development*.

The same elements are elaborated upon by Biesta (2015), who distinguishes:

- *Qualification*: gaining knowledge, skills, dispositions etc. needed to go on and do something, either specific such as a profession, or in general, such as being qualified to live in a complex society.
- *Socialisation*: becoming part of society (existing ways for doing and being) – culture and tradition.
- *Subjectification*: becoming more autonomous and independent in thinking and acting.

The question for a curricular rationale can thus be rephrased as: 'What is the relationship and impact of the subject domain to these general goals of education?' The perceived nature of the discipline is an important influence factor for a general vision of computer science education.

In the introduction of the CAS curriculum document (Computing at School Working Group, 2012), the three general goals are addressed: '*Pupils studying computing gain insight into computational systems of all kinds, whether or not they include computers*' (qualification), '*Education enhances pupils' lives as well as their life skills. It prepares young people for a world that doesn't yet exist, involving technologies that have not yet been invented, and that present technical and ethical challenges of which we are not yet aware*' (socialization) and, less prominently, subjectification: '*This (. . .) makes it an extraordinarily useful and an intensely creative subject, suffused with excitement, both visceral ("it works!") and intellectual ("that is so beautiful")*'.

The CSTA standards contain elements of socialization and a more prominent subjectification rationale:

> K–12 computer science teachers can thus nurture students' interests, passions, and sense of engagement with the world around them by offering opportunities for solving computational problems relevant to their own life experiences.
>
> (CSTA, 2016: 5)

Many educators regard the competence to *express oneself* as important – or even a prerequisite. This self-expression side of subjectification is more prominent in arts-related subjects. If one looks closely, however, this aspect can also be found in computing.

Example: Programming for self-expression

Storytelling is sometimes used in introductory programming (e.g. producing small animations in Scratch by primary school students). Doing so, the students are indeed learning about programming – but the animation itself does not have a particular usefulness, it does not solve a problem. Hence, the value of these tasks is sometimes seen only in its contribution to learning problem-solving techniques. However, based on the general goal of subjectification, the ability to write an animation as a self-expression has value in its own right. Indeed, it could be possible to extend the role of programming to 'expression': the idea that learners learn to program as a means to produce aesthetic expressions (Schulte, 2013), and hence as a contribution to subjectification as the third general goal of education.

In 2002 the British artist Alex McLean won the Transmediale Art Prize in Berlin for the program forkbomb.pl. It is not a piece of software that is useful in a traditional sense in computer science. A fork bomb is a program that replicates (forks) itself until the system resources are exhausted – besides that the program prints a series of 0s and 1s. For more details see the discussion of this code as a piece of art (Mackenzie 2006).

The example of programming as expression is probably somewhat unusual – we used it to illustrate that by reviewing the rationale underlying the curriculum it is possible to discover new aspects of the curriculum or to enrich the curriculum with otherwise overlooked contributions for education.

Besides its role in discovering new curriculum elements, awareness of the underlying rationale is crucial for maintaining the coherence and balance of the components constituting the curricular spider web.

7.3 Curriculum perspectives: Content

In this section we will look at content matter in curricula from a conceptual point of view. The term 'concepts' refers to 'topics and ideas belonging to the subject matter, regardless of the specific skills or attitudes in which they appear' (Barendsen et al., 2015).

A classification of concepts can be a useful way to compare curricula (e.g. on a global level). Barendsen et al. (2015) and Barendsen and Steenvoorden (2016) apply a content analysis method to various curriculum documents. First, literal concepts were extracted from curriculum texts (open coding, see Cohen, Manion and Morrison, 2013). In a second phase, similar concepts were merged into more abstract concept descriptions. The resulting concepts were then grouped into general categories based on the list of so-called knowledge areas of the ACM/IEEE Computing Curricula (2013): Algorithms, Architecture, Modelling, Data, Engineering, Intelligence, Mathematics, Networking, Programming, Security, Society, Usability, and a final Rest category.

The resulting classification can be used to explore the content emphasis in curriculum documents, using the number of occurrences as an indicator of the relative importance of concepts and knowledge categories. Moreover, the frequency distribution and the marked curriculum documents can serve as starting points for a more in-depth comparison of curricula.

Example: Classification of content

Barendsen and Steenvoorden (2016) applied the above method to the curriculum documents of CSTA and CAS, as well as the national curriculum descriptions of France and The Netherlands (before and after the curriculum revision of 2016). The top five knowledge categories are displayed in Table 7.3 (most frequent categories are mentioned first).

Notable aspects include the high scores of the algorithms category, especially in recent curricula. In the French curriculum document, data was most prominent, appearing almost twice as often as concepts in the second category. The engineering and society categories have varying scores. Societal aspects include privacy and in some cases legal and ethical issues.

Table 7.3 Top five knowledge categories in the sample curricula

CSTA	CAS	France	Netherlands 2007	Netherlands 2016
Algorithms	Algorithms	Data	Architecture	Programming
Engineering	Networking	Programming	Data	Engineering
Architecture	Architecture	Architecture	Engineering	Data
Society	Data	Networking	Networking	Society
Networking	Programming	Algorithms	Rest	Architecture

Conceptual choices, priorities and applications can often be explained using Tedre's framework of computing traditions (see Chapter 2). Let us, for example, speculate about typical roles of the concept of the Turing machine in the respective traditions. As an important analytic model, the Turing machine would be a primary concept in any curriculum rooted in the mathematical tradition. In the engineering tradition, however, one could expect it to occupy a more marginal role as a theoretical basis of more prominently visible principles of (non-)computability. In the science tradition, the Turing machines can be expected to serve as a descriptive model for the way computers work.

In a similar way, we can explain some differences in the relative weights of concepts in the above curricula. The CSTA and Dutch documents emphasize the engineering ('making') aspect of computing, which accounts for the relatively high frequencies of engineering and programming concepts. Also, from the more in-depth content analysis, it appears that in the CAS curriculum and French documents, the scientific tradition is more present.

To conclude, analysing the content dimension in terms of concepts and knowledge categories of a curriculum provides a useful way to uncover some underlying principles beneath the selection of content in curricula. In this case it was also useful for discussing and discovering various traditions in otherwise seemingly incomparable documents.

7.4 Curriculum perspectives: Aims and objectives

Curriculum descriptions usually contain learning objectives in terms of knowledge, skills and attitudes, as opposed to just a specification of content matter. Such a description specifies the aims of the curriculum in terms of students' outcomes. To prepare for a proper alignment of the learning objectives with assessment, learning objectives are usually formulated in operational terms (i.e.in terms of observable student behaviour).

Various taxonomies exist for facilitating the formulation of operational objectives[2]. One of the best known of those is Bloom et al.'s (1965) classification:

---

[2] For an elaboration on these taxonomies, see Chapter 16.

- Knowledge (characteristic verbs: define, name)
- Understanding (explain, compare)
- Application (show, solve)
- Analysis (categorize, subdivide)
- Synthesis (construct, design)
- Evaluation (criticize, recommend).

It has been argued that this taxonomy does not fit seamlessly into computer science. Indeed, many 'making' activities will be categorized in the higher Bloom categories (e.g. Lister and Leany, 2003). Johnson and Fuller (2006) propose to add a level 'higher application'. Another possible refinement is provided by the SOLO taxonomy (Biggs and Collis, 1982), distinguishing levels according to the 'scope' of students' skills, varying from a local to a holistic perspective, with the following key aspects:

- Pre-structural: unconnected, unorganized
- Unistructural: local perspective
- Multistructural: multi-point perspective
- Relational: holistic perspective
- Extended abstract: generalization and transfer.

See Chapter 16 for more discussion of the Bloom and SOLO taxonomies. Many authors use complexity by referring to local versus holistic perspectives ('scopes') (e.g. lines in a program versus interactions in a multi-component system) (see Lister et al., 2006; Whalley et al., 2006).

In curriculum specifications we find similar indications. A local perspective applies when using programming constructs such as:

Sequencing (doing one step after another); Selection (if-then-else): doing either one thing or another, and Repetition (Iterative loops or recursion).

CAS, 2012

The following requires a more holistic (in this case, relational) perspective:

Reflect thoughtfully on their program, including assessing its correctness and fitness for purpose; understanding its efficiency; and describing the system to others.

CAS, 2012

An example demonstrating a relationship with CS traditions can be seen in the explanation given by the Dutch national curriculum committee.

Informatics is seen by many as a constructive discipline: a subject area where creating things (mostly digital artefacts) is the key element. In this epistemic view, informatics as a scientific discipline supplies the conceptual and procedural knowledge about such artefacts and the creation process. The 'creation' perspective is an attractive starting point for the subject. (…) Therefore, the committee has decided to position 'design and development' as a central skill in the new curriculum.

Barendsen, Grgurina and Tolboom, 2016:109

One can recognize a strong 'engineering' emphasis, with maths/science as supporting traditions.

In summary, formulating goals and objectives for a given curriculum content is not straightforward. First, taxonomies are useful tools to be precise about the intended outcome levels. In the case of computer science, it is fruitful to complement a purely cognitive framework like Bloom's with domain-specific complexity indicators in SOLO terms. Second, the underlying perception of the nature of the discipline impacts the translation of content into specific learning goals.

7.5 Summary: The role of the teacher: Interpretation and implementation

So far, we have discussed the intended curriculum – in this section we will focus on the implemented curriculum: the ways teachers perceive and put the intended curriculum into action. This process of implementing the curriculum is influenced by a range of teacher factors, like knowledge such as content knowledge (CK) and pedagogical content knowledge (PCK), orientations and beliefs (Shulman, 1986).

The space for teachers to give a personal interpretation in implementing a formal curriculum also became apparent in a PCK study by Rahimi, Barendsen and Henze (2016) in the context of the Dutch formal curriculum, which stresses the engineering perspective as we have seen. In the teachers' PCK, Rahimi et al. found a broad range of goals and objectives connected to the topic 'design and development', ranging from purely conceptual objectives to more practical learning goals.

For computer science education, several studies found a relationship between beliefs and teaching (e.g. Fessakis and Karakiza, 2011; Schulte and Bennedsen, 2006; Bender et al., 2016).

Teachers' *curriculum emphasis* is considered to be one of these beliefs. The idea is that teachers have goals that lie beyond the subject itself; such an emphasis has also the role to send a message about the subject. In a study with Dutch chemistry teachers, Van Driel et al. (2007, 2008) found three different curriculum emphases: fundamental chemistry (FC), chemistry, technology and society (CTS), and knowledge development in chemistry (KDC). FC corresponds to the belief that theoretical notions should be taught first, because such notions can provide a basis for subsequently understanding the natural world and are needed for the students' future education. CTS implies an explicit role of technological and societal issues within the chemistry curriculum. Finally, KDC is connected with the idea that students should learn how knowledge in chemistry is developed in socio-cultural contexts, so that they learn to see chemistry as a culturally determined system of knowledge, which is constantly developing (cf. Barendsen and Henze, 2017).

To our knowledge, this framework has not been studied empirically in computer science education, but we can use the curriculum emphasis still as a framework to discuss how a teacher makes decisions when implementing a curriculum. We can speculate about a version of the framework for computer science: FC is then the idea that the fundamental concepts of computer science should be emphasized, CTS is the notion that the interaction between computing and society should be emphasized, and KDC stresses the way of thinking like a computer scientist. It therefore seems natural that a teacher with a KDC mindset stresses computational thinking, defined in the CSTA curriculum draft as 'a distinct means of analysing and developing solutions to problems that can be solved computationally'. Computational thinking would then be taught with the aim to teach learners to think like a computer scientist. However, from a CTS point of view, a teacher might stress computational thinking as a way to have some impact on society and technology, whereas a teacher with a focus on FC probably would stress the need to first teach fundamental concepts like algorithm as a prerequisite for engaging in computational thinking. Van Driel et al. found in their study that most teachers tend to support all three emphases to some degree, their focus being influenced by their experience and beliefs.

Example activity for teachers: Curriculum implementation

It is likely that your curriculum includes teaching students how the computer works. Implementing this in a sequence of lessons will vary according to whether you think computer science is a mathematical, scientific or engineering discipline (as discussed in Chapter 2). Consider how these different perspectives would influence how you would implement this curriculum topic.

Ni (2011) presents a model of computer science *teacher identity* as a personal factor. This comprises 'Perception of CS', 'Perception of Teaching' and 'Perception of Self as a CS Teacher'. These three perceptions interact with the educational background of the teacher, the curriculum, and (Ni stresses this point) the availability of a CS teacher community.

We have seen that personal factors influence the implementation of formal curricula when it comes to interpreting and elaborating the higher-level learning goals and when making decisions on how to implement the curriculum. Bishop and Whitfield (1972) provide a framework depicting the elements of this decision-making process. It contains a chain of factors, from *background and experience* via *beliefs and values* to *aims and objectives*. A so-called *decision schema* connects these (personalized) aims and objectives to the teaching situation, resulting in *decision and action* (see Borko, Roberts and Shavelson, 2008).

This influence is not only visible in the long-term (deliberate, advised) planning of teacher and student activities, but also plays a role in decision making 'on-the-spot' (i.e. during teaching). In such moments, all threads of the curricular spider web come together.

Being aware of the underlying perspectives, views and emphases in a curriculum and of one's own identity as a teacher can help to reflect on decisions and thus enhance this decision making and ones' own professional identity as a teacher. One aspect of this is the belonging to a community of computer science teachers. As quoted at the beginning of the chapter: curricula in computer science education will continue to evolve. Thus we believe as a teacher you should not only be aware of implementing the curriculum in your classroom, but also be able to participate in refining the formal curriculum.

Key points

- The term 'curriculum' comprises various aspects of teaching and learning (e.g. aims and goals, content, learning activities and so forth). If one changes one aspect, the others will be affected. The visualisation of the components in a 'curricular spider web' emphasizes that the components should be coherent ('aligned') and (to some extent) flexible to be effective.

- The underlying rationale of a curriculum is crucial for alignment of content and internal coherence. In essence, the rationale is the answer to the question: 'Why learn this?' and thus reflects on a general account of the roles and aims of education (e.g. qualification, socialization and subjectification).

- The content of a curriculum can be characterized in terms of concepts and knowledge categories. These provide a way to compare documents that can be disparate in many ways.

- Taxonomies like Bloom's and SOLO can help to formulate aims and objectives in a precise and operational way.

- The intended curriculum is often described as a document on a formal, in practice, national level. On a local level, there is the implemented curriculum: the ways teachers perceive the intended curriculum and put it into action. This provides space for teachers to give a personal interpretation in implementing a formal curriculum, depending on individual perceptions, beliefs and interpretations.

- Teachers' curriculum emphasis is considered to be one of these beliefs (e.g. the idea that the fundamental concepts are the basis of teaching computer science or the notion that the interaction between computing and society is fundamental or the belief that computer science education should stress typical ways of thinking and mindsets).

- To be aware of one's own viewpoints and interpretations of the curriculum, the aspects for analysis mentioned in this chapter could be helpful; they address: (a) underlying educational values (qualification, socialization, subjectification), (b) the curriculum emphasis in one's own teaching as well as an assumed emphasis in curriculum documents (e.g. FC, CTS and KDC), and (c) for the underlying nature of the discipline (e.g. engineering, maths or science).

Further reflection

- Reflect on your local curriculum, standards or guidelines. Which computing traditions and general educational goals are in focus?
- Choose a content area in your current national curriculum and discuss various ways the content can be interpreted, based on different curriculum emphases (e.g. FC, CTS, KDC).
- Choose some goals/aims from your current national curriculum and discuss them with regard to a taxonomy (Bloom, SOLO). Are the intended levels clear and realistic?

References

ACM/IEEE-CS Joint Task Force on Computing Curricula (2013). *Computer Science Curricula 2013* (Tech Rep.). ACM Press and IEEE Computer Society Press.

Barendsen, E and Henze, I (2017). 'Relating Teacher PCK and Teacher Practice Using Classroom Observation' *Research in Science Education* 1–35.

Barendsen, E and T Steenvoorden (2016). 'Analyzing Conceptual Content of International Informatics Curricula for Secondary Education' in A Brodnik and F Tort (eds), *Informatics in Schools: Improvement of Informatics Knowledge and Perception* (Cham, Springer International) 14–27.

Barendsen, E, N Grgurina and J Tolboom (2016). 'A New Informatics Curriculum for Secondary Education in The Netherlands' in A Brodnik and F Tort (eds), *Informatics in Schools: Improvement of Informatics Knowledge and Perception* (Cham, Springer International) 105–117.

Barendsen, E, L Mannila, B Demo, N Grgurina, C Izu, C Mirolo, S Sentance, A Settle and G Stupuriene (2015). 'Concepts in K–9 Computer Science Education' in *Proceedings of the 2015 ITiCSE on Working Group Reports* 85–116.

Bender, E, N Schaper, ME Caspersen, M Margaritis and P Hubwieser (2016). 'Identifying and Formulating Teachers' Beliefs and Motivational Orientations for Computer Science Teacher Education' 41(11) *Studies in Higher Education* 1–16.

Biesta, Gert JJ (2015). *Good Education in an Age of Measurement: Ethics, Politics, Democracy* (Abingdon, Routledge).

Biggs, JB and KF Collis (1982). *Evaluating the Quality of Learning: The SOLO Taxonomy (Structure of the Observed Learning Outcome)* (Cambridge MA, Academic Press).

Borko, H, SA Roberts and R Shavelson (2008). 'Teachers' Decision Making: From Alan J. Bishop to Today' in P Clarkson and N Presmeg (eds), *Critical Issues in Mathematics Education* (Berlin, Springer) 37–67.

Computing at School Working Group (2012). *Computer Science: A Curriculum for Schools*. Available at: www.computingatschool.org.uk/data/uploads/ComputingCurric.pdf

CSTA (2016). [INTERIM] CSTA K–12 Computer Science Standards Revised 2016. Available at: www.csteachers.org/resource/resmgr/Docs/Standards/2016StandardsRevision/INTERIM_StandardsFINAL_07222.pdf

Fessakis, G and T Karakiza (2011). 'Pedagogical Beliefs and Attitudes of Computer Science Teachers in Greece' 4(2) *Themes in Science and Technology Education* 75–88.

Hansen, K-H and J Olson (1996). 'How Teachers Construe Curriculum Integration: The Science, Technology, Society (STS) Movement as Bildung' 28(6) *Journal of Curriculum Studies* 669–682.

Johnson, CG and U Fuller (2006). 'Is Bloom's Taxonomy Appropriate for Computer Science?' in *Proceedings of the 6th Baltic Sea Conference on Computing Education Research*: Koli Calling 2006 120–123.

Lister, R, and J Leaney (2003). 'Introductory Programming, Criterion-referencing and Bloom' 35(1) *ACM SIGCSE Bulletin* 143–147.

Lister, R, B Simon, E Thompson, JL Whalley and C Prasad (2006). 'Not Seeing the Forest for the Trees: Novice Programmers and the SOLO Taxonomy' 38 *SIGCSE Bulletin*, 118–122.

Mackenzie, A (2006). *Cutting Code: Software and Sociality* (New York, NY: Peter Lang).

Ni, L (2011). *Building Professional Identity as Computer Science Teachers: Supporting Secondary Computer Science Teachers through Reflection and Community Building* (New York, NY, ACM Press).

Rahimi, E, E Barendsen and I Henze (2016). 'Typifying Informatics Teachers' PCK of Designing Digital Artefacts in Dutch Upper Secondary Education' in A Brodnik and F Tort (eds), *Informatics in Schools: Improvement of Informatics Knowledge and Perception* (Cham, Springer International) 65–77.

Schulte, C (2013). Reflections on the Role of Programming in Primary and Secondary Computing Education' in *Proceedings of the 8th Workshop in Primary and Secondary Computing Education* (New York, NY: ACM Press) 17–24.

Schulte, C and J Bennedsen (2006). 'What Do Teachers Teach in Introductory Programming? Gehalten auf der ICER '06, (New York, NY: ACM Press) 17–28.

Seehorn, D, S Carey, B Fuschetto, I Lee, D Moix, D O'Grady-Cunniff and A Verno (2011). *CSTA K–12 Computer Science Standards: Revised 2011* (New York, NY, ACM Press).

Shulman, LS (1986). 'Those Who Understand: Knowledge Growth in Teaching' 15(2) *Educational Researcher* 4–14.

Thijs, A and J Van den Akker (2009). *Curriculum in Development* (Enschede, SLO).

Van den Akker, J (2004). 'Curriculum Perspectives: An Introduction' in *Curriculum Landscapes and Trends*. Available at: http://link.springer.com/chapter/10.1007/978-94-017-1205-7_1

Van Driel, JH, AMW Bulte and N Verloop (2007). 'The Relationships Between Teachers' General Beliefs about Teaching and Learning and their Domain-specific Curricular Beliefs' 17(2) *Learning and Instruction* 156–171.

Van Driel, JH, AMW Bulte and N Verloop (2008). 'Using The Curriculum Emphasis Concept to Investigate Teachers' Curricular Beliefs in the Context of Educational Reform' 40(1) *Journal of Curriculum Studies* 107–122.

Whalley, J, R Lister, E Thompson, T Clear, P Robbins and C Prasad (2006). 'An Australasian Study of Reading and Comprehension Skills in Novice Programmers, using the Bloom and SOLO Taxonomies' in *Proceedings of the Eighth Australasian Conference Computing Education*, Hobart, Australia, 243–252.

8

Teaching of Concepts

Paul Curzon, Peter W. McOwan, James Donohue, Seymour Wright and William Marsh

Chapter outline

Chapter synopsis

This chapter overviews a wide range of strategies successfully used for teaching computer science and computational thinking concepts. We review teaching through analogy, various 'unplugged' strategies; strategies based on discourse and writing, contextualized approaches and enquiry-based learning. We give concrete examples based on our practical experience of teaching computing concepts to students of all ages, through projects such as Computer Science for Fun (www.cs4fn.org), and in developing material to support teachers through Teaching London Computing (teachinglondoncomputing.org). We also draw on other existing resources such as CS Unplugged (csunplugged.org) which spawned an interest in kinaesthetic activities stimulating understanding of concepts in concrete ways by making the abstract tangible.

8.1 Introduction

Computing does not just develop sophisticated skills such as programming. It is also a rigorous academic subject akin to physics or history, consisting of a rich conceptual framework, both around programming and more generally. Computational thinking is the core skill set that students develop by studying computing. This too is rich with concepts such as abstraction, decomposition and generalization. Understanding these concepts is an important part of being able to do computational thinking. For many aspects of the subject, a solid understanding of earlier concepts is a prerequisite for understanding later ones (see Meyer & Land, 2006), especially with respect to programming. Similarly, it is easy for students to form faulty mental models of processes and so hold misconceptions about critical concepts. Having ways to give students timely help around threshold concepts and misconceptions is vital.

The learning of concepts is therefore a critical part of the subject. Appropriate pedagogic methods are needed which leave students with a clear understanding of individual concepts, their relationships and of how they fit into broader contexts of the subject. In this chapter we examine a variety of approaches.

8.2 Teaching through analogy and storytelling

Analogy

Many computing concepts have links to everyday objects and real world ideas so the use of analogy is a powerful way to scaffold students' understanding. These can be used as a way to explain the computer science version in a memorable way (see box). We describe many such analogies in Curzon (2014). These can lead directly to role playing approaches where the situations or different approaches are acted out, that we discuss in Section 8.3.

It is important to make clear the boundaries of the analogy and clearly link back to the computing concept. This relates to the educational theory of 'semantic waves' (Maton, 2013; Macnaught et al., 2013) which argues that good teaching involves waves of explanation. First the teacher descends the semantic wave linking from abstract and technical concepts to concrete and everyday concepts. Critically, they then go back up the wave to link back to the technical concepts.

Some apparent computing analogies are more than an analogy at the conceptual level – the computing and real world version are actually identical at the conceptual level. Computation is something that happens in the world not just in computers. For example, a stack of chairs follows the rules of a stack data structure in that chairs can only be added and taken in a last-in-first out manner. It is the implementation of the concepts that differs not the abstract concept itself. Such everyday equivalences make for very powerful explanations.

Examples of analogy for computing concepts

First-in-first-out queue data structures have a direct analogy to what we do in supermarkets. A priority queue might be illustrated by talking about what happens at an upmarket night club where most people queue but celebrities go straight to the front and the arrival of an A-list celebrity leaves minor celebrities waiting. Similarly, a stack of chairs can be used to physically show what kind of queue a stack is, with only the top-most object removable.

The idea that one data structure might be implemented in several completely different ways can also be illustrated with real world examples. Staying with the concept of a first-in-first-out queue, have students consider different situations they have encountered where queues form (a deli counter and a bus stop, perhaps) and explain how they work. Both ultimately work in a first-in-first-out way but may do so with completely different implementations. The bus stop might have people waiting in line: new people join at the back but leave from the front and all shuffle up as someone leaves. The deli counter might have a ticket system. People then take a number and stand anywhere they like. When the number comes up they move forward but no one else moves. Both implementations still implement a queue. Many other implementations exist, showing that one abstract data type can be implemented in many ways.

Key concept: Semantic waves

Semantic waves is a theory about what makes a powerful explanation. It explains a core issue behind how to make many of the approaches described here work (or not work if the approach is not followed). Good explanation starts by introducing technical concepts but then relates them in some way to concrete (or material) situations or contexts that are already understood, before then explicitly linking back to the new concept. This approach is behind successful teaching by analogy, storytelling and successful unplugged teaching.

Storytelling

Storytelling provides a different kind of hook or context to link concepts to (see box). It is important that the stories are engaging and memorable. The place of the concept in the story must also be natural. The links from the story to the technical concepts, again, have to be made clear – travelling the semantic wave. One approach is to tell a story, then have students identify the concepts themselves.

Examples of storytelling

An example of using fiction to teach concepts is in telling the Dr Seuss story of the 'Cat in the Hat' (Dr Seuss, 1958) to explain recursion. In this story a series of ever-smaller cats appear to help solve a problem of a stain on a bath. With the cats representing recursive calls, the story includes analogies for the key concepts underpinning recursion, including base and step cases, and the need to unwind the recursive calls. Linked to the story, these concepts are given a problem-solving context and made memorable.

A non-fiction example is that embodied in the Teaching London Computing 'Searching to Speak' activity (Curzon and McOwan, 2017). This involves the story of how a locked-in syndrome patient was able to write a book despite having total paralysis. You interactively explore with the class how to devise an algorithm for him to communicate when all he can do is blink an eye. The natural human drama involved, together with a twist at the end, makes the story a memorable way to learn about concepts such as divide and conquer.

Invention

Another avenue into concepts is to support students to *invent* the concepts themselves. Other approaches such as puzzles or kinaesthetic activities provide additional scaffolding. For example, to introduce while loops, introduce the need for repetition and have the students invent the actual syntax and structure, based on their earlier understanding of if-statements. We discuss further examples in the subsequent sections.

8.3 Computing unplugged

Unplugged computing (Bell, et al., 2009) involves teaching concepts away from the computer. Unplugged activities provide ways to understand concepts in a constructivist way (Papert and Harel, 1991). As with all approaches based on analogy, it is vital that the links to the concepts demonstrated are clearly made. Without this students can be left understanding the everyday version of the activity but not the computing concept itself. Unplugged activities are a physical, rather than verbal, version of applying semantic waves (Macnaught et al., 2013) where the physical activity is a way of engaging with the concept in a concrete way, before ascending the wave to make the link to the technical concept.

Key concept: Unplugged computing

Unplugged computing involves teaching computing away from computers. Physical objects are used to illustrate abstract concepts. There are a variety of approaches to do this centred around kinaesthetic approaches. Variations include role playing computation, puzzles, games and magic. Much of the strength is in the way intangible abstract concepts are made physical, so can be pointed to, manipulated and questions easily asked about them.

Kinaesthetic activities

In direct kinaesthetic unplugged activities (Curzon et al., 2009) tangible objects are used as representatives of abstract concepts. These can be physically manipulated (e.g. by following an algorithm). In doing so learners are able to see, point to and manipulate objects. This can make it much easier to explore the concepts involved and makes it easier to ask questions about things that aren't understood. A barrier to asking questions is often that the person does not possess the vocabulary to even frame the question. By providing a physical representation, the learner can point to it and ask the question at the level of the analogy rather than having to fully verbalize it at the technical level. This kind of unplugged activity can also be used to encourage students to invent concepts.

Example activity: Kinaesthetic binary search

In the CS Unplugged 'Binary Search' activity (csunplugged, 2008), participants are encouraged to invent binary search. A physical scenario for doing the search is set up with a series of numbered objects placed in order under cups. The student must find a particular object, looking under as few cups as possible. The secret is to check the middle first and use the ball there as a sign post as to which half to then search recursively; if students don't immediately come up with this idea, then can be given scaffolded hints of how to speed up what they are doing.

Role playing computation

The kinaesthetic approach can be taken a step further: role playing computation. Instead of physical objects taking the place of virtual things and the student applying an algorithm to them, the computation now acts on the students themselves. The CS Unplugged 'Beat the clock: Sorting Networks' activity (Bell et al., 2015) is a classic example. Students act as pieces of data that are sorted into order following an algorithm.

Dance and sport can also provide engaging activities. A BBC Live Lesson (*Strictly micro:bit*, 2016) demonstrated why the order of instructions matters in an algorithm, by having dancers dance a dance where the steps had been shuffled. Dance has also been used as a way to visualize sort algorithms. Sort algorithms can alternatively be turned into a sport's day relay race sorting numbered bean bags into order in buckets as fast as possible.

Example activity: Role playing program execution

Assignment is a threshold concept when learning programming. In the Teaching London Computing 'Box Variables' activity (*Box variables*, n.d.) students role play being variables: storage spaces with shredders and photocopiers included. A fragment of code, such as assignments that do a swap, is executed on those variables. This builds a clear mental model of how a sequence of assignments works. It gives a clear, visual illustration of how a single value is *copied* from elsewhere then stored, with old values discarded (*shredded*). It also makes a tangible distinction between names (a label round the person's neck), the variable (the box the person holds) and the value (the thing placed in the box).

Students can role play commands as well as data, wiring them together as in the 'Imp Computer' activity (*Imp computer*, n.d.), to illustrate control structures. Program fragments can be 'compiled' onto a group of students, 'wired' together each acting as a statement or test, following their instruction only when a baton (the program counter) is passed to them.

Puzzles

Computer scientists have long used puzzles as a way of developing computational thinking skills (Harel, 2004, Levitin and Levitin, 2011). Popular logic puzzles including Sudoku can be used as a way to develop logical thinking skills. Variations of many puzzles of the forms found in newspapers and puzzle books can be used to illustrate a wide range of concepts in computer science. Teaching London Computing provides a variety of puzzles for use to illustrate different concepts (*Puzzles*, n.d.).

Puzzles can give a simple, but fun, way to actively work with concepts. An obvious example of this is in understanding concepts related to encryption, by being given ciphertext as a puzzle to decrypt with and without keys. This can lead to active learning around concepts such as encryption, decryption, frequency analysis, cribs, plaintext and ciphertext, encryption keys, symmetric and asymmetric ciphers, as well as different encryption algorithms. Puzzles can also recreate other forms of attack such as man-in-the-middle attacks by setting the puzzle as being to forward an encrypted message with an additional sentence added. A similar approach can be taken with other concepts, turning specific algorithms into puzzles: follow the algorithm to solve the puzzle. For example, compression puzzles are a way to understand concepts around compression of text (*Compression Puzzles*, n.d.).

More general concepts can also be illuminated this way. For example, the simple 'Swap puzzle' (*Swap puzzle*, n.d.) involves swapping the positions of pieces by sliding or jumping them; this can be used to explore not only what is meant by an algorithm, but also how there can be different algorithms that solve the same problem. It also illustrates that such alternatives can take different numbers of steps and so lead to an understanding of concepts linked to the efficiency of algorithms.

Art

Art activities can be linked to some concepts. For example, one CS Unplugged activity involves creating necklaces that encode binary in the colours or shapes of beads. Variations of colour-by-number pixel puzzles (*Pixel Puzzles*, n.d.) can also be used to explore concepts related to image representation. These square grid puzzles, where numbers represent the colour of each square, are a way of introducing bitmap graphics. Interdisciplinary links can also be made to the art movement of Pointilism (painting with lots of small circles) and Roman mosaics/tesserai (pixels as pieces of glass). Variations of these puzzles can illustrate colour depth and image compression. Transmission of images can be introduced using a kinaesthetic activity, transmitting pictures across the room. This gives another example of invention of concepts. Give students the task of transmitting a pixel puzzle drawing across the room by holding up signs with numbers on. Then, encourage them to invent a way of transmitting the image while sending fewer numbers (e.g. invent run-length encoding). Vector graphics can be introduced using pictures created from shapes that can also be set in a puzzle context. Recursion can be introduced using recursive images such as drawings of grass or trees (*Doodle Art*, n.d.). The larger context to this can be CGI (computer-generated imagery) central to the special effects of films and also generative art, where algorithms are used to generate art.

Games

Games of all kinds can provide a way to teach concepts embedded in those games. This extends from simple pencil and paper games to appropriately designed video games. The game can be centrally linked to the concept or just provide an engaging context. For example, the card game Control-Alt-Hack® (www.ControlAltHack.com) is explicitly designed to teach computing concepts. It sets the players as ethical hackers working for a security company to provide security audits. It aims to help players understand wide-ranging security concepts from encryption to social engineering, as they play the game, embarking on security missions. Other games draw on close analogies. For example, playing 20-Questions (*20-questions*, n.d.) can be used to illustrate divide and conquer. If you just name people in turn: 'Is it Adele?', 'Is it Batman?', . . ., doing a linear search through the names of all famous people, you will not win! Playing it well involves finding halving questions. Games can also provide an engaging context as in the Brain-in-a-Bag activity discussed further below, where Snap is used as a game for unplugged brains to play to illustrate neural nets or logic gates (*Brain-in-a-bag*, n.d.).

Magic and mystery

Magic tricks can be used to illustrate a wide range of computing concepts in fun, memorable ways. Challenge the class to work out both how the magic works, and the link to computer science. A trick that magicians call 'self-working' is exactly what a computer scientist calls an algorithm. The trick comprises a series of specific instructions that if followed in the given order always results in a specific, desired magical effect. In a card trick this outcome might be the magical effect that the card you end up with is the one predicted, for example. Computer programs are just algorithms written in a language that a computer, rather than a human magician, can follow with the guaranteed effect of whatever the program is supposed to do. This analogy gives an interesting way to introduce both algorithms and the concepts of computational thinking to the class.

Example activity: A magic trick

Download the teleporting robot jigsaw trick (*Teleporting robot*, n.d.) and cut out the pieces. To do the magic, a very simple three-step algorithm is followed: count the robots, rebuild the jigsaw in a different way, count the robots again. One robot disappears. Everyone can do the trick by following the instructions. The point of algorithms is you need no understanding of what is going on for the correct effect to be guaranteed to happen – that is what computers need in programs as all they do is follow instructions blindly. The magic trick illustrates why algorithms are the basis of computing.

The idea of using a magic trick to teach computing was first used as part of Computer Science Unplugged (e.g. to illustrate error-correcting codes in the Card Flip Magic Activity (Bell et al., 2015)). 'The Magic of Computer Science' series (McOwan and Curzon, 2008; McOwan, Curzon and Black, 2009; Curzon and McOwan, 2015) take easy to perform self-working tricks, showing how the secret techniques can be mapped to many different concepts in computing, such as binary, search algorithms and pattern recognition. Tricks can be used as openers to a study session using the emotional hook and mystery of magic to set the scene for in-depth analysis of the taught concepts.

The way tricks are invented and written down also explores computational thinking concepts such as decomposition (full tricks are built from combinations of smaller techniques), generalization (creating a new trick from the principle of an old one) and evaluation (are you sure enough it works to present it to an audience?).

Presentation matters as much as the algorithm if a trick is to be fit for purpose. This gives a way to introduce concepts around usability (i.e. that programs are fit for purpose). The same understanding of human cognition is as important when presenting a magic trick as when designing software that is easy and intuitive to use (McOwan, Curzon and Black, 2009; Curzon and McOwan, 2015). This provides an avenue into discussing the importance of human factors in computing.

Having mastered the performance and learning opportunities of self-working magic, develop your own lessons based on self-working card tricks, starting with Fulves' (1976) classic self-working tricks series. Diaconis and Graham (2013) take a more detailed dive into the world of mathematical card magic.

Part of the strength of magic tricks as the basis of a strategy for teaching concepts is the mystery involved, which we discuss further below.

8.4 Context-based learning

Context-based learning involves teaching concepts within either real-life or fictitious, but realistic, examples. This involves actively engaging students with the material rather than presenting concepts in an isolated and theoretical manner. If topics can be set in a context that relates to a student's interests and pre-existing knowledge and understanding, then that interest can drive their learning. Several different contexts can be drawn on to support learning of computing concepts.

Within-syllabus context

The most basic context is that of the wider subject itself. The computing syllabus is not just a series of largely self-contained areas. There are rich links between them. Drawing out the connections, and scaffolding students to do so themselves is important. In particular, it is helpful to place more basic topics in a wider context of the subject, so that they are not just abstractions. For example, binary representations are often taught in isolation. They can instead be motivated by the context of networking and how text is represented, allowing messages to be sent between computers. Concept maps, discussed below, can be used by students to draw out wider links across a subject. This relates to the higher levels of the SOLO taxonomy, where being able to form such links is a measure of intellectual progress (Biggs and Collis, 1982).

Technological contexts

In computing, within-syllabus contexts can be extended to real-world technological contexts. Computers are increasingly ubiquitous and so disappearing into the environment. For example, rather than just discuss binary representations of letters and images in the context of networking, such binary representations can be put in the context of how mobile phones represent and send texts. Image representation can be set in the context of how a digital camera works. This draws on a student's curiosity in understanding how technology actually works.

Historical context

An historical context can be used to help understand many concepts. For example, Roman numerals were better for large numbers than the notches in sticks used by shepherds. However, it is hard to do multiplication with Roman numerals, which is why they were eventually replaced. These examples show why number representation matters. Prominence can also be given to the roles of women through the history of computing by telling the stories of Ada Lovelace, Grace Hopper and others. Pre-computer-age historical links can intrigue, combining with the storytelling approach of providing strong narratives (see box).

Example activity: Historical storytelling

Cryptography and steganography date back thousands of years. For example, Mary Queen of Scots was placed under house arrest by Elizabeth I for twenty-one years. Mary became involved in an assassination plot. She communicated with the plotters by hiding messages in casks of ale (steganography) and used a simple substitution cipher. Elizabeth's spy master knew of the plot and his man-in-the-middle attack, intercepting messages, using frequency analysis to read them, and adding text to the end of messages, gave him the evidence he needed to execute the plotters.

Historical approaches can link to history syllabuses. The role of Bletchley Park in cracking cyphers gives new understanding about the actions of allied commanders, and their ability to outmanoeuvre the Nazis.

Cross-curricula context

Computing has rich interdisciplinary links, both drawing on other subjects, and in changing the way they are done. We have already seen links to art and history. Taking a science example, computer scientists have drawn from biology approaches such as neural networks (computing based on the way the brain works) and genetic algorithms (computing based on the way evolution works). Computational modelling can also be used as a method for bringing to life concepts in other subjects. At the same time the concept of computational modelling itself can be explored.

Example of computational modelling

The Teaching London Computing Brain-in-a Bag activity (*Brain-in-a-bag*, n.d.) gives a memorable way to teach how neurons work in biology, and computational modelling and neural networks (or logic gates at a simpler level) in computing. Students role play neurons, passing tubes (neurotransmitters) to connected neurons only when their internal rules allow it. Different students act as sensory, relay and motor neurons. Wired in the right way, the students act as a brain that automatically plays Snap.

Non-computing contexts

Another useful kind of context is that of non-computing contexts. This allows students to understand new abstract concepts in terms of things they already understand or that are physical and tangible and so easier to understand first (i.e. lower down the semantic wave). It draws on constructivist principles and shows how computer science is about much more than computers.

For example, Braille can be used as a way to introduce binary representations. It is a binary system of bumps and no-bumps that was the first practical use of a binary representation of characters. For teaching purposes it is helpful that it is a physical binary representation that students can touch for themselves; it has a real and valuable purpose. Another example of this approach is that of helping people with locked-in syndrome discussed earlier.

Research context

Another way of embedding concepts in context is to use research stories. This is the basis of the *Computer Science for Fun* magazine and website (www.cs4fn.org). It presents research in a fun way, using accessible language. Jargon is kept to a minimum but clear explanations of core computing concepts are embedded in this research context. Topics go beyond the syllabus showing how more basic concepts are the foundation of leading-edge research. This sets concepts into the context of potential future technology. The interdisciplinary aspect of many research stories also gives another way of providing cross-curricular context. For example, a 2016 issue covered generative art inspired by the way ants leave chemical trails and using evolutionary computing techniques. Another discussed an interactive art installation based on bee communication. These pull together topics in computing, electronics, art and biology, showing how artists can be programmers inspired by science. Presented as a desirable magazine, *cs4fn* was originally intended as hobby-mode learning to be read as any other magazine. However, schools use it in many other ways including as set reading in lessons or homework, as a source of ideas for writing, and to support literacy.

8.5 Enquiry-based learning

The way science is traditionally taught is a cause of students' declining interest in STEM with age (Rocard, 2007). Enquiry-based learning, where students are supported to explore topics using real scientific method, has been found to help arrest the decline in student attitudes towards STEM and foster better scientific thinking, while giving a deep way to learn concepts.

TEMI

TEMI (Teaching Enquiry with Mysteries Incorporated) (teachingmysteries.eu) is an enquiry-based learning framework using a mystery as a hook to engage students. It defines enquiry in terms of a student cognitive skill set and uses a stepwise progression to engender confident enquirers. It exploits the affective side of learning, the need to engage emotionally and creatively, that is at the core of all scientific practice. The TEMI framework is based on the 5Es *learning* cycle (Bybee et al., 2006), an effective methodology for teaching concepts where the students do the work.

Key concept: The 5Es learning cycle

The 5Es *learning* cycle involves structuring lessons around the following five stages.

(1) Engage: Students are first hooked. In TEMI this is by the chosen mystery. It generates questions.

(2) Explore: Students then carry out research and experiments, to answer the question(s) identified in the 'engage' phase.

(3) Explain: Students summarize their learning so far. The teacher assesses understanding, possibly intervening to ensure students correctly grasp principles.

(4) Extend: Students use their new learning in a different context, applying the concepts they have learnt about.

(5) Evaluate: Students reflect on what and how they have learnt so they can build on the skills developed. This stage may include formal testing.

A gradual release of responsibilities through the stages structures the learning activity, starting from the teachers acting as model, employing a phased apprenticeship approach where students take responsibility for their own learning, mistakes and successes. Binding TEMI lessons together is showmanship, maintaining a sense of excitement as activities unfold.

Example of a TEMI Lesson

The TEMI lesson 'Your number's divided' (Loziak et al., 2016) is a maths and computing example. Its mystery is based around a magic trick where the magician can know something about a freely chosen six-digit number. The *engage* stage involves performing the trick. Three students choose a three-digit number then double it up (e.g. 123 becomes 123123). You immediately give each a number that divides into their number and they check you are correct. You finish in a flourish making further predictions based on the numbers. In the *explore* phase you do the trick repeatedly allowing the class to collect data and look for patterns, noticing for example, the factors called are always 7, 11, and 13 in some order. In the *explain* step, with teacher support, they note that multiplying those three numbers gives 1001 and multiplying a three digit number by 1001 is the same as duplicating it. The *extend* step involves applying the principle in other contexts such as if the original number is a single digit duplicated three times like 333. At this point it can be linked to the need to calculate prime factors in encryption systems (e.g. for online shopping). In the *evaluate* step students are asked, for example, 'would it work with a 2-digit number, so multiplying by 101?'

This gradually releases responsibility as you first carry out an enquiry step explaining your hypothesis and tests by explaining aloud: 'I do'. The students record your thinking onto a structured worksheet (a 'hypothesizer lifeline') gathering data in the form of numbers. In the next phase students take over and using their sheet, record their hypotheses, tests and results: 'you do'. Ultimately the students are led towards solving the mystery using ideas about prime factorization and number patterns in the multiplication by 1001.

8.6 Enquiry through computational modelling and programming

A way to teach computing concepts with students who can program is to set exercises to write programs that implement them. This can be done in an enquiry-based way. Care needs to be taken to scaffold exercises and ensure they are at appropriate levels for students' programming skill. It forces students to deeply engage with the concepts.

In a similar way, computational modelling can be used as a way to investigate other subjects. The Turtle (Millican, 2016) and Greenfoot (www.greenfoot.org) programming environments come with a variety of examples. For example, by writing a program that simulates Brownian motion, how ants leave trails or the forces acting on a projectile that lead to its trajectory, one gets to better understand that phenomena. This kind of activity can involve programming from scratch or editing parameters on a pre-written simulation. It leads to a better understanding of computational modelling as an investigative tool.

8.7 Discourse and active writing

The approaches discussed so far draw, to a greater or lesser extent, on natural language. We now focus on how it can be used directly to enhance (and assess) learners' knowledge.

Talking as well as doing

Grover and Pea (2013) argue that students gain a better understanding of concepts if 'discourse-intensive pedagogical practices' are used. This involves ensuring tasks are combined both with discussion with peers (hence the importance of group work) and productive teacher-led discussions. This again links to the theory of semantic waves (Macnaught et al., 2013) with the teacher encouraging discussion moving from the concrete activities to the concepts.

Grover and Pea (2013) do this in the context of students using App Inventor to write apps, discussing concepts needed and encountered in the process. The idea is also part of exercises encouraging students to actively look for computing concepts in everyday examples. Furthermore, it is good to encourage students to always explain the programs they write to someone else. Actively explaining how a program works is a powerful way of gaining a deeper understanding of the program and the concepts. This is also a very positive thing to do as part of debugging. Often bugs highlight incorrect mental models of the underlying concepts. Trying to explain how a program works can lead to the student seeing the problem themselves. This extends to explaining algorithms to understand the concepts behind them too.

Short writing activities

Defining and explaining concepts or exploiting concepts when explaining code, are common teaching strategies. Asking learners to do the same is a common form of assessment. The short texts which learners *write* in response give useful snapshots of their knowledge of the concepts concerned. Although a piece of writing can seem to be a static and fixed product, it is actually the embodiment of lots of processes of thinking and composition. Focusing on how a text is composed is a good way to make a student aware of the thinking – the conceptualization – embodied in that writing.

Examples of short writing activities

In the following series of activities, the answers provided by previous students to short assessment questions are used with current students' to revise their conceptual knowledge and focus their attention on how to present their conceptual knowledge effectively in an assessment context. Students involved commented they enjoyed this approach because the teacher 'was testing our understanding, not just telling us things'.

The first approach focuses on 'what makes a good exam answer' to a question such as *'Explain what is meant by a "system call"?'* First review the concepts involved then have students discuss their expectations about the answer in small groups. Next provide five candidates' answers to this question that range from high scoring to low scoring with students role playing being examiners. In their groups they should decide how they would grade the answers using terms like *Poor, Some merit, Good;* and/or by putting them in order. The class then vote on grades and the actual grades/order are shared. Next, the groups discuss the 'criteria' they used to decide on grades. They are likely to generate criteria specific to the particular question. Steer them towards more generic criteria and have them share their thoughts with the whole class, before sharing the criteria used by the examiners, part of which will involve correct concepts and relationships between concepts, and part is to do with the command words (such as 'Explain' or 'Compare') in the question and how these mean that the question predicts the shape of the answer.

As a follow-up, take a student's answer where some of the statements *are* related to the question (although perhaps not exactly accurately) and some *are not*, then present the answer broken up into its separate statements. Students work in groups to identify two statements which deal with concepts relevant to the conceptual field of the question and two that are irrelevant and actually belong to different conceptual fields.

Another exercise is to give students lists of concepts which are related to a question. They allocate the concepts to columns in a table headed: *Most Related, Somewhat Related, Little Related.* Share the students' tables and invite comment and critique.

Understanding concepts involves understanding relationships between concepts. Explain this, then present students with sentences linking concepts in which one of the concepts is omitted (e.g. *'A system call causes a _____'*), together with a mixed-up list of the omitted concept words. In groups they complete the sentences, before discussing the answers.

Concept maps

Concept maps provide a visual way to work actively with concepts and the relationships between them. They can be used both as a way to develop understanding and as a diagnostic test of students' understanding. Both are useful in the teaching of concepts. One of the advantages is that they give a way for students to frame their thoughts and understand when those thoughts are still hazy. They can also be used as a stepping stone towards writing sentences. One simple way to use concept maps is as a variation on writing the relationship statements discussed above. Partially created concept maps must be filled in using a set of given terms. Another is to draw concept maps based on the students' own written answers to questions, then compare these with an expert concept map. This could be used as part of a role playing exercise where the students play the part of an examiner commenting on the work of other students based on the discrepancies to the expert concept map.

Diagnostically, concept maps can be used to identify students who need extra support in an area, or to correct the misunderstandings of individual students face to face. Another variation is for students to be presented with a question and first aim to brainstorm around twenty concepts that are related to the question, before creating a draft concept map from it. Students can also be encouraged to draw links between concept maps drawn for different conceptual areas. By doing activities around concept maps over time, students can start to build up much richer conceptualisations of the subject themselves (Novak and Cañas, 2006).

Program and algorithm comprehension

Programming is a skill. However, it is still important that a strong focus is placed on the deep understanding of underlying concepts. It is easy for students to focus on syntax, seeing the task of learning to program as one of remembering keywords and punctuation. Teaching approaches need to ensure that syntax is seen as the least important issue with the focus being instead on semantics. That involves deeply understanding programming concepts. The many ways to teach concepts already discussed provide an initial way to do this, but with programming, formative assessment based on dry run/tracing is a critically important additional way. The focus of dry run activities and of feedback around them, should not be the final answer but on the program's step-by-step operation.

Key concept: Dry run

Dry-run activities involve working out on paper, step-by-step, the execution of a program, keeping track of the values in variables and the results of tests as each line of a program executes. They help students understand the operational semantics – the step by step workings – of the program and so of the concepts behind the underlying constructs.

Pencil-and-paper dry-run exercises can also be integrated with drama-based unplugged techniques to act out the execution of fragments of code to demonstrate how programming constructs work and so understand the concepts involved.

8.8 Summary

It is easy to fall into the trap of believing that teaching concepts boils down to giving clear definitions for students to learn. This is essentially a transmission model of teaching. We have shown in this chapter that there are many alternative approaches that allow learners to directly engage with concepts in more constructivist ways, building on their existing knowledge and experience. The best approaches combine these techniques giving multiple and rich ways to understand concepts and their inter-relations. The ideas behind semantic waves are key to many of these approaches. They involve in various ways travelling the semantic wave, from technical concept down to everyday experience, but then critically back up the wave with clear links made back to the technical concept.

Key points

- Success in programming and computational thinking skills, as well as computing more generally, is founded on a deep understanding of rich concepts.
- Concepts do not have to be taught using a transmission model of teaching.
- There are a wide variety of constructivist approaches that can be used from analogy-based and unplugged approaches to those built around discourse and active writing.
- Aim to embed discussion within one of the many contexts available for teaching computing concepts, including interdisciplinary approaches.
- Tell stories and use mystery to engage pupils with concepts in memorable ways.
- Use a mixture of approaches and contexts.
- Whatever techniques are used to teach concepts, aim to travel down and then back up the semantic wave.

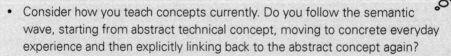

Further reflection

- Consider how you teach concepts currently. Do you follow the semantic wave, starting from abstract technical concept, moving to concrete everyday experience and then explicitly linking back to the abstract concept again?
- Identify concepts you currently teach using simple transmission and explore which if any of the approaches listed apply.
- Identify threshold concepts that students struggle with. Could a targeted change help students overcome the problem?

References

Algorithmic doodle art (n.d.) Available at: https://teachinglondoncomputing.org/algorithmic-doodle-art/

Bell, T, J Alexander, I Freeman and M Grimley (2009). 'Computer Science Unplugged: School Students Doing Real Computing Without Computers' 13(1) *The New Zealand Journal of Applied Computing and Information Technology* 20–29.

Bell, T, IH Witten, M Fellows, R Adams, J McKenzie, M Powell and S Jarman (2015). *CS unplugged*. Available at: http://csunplugged.org/wp-content/uploads/2015/03/CSUnplugged_OS_2015_v3.1.pdf.

Biggs, JB and K Collis (1982). *Evaluating the Quality of Learning: The SOLO Taxonomy* (Cambridge MA, Academic Press).

Bybee, RW, JA Taylor, A Gardiner, P Van Scotter, JC Powell, A Westbrook and N Landes (2006). *The BSCS 5E Instructional Model: Origins and Effectiveness*. Available at: http://science.education.nih.gov/houseofreps.nsf/b82d55fa138783c2852572c9004f5566/$FILE/Appendix%20D.pdf

Compression code puzzles (n.d.). Available at: https://teachinglondoncomputing.org/compression-code-puzzles/

Computational thinking: searching To speak (n.d.). Available at: https://teachinglondoncomputing.org/resources/inspiring-computing-stories/computational-thinking-searching-to-speak/.

csunplugged (2008). *Unplugged: The Show. Part 10: Binary Search – Divide and Conquer* [Video file] Available at: www.youtube.com/watch?v=iDVH3oCTc2c

Curzon, P (2014). *Computing without Computers*, V 0.15. Feb, QMUL. Available at: https://teachinglondoncomputing.org/resources/inspiring-computing-stories/computingwithoutcomputers/.

Curzon, P and PW McOwan (2015). 'The Magic of Computer Science III: Magic meets Mistakes, Machines and Medicine'. QMUL. Available at: https://cs4fndownloads.wordpress.com/magic-computer-science-3/

Curzon, P and PW McOwan (2017). 'The Power of Computational Thinking: Games, Magic and Puzzles to Help You become a Computational Thinker'. World Scientific.

Curzon, P, PW McOwan, QI Cutts and T Bell (2009). 'Enthusing and Inspiring with Reusable Kinaesthetic Activities' 41(3) *ACM SIGCSE Bulletin – ITiCSE '09* 94–98. ACM.

Diaconis, P and R Graham (2013). *Magical Mathematics* (Princeton, Princeton University Press).

Dr Seuss (1958). *The Cat in the Hat Comes Back* (New York, Random House).

Fulves, K (1976). *Self Working Card Tricks* (Mineola, Dover Publications).

Grover, S and R Pea (2013). 'Using a Discourse-intensive Pedagogy and Android's App Inventor for Introducing Computational Concepts to Middle School Students' in *Proceedings of the 44th SIGCSE Technical Symposium on Computer Science Education*, 723–728.

Harel, D and Y Feldman (2004). *Algorithmics: The Spirit of Computing* (Harlow, Addison Wesley).

Levitin, A and M Levitin (2011). *Algorithmic Puzzles* (Oxford, Oxford University Press).

Loziak, D, PW McOwan and C Olivotto (eds), (2016). *The Book of Science Mysteries*, Version 2.0. TEMI. Available at: https://cs4fndownloads.wordpress.com/temi-book-of-science-mysteries/

Maton, K (2013). 'Making Semantic Waves: A Key to Cumulative Knowledge-Building' 24(1) *Linguistics and Education* 8–22.

Macnaught, L, K Maton, JR Martin, E Matruglio (2013). 'Jointly Constructing Semantic Waves: Implications for Teacher Training' 24 *Linguistics and Education* 50–63.

McOwan, PW and P Curzon (2008). *The Magic of Computer Science: Card Tricks Special*, QMUL. Available at: https://cs4fndownloads.wordpress.com/magic-computer-science-1/

McOwan, PW, P Curzon and J Black (2009). *The Magic of Computer Science II: Now We Have Your Attention . . .*, (QMUL). Available at: https://cs4fndownloads.wordpress.com/magic-computer-science-2/

Meyer, JHF and R Land (eds), (2006). *Overcoming Barriers to Student Understanding: Threshold Concepts and Troublesome Knowledge* (London, Routledge).

Millican, P (2016). *The Turtle System: Computer Science across the Curriculum*. Available at: www.turtle.ox.ac.uk/csac

Novak J D and AJ Cañas (2006). *The Theory Underlying Concept Maps and How to Construct Them* (Technical Report No IHMC CmapTools 2006–01) (Pensacola, FL, Institute for Human and Machine Cognition).

Papert, S and I Harel (1991). *Constructionism* (New York, NY, Ablex Publishing).

Pixel puzzle pictures and computational thinking (n.d.) Available at: https://teachinglondoncomputing.org/pixel-puzzles/

Puzzles and computational thinking (n.d.) Available at: https://teachinglondoncomputing.org/puzzles/

Rocard, M (2007). 'Science Education NOW: A Renewed Pedagogy for the Future of Europe' (Brussels, European Commission). Available at: http://ec.europa.eu/research/science-society/document_library/pdf_06/report-rocard-onscience-educationen.pdf.

Strictly micro:bit – Live Lesson (2016). Available at: www.bbc.co.uk/programmes/articles/49tjW0qR05wXrdpK7ZbGTbs/strictly-micro-bit-live-lesson

The Box Variable Activity (n.d.) Available at: https://teachinglondoncomputing.org/resources/inspiring-unplugged-classroom-activities/the-box-variable-activity/

The Brain in a Bag Activity (n.d.) Available at: https://teachinglondoncomputing.org/resources/inspiring-unplugged-classroom-activities/the-brain-in-a-bag-activity/

The Imp Computer Activity (n.d.) Available at: https://teachinglondoncomputing.org/resources/inspiring-unplugged-classroom-activities/the-imp-computer-activity/

The Swap Puzzle Activity (n.d.) Available at: https://teachinglondoncomputing.org/resources/inspiring-unplugged-classroom-activities/the-swap-puzzle-activity/

The Teleporting Robot (and Melting Snowman) Activity (n.d.) Available at: https://teachinglondoncomputing.org/resources/inspiring-unplugged-classroom-activities/the-teleporting-robot-activity/

The 20-Questions Activity (n.d.) Available at: https://teachinglondoncomputing.org/resources/inspiring-unplugged-classroom-activities/the–20-questions-activity/

9

Teaching Programming

Michael E. Caspersen

Chapter outline

Chapter synopsis

The defining characteristic of the computer is its programmability and programming is the essence of computing/informatics. Indeed, computing is much more than programming, but programming – the process of expressing one's ideas and understanding of the concepts and processes of a domain in a form that allows for execution on a computing device without human interpretation – is essential to computing.

Teaching and learning programming is not easy; in fact, it is considered one of the grand challenges of computing education. In this chapter, we describe the nature of the challenge, and we provide a dozen teaching strategies to help overcome the challenge.

For the interested reader, this chapter offers many references to the vast amount of research literature on the topic.

9.1 Introduction

Writing a chapter about the teaching of programming is an intriguing, but for many reasons also a challenging task and entire books could be written on the subject.

One aspect of the challenge is the abundance of programming technologies (programming languages and environments) that can be used for teaching programming. The programming technologies can be categorized according to language paradigm with archetypical subcategories such as procedural, object-orientated, functional, relational and concurrent languages (note that these subcategories are not mutually disjoint; a specific programming language may fit in several categories). Or they can be categorized according to syntactical appearance, i.e. lexical (text-based) or graphical (block-based) languages.

In this chapter, we refrain from using a specific programming technology. This decision has advantages and disadvantages. An advantage is that the chapter is applicable regardless of which language technology you as a teacher intend to use. A disadvantage is the lack of concrete examples, expressed in a specific programming technology that you can apply directly in your teaching.

The first section describes the challenge of teaching programming. In section two, which is the heart of the chapter, we present a dozen teaching strategies that can help overcome some of the challenges of teaching programming. In the third section, we briefly discuss concrete technologies and some contemporary teaching approaches relevant in today's programming classroom.

9.2 Teaching and learning programming is a grand challenge

In some ways, programming education has changed dramatically over the past more than fifty years. From assembly programming via Fortran, Algol, and Pascal to C++, Java, Python, and JavaScript – or from Lisp via Standard ML and Miranda to Scheme and Haskell – we have experienced a rich and successful development in programming language technologies and an accompanying development of teaching practices.

However, in other ways, things have not changed that much and it is still the case that typical introductory programming textbooks devote most of their content to presenting knowledge about a particular language (Robins et al., 2003).

Exposing students to the process of programming is merely implied but not explicitly addressed in texts on programming, which appear to deal with 'program' as a noun rather than as a verb.

But teaching programming is much more than teaching a programming language. Knowledge about a programming language is a necessary but far from sufficient condition for learning the practice of programming. Students also need knowledge about *the programming process*, i.e. how to *develop* programs, and they need to extend that knowledge into *programming skills*.

David Gries pointed this out already in 1974, when he wrote as follows (Gries, 1974, p. 82):

> Let me make an analogy to make my point clear. Suppose you attend a course in cabinet making. The instructor briefly shows you a saw, a plane, a hammer, and a few other tools, letting you use each one for a few minutes. He next shows you a beautifully-finished cabinet. Finally, he tells you to design and build your own cabinet and bring him the finished product in a few weeks. You would think he was crazy!

Clearly, cabinet making cannot be taught simply by teaching the tools of the trade and demonstrating finished products, but neither can programming.

Nevertheless, judged by the majority of past as well as contemporary textbooks, this is what is being attempted. In (Kölling, 2003), a survey of thirty-nine major selling textbooks on introductory programming was presented. The overall conclusion of the survey was that all books are structured according to the language constructs of the programming language; the process of program development is often merely implied rather than explicitly addressed.

A typical structure of a section on a specific language construct (e.g. the while loop), is the presentation of a problem followed by a presentation of a program to solve that problem and a discussion of the program's elements. From the viewpoint of a student, the program was developed in a single step, starting from a problem specification and resulting in a working solution.

This pattern of introducing material creates – unintentionally – the illusion that programming is trivial and straightforward. The fact that we all, when we start addressing a problem, start with incomplete and incorrect programs, which we then gradually modify by extending, refining and restructuring our implementation until we arrive at an acceptable solution, seems to be swept under the carpet as if it was an embarrassing secret that must not be mentioned. While the ultimate solution to the problem is explained in detail, the process – how we go about developing the solution – is almost entirely neglected in textbooks and beginners' courses (Caspersen and Kölling, 2009).

Essentially, programming is one of the best-kept secrets of programming education!

As mentioned, David Gries pinpointed this already in 1974, but it is still an issue, and this is the reason why, to this day, teaching and learning programming is still considered one of computing education's grand challenges (McGettrick et al., 2005). In the report, the authors write:

> Major concerns exist among the academic community internationally that when we set out to teach programming skills to students, we are less successful than we need to be and ought to be [...]. The particular concern is that, after more than forty [now fifty] years of teaching an essential aspect of our discipline to would-be professionals, we cannot do so reliably. Indeed, there are perceptions that the situation has become worse with time.

In a time where computing/informatics education is becoming general education for all and students don't choose to learn programming out of personal interest, the challenge not only persists, but is reinforced.

According to du Boulay (1989), the difficulties of novices learning programming can be separated into five partially overlapping areas:

- Orientation: Finding out what programming is for.
- The notional machine: understanding the general properties of the machine that one is learning to control.
- Notation: Problems associated with the various formal languages that have to be learned, both mastering syntax and semantics.
- Structure: The difficulties of acquiring standard patterns or schemas that can be used to achieve small-scale goals such as computing the sum using a loop or implementing a 0..* association between two classes.

- Pragmatics: The skill of how to specify, develop, test, and debug programs using whatever tools are available.

The good news is that there are some relatively simple and effective strategies – or didactical principles – that help alleviate the challenge; we organize these strategies into four categories:

- Progression
  - Be application-orientated
  - Let students progress from consumer to producer (use-modify-create)
  - Organize the progression in terms of complexity of tasks, not complexity of language constructs.

- Examples
  - Provide exemplary examples
  - Provide worked examples
  - Establish motivation through passion, play, peers and meaningful projects.

- Abstraction and patterns
  - Reinforce specifications
  - Reinforce patterns
  - Reinforce models and conceptual frameworks (program *into* a language).

- Process
  - Reveal process and pragmatics
  - Provide scaffolding through stepwise self-explanations
  - Apply and teach incremental development through stepwise improvement (i.e. extend, refine, restructure).

These teaching strategies are described in detail in the next section. However, while the strategies help overcome many aspects of the challenge of teaching and learning programming, it still persists (Gries, 1974, p. 5):

> Programming is a skill, and teaching such a skill is much harder than teaching physics, calculus, or chemistry. People expect a student coming out of a programming course to be able to program any problem. No such expectations exist for a calculus or chemistry student. Perhaps our expectations are too high.
>
> Compare programming to writing. In high school, one learns about writing in several courses. In addition, every college freshman takes a writing course. Yet, after all these courses, faculty members still complain that students cannot organise their thoughts and write well! In many ways, programming is harder than writing, so why should a single programming course produce students who can organise their programming thoughts and program well.

Is writing hard? Is teaching writing hard? Well, clearly it depends a great deal upon what you are trying to (teach your students to) write.

Writing a novel, a textbook or a dissertation is very hard and it is hard to teach how to do so. Writing an article, a feature or a report is also fairly hard and hard to teach. Writing a birthday greeting, a to-do list or a text message is much easier and requires very little instruction apart, of course, from learning the basics of (reading and) spelling.

Learning programming is not very different from learning writing. Most of the time, programming is creative and fun. However, like writing, programming is not trivial, and we teachers must embrace the challenge with enthusiasm but also with a humble attitude and reasonable expectations.

9.3 Strategies for teaching programming

In this section, we describe twelve teaching strategies or didactical principles, organized into four categories. The strategies, which are all backed by research and experience, can help to overcome some of the challenges of teaching and learning programming.

Progression
Be application orientated

Traditionally, introductory programming courses apply a bottom-up approach, in the sense that pupils are introduced to basic and foundational concepts and expected to master these before more advanced concepts and principles are introduced. Hence, in a traditional programming course, pupils are often trained in constructing a trivial program as the very first activity, and then later on are trained in adding more layers of complexity to a system in terms of user interfaces, databases, etc. For the technically inclined pupils this may be a feasible approach, but for a more general audience, this could pose severe motivational problems, as we are dealing with a wider range of pupils with much more diverse interests and backgrounds.

There is an even more important reason why a traditional bottom-up approach is fallible. For a general audience, we are not aiming at developing detailed and concrete competences in a specific programming technology; instead, we are aiming at developing interest, critical thinking, creativity and broader skills in programming and computational thinking and practice. Therefore, we recommend an application-orientated top-down approach. This implies to start various teaching activities by introducing toy versions of well-known or familiar applications, which is then split apart for conceptual and/or technical examination, evaluation and modification.

For motivational reasons, we recommend applications based on the criteria, that they must, by themselves, be naturally appealing to pupils in the relevant age range. Applications, which they find interesting to use and hopefully to examine and improve. Examples could include pedagogical lightweight versions of Facebook, iTunes/Spotify, YouTube, Twitter, Blogs, Photoshop, Instagram and similar applications. Or it could be something embedded in a physical context based on Internet of Things (e.g. wearables and smart clothes). But these are just examples; in general, the choice of application types depends on the specific context and target group (Caspersen and Nowack, 2013).

For a specific technology like Scratch, there are a great number of approaches and domains that have inspired educators and researchers to develop teaching materials (e.g. a data-driven approach (Dasgupta and Resnick, 2014), a creativity and maker driven approach (Brennan et al., 2014) and a computing concept driven approach (Armoni and Ben-Ari, 2010; Meerbaum-Salant et al., 2013)).

Let students progress from consumer to producer (use-modify-create)

In (Pattis, 1990), the author introduces the *call before write* approach to teaching introductory programming, arguing that it 'allows students to write more interesting programs early in the course and it familiarizes them with the process of writing programs that call subprograms; so it is more natural for them to continue writing well-structured programs after they learn how to write their own subprograms'.

In (Meyer, 1993), the author introduces the notion of the *inverted curriculum* as follows: 'This proposal suggests a redesign of the teaching of programming and other software topics in universities on the basis of object-oriented principles. It argues that the new 'inverted curriculum' should give a central place to libraries, and take students from the reuse consumer's role to the role of producer through a process of 'progressive opening of black boxes'.

In (Schmolitzky, 2005), the author briefly mentions the notion of *consuming before producing* by providing three specific examples. One example is: 'BlueJ allows beginning with an object "system" with just one class where students just interactively use instances of this class (they *consume* the notion of interacting with an object via its interface). *Producing* the possibility of interacting with an object, on the other hand, requires more knowledge about class internals and should thus be done after the principle of interaction with objects is well understood.'

The *consume-before-produce* principle is applicable to a wide number of topics (e.g. code, specifications, class libraries and frameworks/event-driven programming).

Code: The principle may be applied with respect to the way students write code at three levels of abstractions: method level, class (or module) level and modelling level as follows: (1) *Use methods* (as indicated above, Blue J allows interactive method invocation on objects without writing any code). At this early stage, students can perform experiments with objects in order to investigate the behaviour and determine the actual specification of a method. (2) *Modify methods* by altering statements or expressions in existing methods. (3) *Extend methods* by writing additional code in existing methods. (4) *Create methods* by adding new methods to an existing class. This may also be characterized as *extend class*. (5) *Create class/module* by adding new classes/modules to an existing model. This may also be characterized as *extend model*. (6) *Create model* by building a new model for a system to be implemented.

Specifications: Specifications and assertions can be expressed in many ways (e.g. as Javadoc, test cases, general assertions in code, loop invariants, class invariants and system invariants (constraints in the class model, for instance a specific multiplicity on a relation between two classes)). In all cases, students are gradually exposed to reading and comprehending specifications prior to producing specifications themselves.

Class libraries: Not many years ago, the standard syllabus for introductory programming courses encompassed implementation of standard algorithms for searching and sorting as well as implementation of standard data structures such as stacks, queues, linked lists, trees and binary search trees.

These days, standard algorithms and data structures are provided in class libraries, ready to be used by programmers. By using class libraries that provide advanced functionality, students can do much more interesting things more quickly. Also, experience as consumer presumably motivates learning more about principles and theory behind advanced data structures and packages for distributed programming, etc.

Consequently, algorithms and data structures are one of the areas where we can sacrifice material to find room for all the new things that make up a modern introductory programming course.

Frameworks/event-driven programming: Sometimes, even using a piece of software can be a daunting task. Frameworks are examples of such complex pieces of software.

Frameworks may constitute a part of an introductory programming course, but in order to ease comprehension of a complex framework with call-back methods (inversion of control), it helps to provide a stepping stone in the form of a small and simple framework, which students consume by making a few simple instantiations. After the road has been paved, you may provide a more general taxonomy for frameworks/event-based programming, which is now more easily understood and grasped in the context of the simple toy framework. With the concrete experiences and the taxonomy in the bag, students are prepared to embark on using more complex frameworks.

Christensen and Caspersen (2002) provide a more thorough discussion of an approach to teaching frameworks and event-based programming in introductory programming courses.

Use-Modify-Create: In Lee et al. (2011), the authors describe how CT takes shape for middle and high school youth in the US. They propose using a three-stage progression for engaging youth in CT. This progression, called Use-Modify-Create, describes a pattern of engagement that was seen to support and deepen youths' acquisition of CT (see also Chapter 3, Computational Thinking).

In Caspersen and Bennedsen (2007), the authors describe a similar three-stage progression for working with programs, called Use-Extend-Create. Caspersen and Nowack (2013) also describe Use-Modify-Create as a specialisation of Consumer-to-Producer. A more elaborate or fine-grained version is Use-Alter-Test-Modify-Assess-Refine-Evaluate-Create.

Lee et al. (2011) conclude that the Use-Modify-Create progression is a useful framework for educators and researchers that are looking at how computational thinking develops and how that development can be supported.

Organize the progression in terms of complexity of tasks, not complexity of language constructs

Typically, progression in introductory programming courses is dictated by a bottom-up treatment of the language constructs of the programming language being used, and this is the way most textbooks are structured. We hold, as a general principle, that the progression in the course is defined in terms of the complexity of the worked examples presented to the students and the corresponding exercises and assignments.

Schmolitzky (2005) sketches eleven complexity levels of object systems used in software engineering education. The levels range from single class programs to programs with several packages of classes.

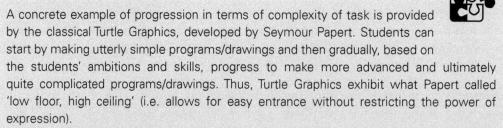

Example: Progression

A concrete example of progression in terms of complexity of task is provided by the classical Turtle Graphics, developed by Seymour Papert. Students can start by making utterly simple programs/drawings and then gradually, based on the students' ambitions and skills, progress to make more advanced and ultimately quite complicated programs/drawings. Thus, Turtle Graphics exhibit what Papert called 'low floor, high ceiling' (i.e. allows for easy entrance without restricting the power of expression).

Another example is to let the progression be defined in terms of complexity of program structure or architecture (e.g. classes and their relationship) by starting with very simple programs with simple functionality and only few components with very simple relationships and then progress to more complex programs with increasingly complex structure and richer functionality. This could be starting with a program with just one component (representing, say, a die, a date, a person, an image, a song, etc.); then work with programs with two components (representing, say, a die and a diecup, a date and a clock, a person and a party, a song and a playlist, etc.) and then go on to work with programs with many components and more complex structure (e.g. a game, music player, an image processing app, etc.). See (Bennedsen and Caspersen, 2004b) for further details.

It is, of course, possible to turn things around and start out using a more complex app, then zoom in and work on a smaller part, perhaps just one component, while modifying this.

Examples

Provide exemplary examples

Examples are important teaching tools. Research in cognitive science confirms that 'examples appear to play a central role in the early phases of cognitive skill acquisition' (VanLehn, 1996). An alternation of worked examples and problems increases the learning outcome compared with just solving more problems (Sweller and Cooper, 1985; Trafton and Reiser, 1993).

Students generalize from examples and use them as templates for their own work. Examples must, therefore, be both easy to generalize and consistent with current learning goals.

By perpetually exposing students to 'exemplary' examples, desirable properties are reinforced many times. Students will eventually recognize patterns of 'good' design and gain experience in telling desirable from undesirable properties. Trafton and Reiser (1993) note that in complex problem spaces, '[l]earners may learn more by solving problems with the guidance of some examples than solving more problems without the guidance of examples.'

With carefully developed examples, teachers can minimize the risk of misinterpretations and erroneous conclusions, which otherwise can lead to misconceptions. Once established, misconceptions can be difficult to resolve and hinder students in their further learning (Clancy, 2004; Ragonis and Ben-Ari, 2005). See also Chapter 13, in which Juha Sorva details many different misconceptions.

A good example must be understandable by students. Otherwise, they cannot construct an effective mental model of the program and it becomes even more difficult to learn how to write a program that a computer can understand. Without 'understanding', knowledge retrieval works only on an example's surface properties, instead of on its underlying structural and conceptual properties (Trafton and Reiser, 1993; VanLehn, 1996).

Furthermore, a good example must effectively communicate the concept(s) to be taught. There should be no doubt about what exactly is exemplified. The structural form of information affects the form of the knowledge encoded in human memory. Conceptual knowledge is improved by best examples and by expository examples, where the best example represents an average, central, or prototypical form of a concept. To minimize cognitive load, an example should exemplify only one new concept (or very few) at a time.

The two example properties (1) understandable by students and (2) effectively communicate the concept(s) to be taught might seem obvious. However, the recurring discussions about the harmfulness or not of certain common examples show that there is quite some disagreement in the teaching community about the meaning of these properties. For further details, including many more references, see (Börstler et al., 2007; 2011; 2015).

Provide worked examples

Studies of students in a variety of instructional situations have shown that they prefer learning from examples rather than learning from other forms of instruction. Students learn more from studying examples than from solving the same problems themselves.

A Worked Example (WE), consisting of (1) a problem statement and (2) a procedure for solving the problem, is an instructional device that provides a problem solution for a learner to study (Atkinson et al., 2000; Chi et al., 1989; LeFevre and Dixon, 1986). WEs are meant to illustrate how similar problems might be solved and are effective instructional tools in many domains, including programming. WEs combined with faded guidance is particularly effective (Caspersen and Bennedsen, 2007).

Atkinson et al. (2000) emphasize three major categories that influence learning from worked examples; Caspersen and Bennedsen (2007) present the categories as how-to principles of constructing and applying examples in education: (1) How to construct examples; (2) How to design lessons that include examples; and (3) How to foster students' thinking process when studying examples. We return to the latter below in sub-section 'Provide scaffolding through stepwise self-explanations'.

Bennedsen and Caspersen (2004a) illustrate implicitly how WEs can be used to teach programming using a systematic, model-based programming process. Caspersen and Bennedsen (2007) present an instructional design for an introductory programming course based on thorough use of WE and Caspersen (2007) provides an overview of WE literature related to programming education as well as a survey of the related cognitive load theory (CLT).

Establish motivation through passion, play, peers and meaningful projects

Mitch Resnick and his research group at the Lifelong Kindergarten at the MIT Media Lab have been developing new technologies, activities, and strategies to engage young people in creative learning experiences (Resnick, 2014). Their approach is based on four core elements, sometimes called the Four P's of Creative Learning:

- *Projects*. People learn best when they are actively working on meaningful projects – generating new ideas, designing prototypes, refining iteratively.
- *Peers*. Learning flourishes as a social activity, with people sharing ideas, collaborating on projects, and building on one another's work.
- *Passion*. When people work on projects they care about, they work longer and harder, persist in the face of challenges, and learn more in the process.
- *Play*. Learning involves playful experimentation – trying new things, tinkering with materials, testing boundaries, taking risks, iterating again and again.

A mantra of the group's work is 'low floor, wide walls, high ceiling'. This is a design principle for technologies to support learning and education and for Scratch in particular, but it can also be used as a design principle for projects to enable diversity in the student population. 'Low floor' means that it should provide easy ways to get started. 'High ceiling' means that it should provide ways to work on increasingly sophisticated aspects over time. But it is not enough to provide a simple pathway from low floor to high ceiling; we also need to provide wide walls so kids can explore multiple pathways from floor to ceiling.

Example

In this example, WE and faded guidance is applied in five stages as follows:

1 In a video, present development of a player with two components, Playlist and Track. [A complete WE]
2 In a lecture, present (a partial) development of a similar example (i.e. with same structure but different cover story). This could be, say, a simple banking system with components Account and Transaction. [A partial WE]
3 In a lab session, students use, modify and extend both examples.
4 In an exercise, students extend the player by adding an Image component that allows several images to be displayed when a Track is played.
5 In an assignment, students implement a similar system (again, similar structure, but different cover story), say, a notebook app with Notes, Keywords, Contacts, etc.

The specific activities can of course be anything else than the specific components mentioned (Playlist, Track, etc.). It could, for instance, be how to make very small program fragments in a specific programming language (say, Scratch, Alice, AgentSheets, Python,

Java or JavaScript), how to make stories or animations in Scratch (Brennan et al., 2014), how to make games and simulations in AgentSheets (Repenning et al., 2015; AgentSheets, 2017) or how to make apps in App Lab (App Lab, 2017).

Abstraction and patterns

Reinforce specifications

In programming, it is essential, at many levels of abstraction, to be able to distinguish and separate *what* a program part does from *how* it does it. A description of what a program does is called a specification; the implementation (i.e. the actual code of the program) is the ultimate description of how it does it. Typically, one specification has many implementations (i.e. there may be many concrete ways to obtain a desired outcome (to meet a specification).

A specification may be expressed as a name of a function, as a comment in natural text, or in a more formal way. The concrete syntactic expression of a specification is not essential; it is the notion of specification itself and the ability to separate specification from implementation that is essential. As Pattis (1990) points out: 'the linguistic ability to cleanly separate a subprogram's specification from its implementation is required to practice the "call before write" approach'.

We therefore hold as principle that the notion of specification is treated as a first-class citizen in introductory programming courses. See (Caspersen, 2007) for more on this.

Reinforce patterns

A pattern captures and describes (the essence of) a recurring structure or process in a given domain. In music, there are patterns of chords that, with minor or major variations of the melody, are used again and again (search the web for 'three chords' or 'four chords' and see for yourself). This is also the case in programming where programming patterns are used again and again to obtain variations of essentially the same structure or process.

The fundamental motivation for a pattern-based approach to teaching programming is that patterns capture chunks of programming knowledge. According to cognitive science and educational psychology, explicit teaching of patterns reinforces schema acquisition as long as the total cognitive load is 'controlled'.

We reinforce patterns at different levels of abstraction including elementary patterns, algorithm patterns and design patterns, but equally important, we provide a conceptual framework for object orientation that qualifies modelling and programming and increases transfer. Furthermore, we stress coding patterns for standard relations between classes (Knudsen and Madsen, 1988; Madsen et al., 1993; East et al., 1996; Muller, 2005; Caspersen, 2007; Caspersen and Bennedsen, 2007).

Reinforce models and conceptual frameworks (program into a language)

The so-called Sapir-Whorf hypothesis from linguistics states that *language defines the boundaries of thought*. Programming languages are artificial and simple so if a programmer's thoughts are nurtured only via the constructs of a specific programming language, these will be severely constrained and have very limiting boundaries.

All programming languages have limitations; we overcome these by thinking and designing in terms of richer and more appropriate concepts and structures which we then simulate in the technology at hand.

In the early days of assembly programming, programmers used jump and compare instructions to *simulate* selection and iteration. This was also the case for the earliest high-level languages with goto statements as the only control structure. Then, control structures for selection and iteration were developed.

Similarly, in the early days of programming, there was no programming language support for arrays (lists) and records (tuples). Consequently, these had to be simulated through careful and minute programming activities.

As long as there was no support for subprograms, but the notion was conceived, programmers had to simulate call and return (and in the general case maintain not only one, but a stack of return addresses).

When there was no support for classes, but the notion of abstract data type was conceived, programmers had to simulate this, again through structured and minute programming activities.

The historic development of programming languages can be viewed as a constant interplay between programming language constructs and architectural abstractions. Limitations in programming languages generate new concepts and architectural abstractions, which can be simulated in existing programming languages. Gradually, these architectural abstractions find their way into mainstream languages, but only to generate more advanced needs and foster new architectural abstractions.

In object-orientated programming, UML and similar modelling languages provide a richer conceptual framework than most object-orientated programming languages support. For example, the notion of association (a special relation between program components) is not directly supported but has to be simulated through structured and minute programming activities. In principle, this is exactly the same situation as simulation of a while loop with goto statements.

When teaching programming, it is important to provide a conceptual framework which is richer than the concrete programming language being used. Programming should not be done *in* a language, but *into* a language.

Conceptual modelling. As a foundation for informatics/computing, we recommend a general introduction to conceptual modelling. Unfortunately, there are no introductory texts on the subject, but Kristensen and Østerbye (1994, section 3) provide a nice section on the subject; the authors present the topic in the context of object-orientated programming languages, but it has much wider applications and implications.

The exposition in Kristensen and Østerby (1994), which originates from (Madsen, Møller-Perdersen and Nygaard, 1993), presents a model of abstraction consisting of three abstraction processes (and their inverses): classification (exemplification), aggregation (decomposition) and generalization (specialization). The model may not be complete, but it has shown its applicability in many cases, including data modelling and object-oriented modelling, but it has the potential to become a much more general framework for informatics and computational thinking. The current focus on computational thinking emphasize abstraction and decomposition as major aspects (Grover and Pea, 2013); however, the above-mentioned framework for conceptual modelling provides a richer and more general approach.

Sowa (1984) is a bold, provocative synthesis of logic, linguistic, and artificial intelligence research, which provides a broader approach to the topic but with a very different perspective.

There are many learning-theoretic arguments for adopting a conceptual framework approach (e.g. a model-driven approach to programming). We provide two (for more details, see (Caspersen, 2007)):

1 Because of their generic nature, the abstract models directly support schema creation and transfer: 'Well-designed learning environments for novices provide *metacognitive managerial guidance* to focus the students' attention and *schema substitutes* by optimizing the limited capacity of working memory in ways that free working memory for learning. Good instruction will segment and sequence the content in ways that reduce the amount of new information novices must process at one time and, as much as possible, reinforce domain patterns to support schema acquisition and improve learning.'

2 Variation of form (e.g. cover story) can help novices realize that there is a many-to-one relationship between form and problem type: when students see a variety of cover stories used for identical or similar structures (of class models), they are more likely to notice that surface features are insufficient to distinguish among problem types and that problem categorization according to structural similarities (patterns) is imperative to enable reuse of solution schemas (Quilici and Mayer, 1996).

Models provide an excellent overview and generic approach to introductory programming. If pedagogical development tools (e.g. BlueJ and DrJava) more completely supported integration of code and UML-like models, we conjecture that the effect would be even better.

Example: Elementary patterns

Elementary patterns (i.e. those for elementary program structures) exist in a number of variations (e.g. roles of variables (Sajaniemi, 2008), selection patterns (Bergin, 1999) and loop patterns (Astrachan and Wallingford, 1998)).

Roles of variables represent programming knowledge that can be explicitly taught to students and which are easy to adopt in teaching. A number of roles for variables was identified and described by Sajaniemi (2008) (e.g. fixed value, organizer, stepper, most-recent holder, one-way flag, most-wanted holder etc).

Bergin (1999) divides selection patterns in three categories: basic selection patterns, strategy patterns and auxiliary patterns. Examples of basic selection patterns are: Whether or Not and Alternative Action, examples of strategy patterns are Short Case First and Default Case First and examples of auxiliary patterns are Positive Condition and Function for Positive Condition.

Astrachan and Wallingford (1998) present a number of loop patterns related to sweeping over a (linear) collection of data. Examples of elementary loop patterns are Linear Search, Guarded Linear Search, Process All Items and Loop and a Half.

Process

As mentioned in section 9.1, the process of programming is one of the best-kept secrets of programming education. Exposing students to the process of programming is merely implied but not explicitly addressed in texts on programming, which appear to deal with 'program' as a noun rather than as a verb.

Thus, students are left on their own to find their process of programming. For novices, this inevitably becomes a random walk, which leaves the students to struggle with all the details and complexity of developing well-functioning programs.

Instead of leaving the students on their own we, as educators, must help students to develop a systematic process to learning programming; instead of leaving the students to random walks, we must provide guided tours for proper program development.

This section deals with process from three perspectives: how to reveal the programming process, how to facilitate process-based self-explanations and how to conceptualize the programming process as consisting of three independent (but of course-related) activities: extension, refinement and restructuring – Stepwise Improvement.

Reveal process and pragmatics

Programming is a process, so it is important that students are exposed to the different activities in programming and their interconnections.

Revealing the programming process to beginning students is important, but traditional static teaching materials such as textbooks, lecture notes, black-boards or slide presentations, etc, are insufficient for that purpose. They are useful for the presentation of a product (e.g. a finished program) but not for the presentation of the dynamic process used to create that product.

Besides being insufficient for the presentation of a development process, the use of traditional materials has another drawback. Typically, they are used for the presentation of an ideal solution that is the result of a non-linear development process. Like others (Soloway, 1986; Spohrer and Soloway, 1986) we consider this to be problematic. The presentation of the product independently of the development process will inevitably leave the students with the false impression that there is a linear and direct 'royal road' from problem to solution. This is very far from the truth, but the problem for novices is that when they see their teacher present clean and simple solutions, they think they themselves should be able to develop solutions in a similar way. When they realize they cannot do so, they blame themselves and feel incompetent. Consequently, they will lose confidence and, in the worst case, their motivation for learning to program.

Besides teaching the students about tools and techniques for the development of programs (e.g. a programming language, an integrated development environment also known as IDE, or programming techniques) we must also teach them about the programming process. This can include the task of using these tools and techniques to develop the solution in a systematic, incremental and typically non-linear way. An important part of this is to expound and to demonstrate that:

- many small steps are better than a few large ones
- the result of every little step should be tested
- prior decisions may need to be undone and code refactored
- making errors is common also for experienced programmers
- compiler errors can be misleading/erroneous
- online documentation for class libraries provide valuable information, and
- there is a systematic, however non-linear, way of developing a solution for the problem at hand.

We cannot rely on the students to learn all of this by themselves, but by using an apprenticeship approach we can show them how to do it. Worked Examples are highly suitable for this purpose and they can be effectively communicated via process recordings. For many more details on this see (Bennedsen and Caspersen, 2005).

Provide scaffolding through stepwise self-explanations

The message from the large amount of self-explanation literature is clear: students who self-explain outperform students who do not. Furthermore, there are different forms of self-explanation, and students often fail to self-explain successfully; most learners self-explain in a passive and superficial way (Chi, 1989; VanLehn, 1996). A good deal of self-explanation research has been conducted in the context of programming education (e.g. Pirolli, 1991; Pirolli and Recker, 1994).

Self-explanations provide guidance regarding the way that students can study and understand instructional material. Clark, Nguyen and Sweller (2005) defined self-explanation as 'a mental dialog that learners have when studying a worked example that helps them understand the example and build a schema from it'. According to Chiu and Chi (2014), the activity of self-explaining promotes learning through elaboration of information being studied, associating this new information with learners' prior knowledge, making inferences and connecting two or more pieces of the given information.

The benefits of self-explanations were first shown by Chi et al. (1989). They found that good students, who self-generated a greater number of explanations while studying examples in the physics domain, scored better at problem solving when compared to poor students. Good students' explanations provided justifications for steps in the examples and related those steps to the concepts presented in the instructional material. Those students also monitored their understanding while studying the examples.

More information on self-explanation and stepwise self-explanation (a specialization of self-explanation related to Stepwise Improvement) can be found in Caspersen (2007) and Aureliano et al. (2016).

Apply and teach incremental development through Stepwise Improvement (i.e. extend, refine, restructure)

In traditional stepwise refinement (Dijkstra, 1969; Wirth, 1971; Back, 1978; Morgan, 1990; Back, 1998), programming is regarded as the one-dimensional activity of refining abstract programs (i.e. programs containing non-executable specifications) to concrete programs (i.e. executable code) through a series of behaviour-preserving program transformations. The fundamental assumption of traditional stepwise refinement is that the complete specification, the requirements, are known and addressed from the outset. Typically, stepwise refinement is described as a strict 'top-down' process of programming.

Programming by Stepwise Improvement (Caspersen, 2007), however, is characterized as an explorative activity of discovery and invention that takes place in the three-dimensional space of *extension, refinement* and *restructuring*. Extension is the activity of extending the specification to cover more (use-) cases; refinement is the activity of refining abstract code to executable code in order to meet the current specification; and restructure is the activity of improving non-functional aspects of a solution without altering its observable behaviour, such as design improvements through refactoring, efficiency optimizations, or portability improvements.

A very simple example of Stepwise Improvement is the development of an app that can show a date and advance to the next/previous date by pushing dedicated buttons in the user interface. Such an app can be developed according to Stepwise Improvement in the following extension steps:

1 Construct (part of) the user interface, no functionality.
2 Make the app work except for the last day of a month (assume thirty days in every month and ignore leap years).
3 Make the app work for variable number of days per month.
4 Make the app work for leap years (except centuries).
5 Make the app work for centuries (except four-centuries).
6 Make the app work for four-centuries.

By breaking the problem down like this, and developing the program in a number of increments/iterations where the specification is gradually extended, the programming task becomes much more manageable. It allows for a success/celebration every time a new version is finished.

There are many pedagogical advantages by organizing students' programming process according to Stepwise Improvement.

Stepwise Improvement captures modern software development methods in the sense that different methods place different emphasis on the order of the activities described. Waterfall methods are characterized by a strict separation of the activities (extension first, refinement and restructure later) whereas agile methods allow a much more fine-grained interleaving of the activities.

The traditional approach to programming education is to invite the students for a random walk in the aforementioned three-dimensional space of extension, refinement and restructuring. Students are shown a few finished programs and told to solve programming problems on their own.

The Stepwise Improvement approach to programming education offers an alternative to random walks by suggesting guided tours. By providing guidance and scaffolding with respect to all dimensions involved, we can ensure that students exercise the important aspects of programming while keeping the cognitive load within the bounds where learning outcome is optimized.

From the Stepwise Improvement framework, Caspersen and Kölling have designed a novice's process of (object-oriented) programming called STREAM (Caspersen and Kölling, 2009).

9.4 Summary: In the classroom

Programming languages and integrated development environments

For practical teaching in the classroom, specific technologies (e.g. programming languages and development environments) must be chosen.

A number of integrated development environments (IDEs), micro worlds and tools have been developed to support various aspects of programming and program development for novices. There are block-based tools, text-based tools, automatic assessment tools and visualisation tools, to name but a few.

There is an abundance of block-based educational tools (e.g. (in alphabetical order) AgentSheets, Alice, Bubble, Kodu, Kojo, Scratch); see Visual programming language (2017) for more details and references.

Similarly, there are a great number of text-based programming languages used in education (e.g. Java, Processing, Python, JavaScript, Scheme).

For most of these languages, there is also an abundance of associated IDEs (e.g. for Java (BlueJ, DrJava, JGrasp, Android Studio, Eclipse, IntelliJ and NetBeans), Python (PyCharm, PyDev, LiClipse and Thonny) and Scheme/Racket where DrScheme is the predominant option).

Some research groups work on providing smooth transitions from block-based to text-based languages, particularly for the frame-based editing approach for Stride, a simplified variant of Java (see Price and Barnes, 2015; Kölling, Brown and Altadmri, 2017). Others do research to compare conceptual understand in block-based versus text-based languages (Weintrop and Wilensky, 2015).

Teaching approaches

A number of approaches to organizing teaching have been developed and refined in recent years; we'll mention just a few of these.

Parson's Problems is a teaching approach to help students acquire competence with the structural syntax of programming languages. Instead of requesting students to write, on their own, statements and expressions of programs, the Parson's Problems approach provides fully programmed alternatives for the students to choose from. Apart from freeing the students from struggling with concrete syntax, this approach has the advantage of requiring the students to read and comprehend code. This is an excellent way to provide scaffolding early in the process of learning programming. For further details see Parsons and Haden (2006) and Denny (2008).

Pair programming is another approach that has gained popularity in recent years. An excellent exposition can be found in Braught et al. (2011). Porter et al. (2013) highlight three teaching approaches that can improve computing education in general and programming education in particular: pair programming, peer instruction and media computation. Although the research for these was carried out in higher education, they are starting to be used in school computer science education.

Key points

- Teaching and learning programming is a grand challenge.
- In a time where computing/informatics education is becoming general education for all and students don't choose to learn programming out of personal interest, the challenge not only persists, but is reinforced.
- Exposing students to the process of programming is merely implied but not explicitly addressed in texts on programming, which appear to deal with 'program' as a noun rather than as a verb.
- Some relatively simple and effective teaching strategies can help alleviate and overcome the challenge:

  - Progression: Be application-oriented; Let students progress from consumer to producer (use-modify-create); Organize progression in terms of complexity of task, not complexity of language constructs
  - Examples: Provide exemplary examples; Provide worked examples; Establish motivation through passion, play, peers and menaningful projects
  - Abstraction and patterns: Reinforce specifications; Reinforce patterns; Reinforce models and conceptual frameworks (program *into* a language)
  - Process: Reveal process and pragmatics; Provide scaffolding through stepwise self-explanations; Apply and teach incremental development through stepwise improvement (i.e. extend, refine, restructure).

Further reflection

- The use of examples is important in helping students to improve their programming skills. Consider how worked examples could be used in your classroom to support a particular programming topic.
- Considering all the strategies presented in this chapter, how do you think these could be incorporated at different points with young, beginner programmers, to enable *progression* in programming?

References

AgentSheets (2017). *AgentCubes*. Available at: www.agentsheets.com

App Lab (2017). *App Lab*. Available at: https://code.org/educate/applab

Armoni, M and M Ben-Ari (2010). *Computer Science Concepts in Scratch*, Licensed under Creative Commons. Available at: https://stwww1.weizmann.ac.il/scratch/scratch_en/

Astrachan, O and E Wallingford (1998). *Loop Patterns*. Available at: https://users.cs.duke.edu/~ola/patterns/plopd/loops.html

Atkinson, RK, SJ Derry, A Renkl and D Wortham (2000). 'Learning from Examples: Instructional Principles from the Worked Examples Research', 70 *Review of Educational Research*181.214.

Aureliano, VCO. PC de AR Tedesco and ME Caspersen (2016). 'Learning programming through stepwise self-explanations' in *Proceedings of the 11th Conferencia Iberica de Sistemas y Technologias de Information*.

Back, R.-J. (1978). *On the Correctness of Refinement Steps in Program Development*, Department of Computer Science, University of Helsinki, Helsinki, Finland.

Back, R.-J. (1998). *Refinement Calculus: A Systematic Introduction* (Berlin, Springer-Verlag).

Bennedsen, J and ME Caspersen (2004a). 'Programming in Context – A Model-First Approach to CS1' in *Proceedings of the Thirty-fifth SIGCSE Technical Symposium on Computer Science Education*, SIGCSE 2004, 477–481.

Bennedsen, J and ME Caspersen (2004b). 'Teaching Object-oriented Programming – Towards Teaching a Systematic Programming Process' in *Proceedings of the Eighth Workshop on Pedagogies and Tools for the Teaching and Learning of Object-Oriented Concepts*, 18th European Conference on Object-Oriented Programming.

Bennedsen, J and ME Caspersen (2005). 'Revealing the Programming Process' in *Proceedings of the Thirty-sixth SIGCSE Technical Symposium on Computer Science Education*, SIGCSE 2005, 186–190.

Bergin, J (1999). *Patterns for Selection*. Available at: www.cs.uni.edu/~wallingf/patterns/elementary/papers/selection.pdf

Börstler, J, ME Caspersen and M Nordström (2007). *Beauty and the Beast – Toward a Measurement Framework for Example Program Quality*. Tech. Rep. UMINF-07.23, Dept. of Computing Science, Umeå University, Umeå, Sweden.

Börstler, J, ME Caspersen and M Nordström (2015). 'Beauty and the Beast: On the Readability of Object-Oriented Example Programs', *Software Quality Journal*, Springer-Verlag.

Börstler, J, M Nordström and JH Paterson (2011). 'On the Quality of Examples in Introductory Java Textbooks', 11 *Transactions on Computing Education* 1–21.

Braught, G, T Wahls, and LM Eby (2011). 'The Case for Pair Programming in the Computer Science Classroom', 11(1) *ACM Transactions on Computing Education* 1–21.

Brennan, K, C Balch and M Chung (2014). *Creative Computing*, Harvard Graduate School of Education. Available at: http://scratched.gse.harvard.edu/guide/

Caspersen, ME (2007). *Educating Novices in the Skills of Programming*, DAIMI PhD Dissertation PD-07-4, Department of Computer Science, Aarhus University, Denmark. Available at: www.cs.au.dk/~mec/dissertation/Dissertation.pdf

Caspersen, ME and J Bennedsen (2007). 'Instructional Design of a Programming Course – A Learning Theoretic Approach' in *Proceedings of the 2007 International Workshop on Computing Education Research*, ICER 2007, Atlanta, 111–122.

Caspersen, ME and M Kölling (2009). 'STREAM: A First Programming Process', 9(1) *ACM Transactions on Computing Education* 1–29.

Caspersen, ME and P Nowack (2013). 'Computational Thinking and Practice – A Generic Approach to Computing in Danish High Schools' in *Proceedings of the 15th Australasian Computer Education Conference*, Adelaide, South Australia, 137–143.

Chi, MTH, M Bassok, L Lewis, M Reimann and R Glaser (1989). 'Self-explanations: How Students Study and Use Examples in Learning to Solve Problems', 13 *Cognitive Science* 145–182.

Chiu, JL and MTH Chi (2014). 'Supporting self-explanation in the classroom' in A Benassi CE Overson and CM Hakala (eds), '*Applying Science of Learning in Education: Infusing Psychological Science into the Curriculum*'. Available at: http://teachpsych.org/ebooks/asle2014/index.php

Christensen, HB and ME Caspersen (2002). 'Frameworks in CS1 – A Different Way of Introducing Event-Driven Programming' in *Proceedings of the Seventh Annual Conference on Innovation and Technology in Computer Science Education*, June, Aarhus Denmark, 24–26.

Clancy, M. (2004). 'Misconceptions and Attitudes that Interfere with Learning to Program' in S Fincher and M Petre (eds), *Computer Science Education Research* (Abingdon, Taylor & Francis) 85–100.

Clark, RC, F Nguyen and J Sweller (2005). *Efficiency in Learning: Evidence-Based Guidelines to Manage Cognitive Load* (Chichester, Wiley).

Dasgupta, S and M Resnick (2014). 'Engaging Novices in Programming, Experimenting, and Learning with Data', 5(4) *ACM Inroads* 72–75.

Denny, P (2008). 'Evaluating a New Exam Question: Parsons Problems' in *Proceedings of the Fourth international Workshop on Computing Education Research*, 6–7 September 2008, Sydney Australia 113–124.

Dijkstra, EW (1969). *Notes on Structured Programming*, EWD 249.

du Boulay, B (1989). 'Some Difficulties of Learning to Program', in *Studying the Novice Programmer* (Hillsdale, NJ, Lawrence Erlbaum) 57–73.

East, JP, SR Thomas, E Wallingford, W Beck and J Drake (1996). 'Pattern-based Programming Instruction' in *Proceedings of the ASEE Annual Conference and Exposition,* Washington DC.

Gries, D (1974). 'What Should we Teach in an Introductory Programming Course?' in *Proceedings of the Fourth SIGCSE Technical Symposium on Computer Science Education*, New York, 81–89.

Grover S and R Pea (2013). 'Computational Thinking in K-12: A Review of the State of the Field', 42(1) *Educational Researcher* 38–43.

Knudsen, JL and OL Madsen (1988). 'Teaching Object-Oriented Programming is More than Teaching Object-Oriented Programming Languages' in *ECOOP '88 European Conference on Object-Oriented Programming*, Oslo, 15–17 August 1998, 21–40.

Kölling, M (2003). *The Curse of Hello World.* Invited Lecture at *Workshop on Learning and Teaching Object-orientation – Scandinavian Perspectives*, Oslo.

Kölling, M, N Brown and A Altadmri (2017). 'Frame-Based Editing', *Journal of Visual Languages and Sentient Systems.*

Kristensen, B.B. and Østerbye, K. (1994). 'Conceptual Modeling and Programming Languages' 29(9) *ACM SIGPLAN Notices* 81–90.

Lee, I, F Martin, J Denner, B Coulter, W Allan, J Erickson, J Malyn-Smith and L Werner (2011). 'Computational Thinking for Youth in Practice', 2(1) *ACM Inroads*, 32–37.

LeFevre, J and P Dixon, (1986). 'Do Written Instruction Need Examples?', 3 *Cognition and Instruction* 1–30.

Madsen, OL, B Møller-Pedersen and K Nygaard (1993). *Object-Oriented Programming in the BETA Programming Language* (Wokingham, Addison-Wesley/ACM).

McGettrick, A, R Boyle, R Ibbett, J Lloyd, G Lovegrove and K Mander (2005). 'Grand Challenges in Computing: Education – A Summary', 48(1) *The Computer Journal* 42–48.

Meerbaum-Salant, O, M Armoni and M Ben-Ari (2013). 'Learning Computer Science Concepts with Scratch', 23(3) *Computer Science Education* 239–264.

Meyer, B (1993). 'Towards an Object-Oriented Curriculum' 6(2) *Journal of Object-Oriented Programming* 76–81.

Morgan, C (1990). *Programming from Specifications* (Upper Saddle River NJ, Prentice-Hall).

Muller, O (2005). 'Pattern-Oriented Instruction and the Enhancement of Analogical Reasoning' in *Proceedings of the 2005 International Workshop on Computing Education Research* Seattle, WA, 57–67.

Parsons, D and P Haden (2006). 'Parson's Programming Puzzles: A Fun and Effective Learning Tool for First Programming Courses' in *Proceedings of the Eighth Australasian Conference on Computing Education*, Hobart, Australia, 157–163.

Pattis, RE (1990). 'A Philosophy and Example of CS-1 Programming Projects', *Proceedings of the Twenty-First SIGCSE Technical Symposium on Computer Science Education*, Washington DC, 34–39.

Pirolli, P (1991). 'Effects of Examples and Their Explanations in a Lesson on Recursion: A Production System Analysis', 8(3) *Cognition and Instruction* 207–259.

Pirolli, P and M Recker (1994). 'Learning Strategies and Transfer in the Do-main of Programming' 12(3) *Cognition and Instruction* 235–275.

Porter, L, M Guzdial, C McDowell and B Simon (2013). 'Success in Introductory Programming: What Works?', 56(8) *Communications of the ACM* 34–36.

Price, TW and T Barnes (2015). 'Comparing Textual and Block Interfaces in a Novice Programming Environment' in *Proceedings of the Eleventh Annual International Conference on International Computing Education Research*, Omaha, 9–13 August 2015, 91–99.

Quilici, JL and RE Mayer (1996). 'Role of Examples in How Students Learn to Categorize Statistics Word Problems', 88 *Journal of Educational Psychology* 144–161.

Ragonis, N and M Ben-Ari (2005). 'A Long-Term Investigation of the Comprehension of OOP Concepts by Novices' 15(3) *Computer Science Education* 203–221.

Repenning, A, DC Webb, KH Koh, H Nickerson, SB Miller, C Brand, AR Basawapatna, F Gluck, R Grover, K Gutierrez and N Repenning (2015). 'Scalable Game Design: A Strategy to Bring Systemic Computer Science Education to Schools through Game Design and Simulation Creation' 15(2) *ACM Transactions on Computing Education* 1–31.

Resnick, M (2014). 'Give P's a Chance' in *Proceedings of Constructionism and Creativity Conference*, Vienna, Austria.

Robins, A, J Rountree and N Rountree (2003). 'Learning and Teaching Programming: A Review and Discussion', 13(2) *Journal of Computer Science Education* 137–172.

Sajaniemi, J (2008). *Roles of Variables*. Available at: www.cs.joensuu.fi/~saja/var_roles/

Schmolitzky, A (2005). 'Towards Complexity Levels of Object Systems used in Software Engineering Education' in *Proceedings of the Ninth Workshop on Pedagogies and Tools for the Teaching and Learning of Object-Oriented Concepts*, 19th European Conference on Object-Oriented Programming. Available at: https://tinyurl.com/yd9vv5w6

Soloway, E (1986). 'Learning to Program = Learning to Construct Mechanisms and Explanations', 29(9) *Communications of the ACM* 850–858.

Spohrer, JC and E Soloway (1986). 'Novice Mistakes: Are the Folk Wisdoms Correct?' 29(7) *Communications of the ACM* 624–632.

Sweller, J and G Cooper (1985). 'The Use of Worked Examples as a Substitute for Problem Solving in Learning Algebra', 2 *Cognition and Instruction* 59–89.

Trafton, JG and BJ Reiser (1993). 'Studying Examples and Solving Problems: Contributions to Skill Acquisition', Technical Report, Naval HCI Research Lab, Washington DC, USA.

VanLehn, K (1996) 'Cognitive Skill Acquisition', 47 *Annual Review of Psychology* 513–539.

Visual programming language (2017). *Visual Programming Language.* Available at: https://en.wikipedia.org/wiki/Visual_programming_language

Weintrop, D and U Wilensky (2015). 'Using Commutative Assessments to Compare Conceptual Understanding in Blocks-Based and Text-Based Programs' in *Proceedings of the Eleventh Annual International Conference on International Computing Education Research* 9–13 August 2015, Omaha, Nebraska, 101–110.

Wirth, N (1971). 'Program Development by Stepwise Refinement' 14(4) *Communications of the ACM* 221–227.

10

Teaching Computing in Primary Schools

Tim Bell and Caitlin Duncan

Chapter outline

Chapter synopsis

With the introduction of computing into the curriculum in primary schools in many countries and as informal learning opportunities in others it is important to consider pedagogy and learning of computer science for children approximately aged 5–12. In this chapter we will summarize current research in this area and draw on our own experiences, in New Zealand, of working with younger children.

10.1 Introduction

The benefits, goals and teaching strategies for computing education have been presented and discussed in previous chapters, but suitable classroom pedagogy is something that changes considerably from early school years through to the end of high school. Extending computing to the primary years of school (students of approximately ages 5 to 12 years old) presents unique challenges, but also opportunities. In this chapter we will look at what computing would look like in a primary school and why one would want it to be taught at that level. We focus on elements relating to computational thinking and concepts from computer science.

To avoid this new subject at primary school coming across as a seemingly unrelated collection of topics, it is useful to be aware of what the *big ideas* are that we want students to take away from their learning (Bell, 2016). For example, many primary school students learn a programming language such as Scratch, but what are the real concepts that we want them to take away from this? In ten years' time it is unlikely that they will need to know the colour of an arithmetic operator or the name of the command for storing a value into a variable. Likewise, many curricula include converting binary numbers to decimal, but in practice few people may ever have to do that. Yet there is value in working with both Scratch programming and binary numbers. Looking for the big picture will be a theme of this chapter, since we need to appreciate the overarching goals to be able to make sense of the small details that appear in the classroom. This will raise ideas such as the concept of teaching computational thinking, and how the ideas can be made suitable for this age group.

Common concerns around incorporating these subjects into primary school are that these concepts are too advanced and are unsuitable for this age group and that teachers are already working with a 'crowded curriculum', so this subject will just become another add-on that there isn't time to teach. There is also, as in all school levels, the challenge of providing large-scale and sustainable professional development, resources and support to teachers, although these challenges can be overcome (Brown et al., 2014; Falkner, Vivian and Falkner, 2014; Schulte, Hornung and Sentance, 2012; Bell, Duncan and Atlas, 2016). Successful computer science education in primary school is not only achievable, but can also help teachers to engage students with integrated (cross curricula) learning (Duncan, Bell and Atlas, 2017).

Computational Thinking has been described in previous chapters, and through this chapter we will connect this definition with primary school curriculum in our examples. Before defining and exploring these ideas carefully, we begin with a case study to give us something concrete to illustrate the principles and ideas that we will introduce.

10.2 Case study one: Binary representation

Data representation and 'binary numbers' are topics that deserve to be understood by students, as binary representation is fundamental to how *everything* is stored and communicated on digital devices. In fact, one of the defining differences about digital technology is in its name: everything is represented by digits!

Phrases like 'data representation' and 'binary numbers' may sound technical, and even scary, to those who are not familiar with the topics, and jargon such as this frequently puts teachers off approaching the subject of computer science. One of the keys to making computer science and Computational Thinking work in primary skill is by making it explicit that much of this jargon can be seen simply as complicated words for simple ideas; every specialist field needs technical language to avoid having to use long-winded descriptions of commonly used ideas.

Example: Teaching binary representation to early primary children using CS unplugged

This activity is a shortened version of the open-source lesson plans at CSUnplugged.org.

Create a set of 5 cards, with dots on one side and nothing on the other. The cards have 1, 2, 4, 8 and 16 dots respectively.

Placing them *from right to left*, show the students the 1-dot and 2-dot cards.

Ask the class what the number of dots on the next card will be. Get them to explain why they think that. Most students will say 3, but silently place the 4-dot card to the left of the 2-dot card, and let them try to see the pattern. Usually some students will complain that you've missed out the three, but simply indicate that you haven't made a mistake.

Ask what the next card is and why. At this point it is common for students to guess that it is 6 (since it follows the numbers 2 and 4). However, if you let them think about it a little more, some will usually come up with 8 and these students should be able to convince the others that they are correct.

Students should be able to work out the fifth card (16 dots) without help.

Tell the students that the rule is that a card either has the dots fully visible or is turned over so that none of them are visible. If we can turn cards on and off by showing the front and back of the card, how would we show 9 dots? Begin by asking if they want the 16 card (they should observe that it has too many dots, so should be flipped over) then the 8 card (they will likely reason that without it there aren't enough dots left without it) then 4, 2 and 1. Without being given any rules other than each card being visible or not, students will usually come up with the representation of the number 9 as 'hidden-visible-hidden-hidden-visible' (i.e. the 8 and the 1 are visible, making 9 dots).

Now ask 'How would you make the number 21?' (Again, start by asking if they want the 16 card, and so on from left to right.)

Using this scaffolding, students have discovered for themselves an algorithm for converting numbers to a binary representation. The representation can then be tested by using different wording for the two sides of the card; for example, the teacher could say they are thinking of the month 'no, yes, no, yes, no', which corresponds to the number 10, and students will readily translate to 'October'. It is a small step from here to using 1 and 0 to represent yes and no.

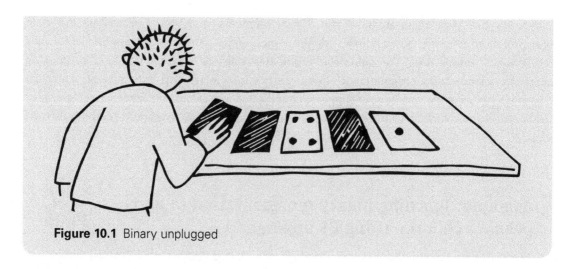

Figure 10.1 Binary unplugged

The binary representation activity shows how the concept of representing numbers and letters in binary can be communicated to relatively young students using just a set of five cards (Figure 10.1). Notice the way it is taught, with students constructing the concepts themselves, rather than simply being told how things work. For example, once students have seen the sequence of 1, 2 and 4 dots, they will be able to work out what the next card is, without being told explicitly; in fact, not only do they work out the value, but they construct the rule (doubling) for themselves. In doing this, students are also demonstrating the CT skills of logical reasoning and pattern recognition.

The terms 'zero' and 'one' for the two symbols isn't mentioned until later, which emphasizes that they are an arbitrary abstraction for what is actually happening – on a hard disk the two symbols would be two directions of magnetization; in computer memory it would be the presence of absence of electrical charge. The important thing isn't what the two symbols *are*, it is the fact that using *any* two different *things* allows us to represent any type of data (already in this activity the binary values have been used to represent integers and months). An important observation is that with the card activity, it's very easy to see which way around a card is, even from a distance, and other representations can be explored, such as high and low notes to indicate which way up a card should be placed. This emphasizes the value of having just two symbols: as long as there is a clear distinction between the two representations, it is very simple to work with.

Sometimes 'binary numbers' are taught as simply converting conventional decimal numbers to a representation with zeroes and ones, which can be conveniently assessed in exams. In fact, computer scientists rarely convert numbers between binary and decimal; the real concepts at play here are much deeper. However, one of the key ideas that students can take away from the activity above is that:

Anything stored on a computer can be represented using just two symbols.

This is a powerful concept and is easily demonstrated to students using the month example. Without explanation, the teacher says something like: 'The month I was born in is no-no-yes-yes-yes' (choosing the cards from left to right), which students could translate to 00111, or the decimal number 7, but are more likely to call out that it is 'July'. This gives the opportunity to point out that a new type of data (months in the range January to December) can be represented by simply saying yes and no. From a computational thinking point of view, this is an application of abstraction; the name 'July' carries a lot of extra information and history (e.g. it was named after Julius Caesar) but for practical purposes (such as working out how long it is until my birthday) abstracting the word to the number 7, or binary representation 00111, is sufficient.

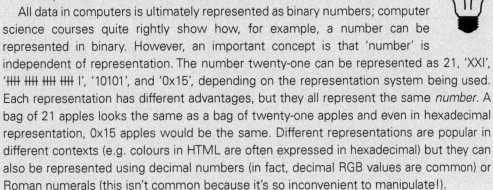

Key concept: Data representation

Are binary numbers different from decimal and hexadecimal numbers?

All data in computers is ultimately represented as binary numbers; computer science courses quite rightly show how, for example, a number can be represented in binary. However, an important concept is that 'number' is independent of representation. The number twenty-one can be represented as 21, 'XXI', 'ⅢⅢ ⅢⅢ ⅢⅢ ⅢⅢ I', '10101', and '0x15', depending on the representation system being used. Each representation has different advantages, but they all represent the same *number*. A bag of 21 apples looks the same as a bag of twenty-one apples and even in hexadecimal representation, 0x15 apples would be the same. Different representations are popular in different contexts (e.g. colours in HTML are often expressed in hexadecimal) but they can also be represented using decimal numbers (in fact, decimal RGB values are common) or Roman numerals (this isn't common because it's so inconvenient to manipulate!).

Another important concept is around the range of values being represented by a given number of bits. The activity above uses five cards, and can represent the values from 0 to 31. This gives 32 *different* values (a concept that may be a challenge for some students to come to grips with). With some guidance, students should be able to extend this idea to 6 cards, which represent the values from 0 to 63, giving 64 different values. The principle that this has started to expose is:

Each extra bit added to a binary representation doubles the range of values that can be represented.

This observation comes up in many different areas. For example, 5 bits are sufficient to represent the letters of the English alphabet (there are 26 letters, compared with the 32 combinations available) but to represent the approximately 100 characters used on an English computer keyboard (including upper and lower case, punctuation and other symbols), 7 bits are needed (which allow for 128 different characters). Extending this to languages such as Chinese that have tens of thousands of symbols, one might expect that a very large number of bits is needed for each character. In fact, 16 bits for each character allows for 65,536 different symbols, and is sufficient for most documents. The same also applies to representing colours. It is generally accepted that the human eye can distinguish a few million different colours; a 24-bit representation of colour allows a digital device to store over 16 million different colours, so in principle it is more accurate than the human eye can perceive.

Relating the technical idea of binary numbers to helping humans communicate in their own language or perceive the colours in images accurately, give meaning to what can appear to be a purely technical concept. This isn't just a motivating example; it is the whole point of binary representation: to be able to store things as diverse as words, images, sounds and financial information at a level of accuracy that matches human need.

> ### Key concept: Digital systems should be designed for humans
>
> The above example makes the point that binary numbers relate directly to human needs and values. This applies to most technical areas of computing: interfaces need to be designed to interact well with the way that the user thinks and works and programs need to be written in a way that if another human has to read it, they can do so easily. Computer systems need to be designed to be reliable so that people aren't constantly wasting their time having to get material from backups or asking for a repeated download. Networks need to operate at a human timescale – we are used to communicating and thinking at the level of around one second; if a system constantly takes thirty seconds to respond it will be frustrating to use. We could use the mantra: Computer programs aren't written for computers; they are written for humans.

One topic that highlights how we need to focus on the big picture is the teaching of sorting algorithms. Often these seem to be taught as a 'laundry list' of methods for students to know, but very few software developers will ever end up writing a sorting algorithm. They provide an excellent platform for exploring the performance of different algorithms for the same task, starting with the idea that the time taken is rarely proportional to the amount of input (even though taking twice the time to sort twice as many values might seem like a reasonable assumption). This can be demonstrated at primary school level using a simple unplugged approach with balance scales.[1]

At a more advanced level, sorting algorithms enable us to explore best, average and worst cases; tradeoffs between space usage and speed; and also techniques that can be used in algorithms, such as divide and conquer, priority queues, merging and partitioning. But stepping back to the bigger picture, the key is that fast algorithms make for better computer programs for humans, because the system responds faster, uses less power and is less wasteful of computer resources.

In the end, digital systems are built to help humans. When teaching computing, it is important to have this as a central theme to motivate students and to prevent students from focusing on the technology for its own sake.

10.3 Computational thinking, computer science and programming at the primary school level

A computing curriculum should support the development of CT skills. But what are these skills, why are they useful, and what do they look like in primary school? As discussed in Chapter 3, CT has been defined in many different ways, although the varying definitions are broadly in agreement.

---

[1] See http://csunplugged.org/sorting-algorithms/

Here we shall draw on two of the most widely accepted definitions of general Computational Thinking (Wing, 2014; CSTA, 2011) and primary education specific CT (CAS Barefoot, 2015).

The value of being able to work with computational ideas is applicable beyond being able to program; conversely, this can be learnt in areas other than programming (such as the 'Unplugged' example above). However, converting an idea to a program and getting it to work on an autonomous device fully exercises one's ability to be precise in the expression of the steps needed to solve a problem. Tedre and Denning (2016) provide a useful history of CT and also draw attention to the evidence for what it does and does not achieve. From the evidence provided, CT can be seen as a useful framework to help us recognize activities that address the gap that currently exists in many education systems, but it shouldn't be touted as either a revolutionary new method that can address all aspects of learning, or reduced to simply learning to write computer programs.

In the following we catalogue the current general range of skills that are seen as part of CT and reflect on how an activity such as the binary number one can exercise these aspects of CT for students at a primary school level.

Algorithmic thinking

Algorithmic thinking supports students to follow algorithms, and to create algorithms to solve problems by breaking them down into steps.

In our binary example, students practise and develop algorithmic thinking skills as they learn (by constructing the knowledge themselves) an algorithm for converting decimal numbers to binary and practise following this algorithm. The algorithm they are likely to come up with can be articulated as:

- Find out the number of dots that is to be displayed. (We'll refer to this as the 'number of dots remaining', which initially is the total number to be displayed.)
- For each card, from the left to the right (i.e. 16, 8, 4, 2 then 1):
  - If the number of dots on the card is more than the number of dots remaining:
    - Hide the card
  - Otherwise:
    - Show the card
    - Subtract the number of dots on the card from the number of dots remaining.

When looking for evidence of students' algorithmic thinking skills, teachers can observe how methodical students are in their approach to the task. Do they start with the leftmost card and move one card at a time to the right, rather than choosing cards at random and flipping them on and off until they get the right number? Do they recognize that if they follow this method correctly it will always give the correct answer?

Abstraction

Abstraction is about simplifying things by identifying what is and is not important, and removing all specific details and patterns that will not help us solve our problem.

The binary activity requires students to work with several abstractions, including using numbers to represent months, cards to represent the digits 0 and 1, and even the terms 'zero' and 'one' to represent the two different states that the digits can be in. All of these values and terms can be absorbed within a higher level abstraction – that any and all types of digital data can be represented using just two different states.

Binary number representation itself is an abstraction! It hides the complexity of the electronics and hardware inside a computer that store data. We can use binary digits to represent any type of data stored on a computer. When we represent other forms of data (such as letters, images and sound) we also use abstraction because we hide the details of all the binary numbers underneath and just look at the whole piece of data.

Teachers can identify students' use of abstraction by seeing if there are students that can represent binary numbers using things other than '1s and 0s', 'black and white', and 'off and on' (e.g. using happy and sad faces, or using people standing up or sitting down). If they are able to interchange terms like 'black' and 'white' with 0 and 1 without students being confused or concerned by the difference, they are exercising abstraction.

Decomposition

Decomposition involves breaking down problems into smaller and smaller steps. To do this we look at the big picture of the problem and think about each of the smaller individual problems we need to solve before we can solve the whole big problem.

When students follow the process of converting between binary and decimal numbers they must decompose this to a series of small steps and work with one bit at a time. The questions 'Should this be 1 or 0' for each of the dot cards is decomposing the problem to a series of questions. This process needs to be decomposed to this level because while a human *might* be able to glance at a number and see all 5 bits at once and add them all together, a computer (and the algorithm that it is running) needs to have the process broken down into much smaller and simpler steps.

Teachers can see students exercising this if they are focusing on each individual bit at a time, rather than being overwhelmed by trying to work it all out in one go.

Generalizing

Generalizing is also sometimes referred to as 'pattern recognition and generalization'. Generalization is taking a solution (generally an algorithm) or part of a solution, to a problem and generalizing it, so it can be applied to other similar problems/tasks. Spotting patterns and recognizing similarities is an important part of this process.

For the binary number activity, students explored representing numbers up to 31, but from there should be able to generalize how the representation could represent larger numbers. Students can usually quickly recognize that the card to the left of the 16-dot one would have 32 dots, and then apply the same algorithm to work out the representation of a value such as 45. Students with more advanced pattern recognition ability will quickly identify these.

Evaluation

Evaluation is about identifying the possible solutions to a problem and judging which is the best to use. When judging our solutions we need to think about a range of factors (e.g. how much time it will take these processes to solve the problem) and will it reliably solve the problem.

For the binary numbers, students can evaluate how many different values can be represented with 5 dots, then with 6 dots, and more. The result of this evaluation is that they should see the exponential growth in the range of values as the number of bits increases.

Teachers could use questions to help students in their evaluations (e.g. how many different numbers could be represented with 4 bits? With 6 bits? With 8 bits)? Each time we add a bit what does that do to the number of values we can represent? If we need to represent 1,000 different values then how many bits will we need to use?

Logic

When trying to solve problems we need to think logically. Logical reasoning is about trying to make sense of things by observing, thinking about the facts and rules that you know are correct and using logic to deduce more rules and information from these. In order to evaluate how many numbers can be represented with a certain number of bits or how many bits are needed to represent a number (as described above) students must apply logical thinking skills

Logical thinking is also applied when students work out whether we have a card visible or not. For example, if we are representing the number 21 and are asking if we should use the 16-dot card, students will usually be able to reason that we *must* use it, since there are only 15 dots remaining on the other cards, and that wouldn't be enough to get 21 in total. Teachers can also challenge students to explain why it is necessary to have a 1-dot card, the answer to which is without having a 1 bit it is impossible to represent odd numbers since all the other cards have an even number of dots.

10.4 Reasons for introducing computing in primary school

There are several positive consequences of having this experience in pre-adolescent years (Duncan, Bell and Tanimoto, 2014):

- Exposing students to the concepts and ideas earlier, before misconceptions about the nature of the subject set in (e.g. 'It's just for boys', 'It's about sitting in front of a computer and using it all day'); these misconceptions potentially damage students' (particularly girls') views of their competence in computing.
- Increased diversity by giving as many students as possible exposure and experience in computing, not just those with a special interest or extra opportunities. At primary school age

students are less concerned about peer pressure, and make decisions based more on their own interest in a topic rather than stereotypes; this is discussed further in Chapter 9, where it is pointed out that teachers have an important role in determining who gets engaged with this subject, and how early experiences are particularly influential.

- Helping students to become well informed citizens and empowering them in the digital world, so they can be *creators*, not just *users* of technology.
- It provides a chance for students to learn the kinds of underpinning skills needed to be good at programming and computing in general, particularly maths and communication skills, which are harder to pick up if a student develops a passion for computing later in their career.
- Natural languages are learned most easily before puberty and while the same has not yet been fully established for programming languages, students do have more time and curiosity to learn this skill at an early age. For example, Siegmund et al. (2014) used fMRI and found a strong relationship between understanding program code and natural language processing.
- Computational thinking and programming provide good opportunities for an integrated curriculum, where students can learn topics as diverse as maths, literacy and music in ways that can be deeper than learning the topics in isolation (Duncan, Bell and Atlas 2017).

10.5 The bigger picture

Having looked at some specific examples and considered the role of CT in the curriculum, we should take a step back and think again about why particular topics appear in the curriculum. We begin by thinking about the ecosystem surrounding digital devices, so that we have a benchmark against which to compare curriculum topics.

Figure 10.2 shows a model of digital systems based on six key elements (Duncan and Bell, 2015). The 'digital device' would traditionally be a computer, but it could also be a smartphone, tablet or even an embedded device such as a burglar alarm or cash register, right through to a supercomputer. All of these devices run 'applications', otherwise referred to as software, apps or firmware; examples would be a word processor, clock, web browser or weather simulator, but also include hidden software such as a printer driver and auto-pilot or a computer controlling the fuel mixture in a car. These applications apply an algorithm to data; this might be as simple as incrementing the number of steps taken in a personal fitness device or as complex as predicting the weather one week from now. A key is that the *algorithm* is just the process that happens (such as adding one to the number of steps taken, matching two DNA sequences, putting some e-mails into date order or working out the time in the current timezone) but to 'put wheels' on the algorithm, someone needs to create a program that physically operates on the data. Many students may not even be aware that all these things are running computer programs; the tools in common use, including search engines and social networks, can appear as monolithic entities rather than some 'code' that someone has written.

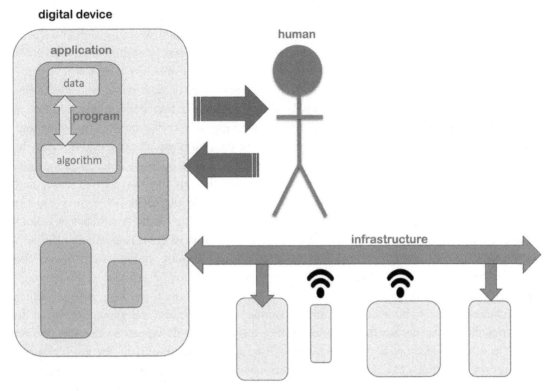

Figure 10.2 A model of digital systems

The most important component of the system is the human; in general software and hardware are created to address a human need, which might be as trivial as entertainment through a small game or animated movie, through to making sure than an airplane flies safely in the most difficult conditions, cars can avoid collisions, or food can be delivered to a population economically and quickly. In all these cases, the interface to the human is crucial; a confusing interface can lead to disaster in transportation and a delightful interface enables the software and its associated hardware to be sold at a premium. Finally, very few digital devices exist in isolation, they are connected through some sort of infrastructure, whether it is the Internet, a local area network, a small personal network such as Bluetooth, or a 'sneakernet' where a memory card or disk is physically moved between devices such as from a camera to a computer.

The six components in Figure 10.2 account for the huge range of digital systems that students are likely to encounter and provide a model for the knowledge that students will need to fully understand a system and be able to design their own digital artefacts. A complaint about older curricula is that they focus primarily on the applications and the data, algorithms, programs and infrastructure are treated as a black box, while the human is expected to conform to the system, rather than viewing the interface critically and considering what is good about it and what might be improved.

This provides us with a bigger picture: if we can explicitly expose students to all six elements of digital systems in a form that is meaningful in their world, then we can give them a better understanding of how it all works and empower them to be creators rather than consumers. This now puts a topic such as 'binary numbers' in context: it is about how data is represented on computers and learning how to represent different types of data using only two values enables students to appreciate the implications of such a representation. For example, students can appreciate that the same hardware can be used for working with a wide variety of information – some of the most common types of information are text, numbers, images, sound, video, but a device might also be storing and processing things such as location and movements or even touch or smell! In the context of programming, not only is the data that the program manipulates represented using digits, but the general purpose nature of digital devices becomes apparent when we realize that programs themselves are represented using digits. Whether it is a block-based or text-based language or a compiled program (which is sometimes explicitly referred to as the 'binary', even though the human readable versions are also stored using binary) they are all represented using digits. Because all of these things can be reduced to binary digits (usually referred to as zeroes and ones) we are able to build multi-purpose devices, such as smartphones that can be a camera, audio recorder, e-mail system and game console at the same time; it means that storing and transmitting this data can all happen on the same system, which is why cloud storage and the Internet have become so important for a wide variety of purposes. Inventions like flash memory open new possibilities for photographers, musicians and seismologists alike because the same physical memory can be used for such different purposes.

Moving back to the bigger picture of a device, and the view that the human is the most important part of a computer system, we become aware that as students learn about programming, they need to always have the human in mind (see chapter 5 in this book for a discussion of this bigger picture). This can be as trivial as thinking about how a response will affect the user, such as responding with a rather humiliating 'You are wrong!!!' to an incorrect answer to a quiz question, to making users wait unnecessarily because the programmer couldn't be bothered to use a more efficient algorithm. Primary school computing is an important opportunity to help students learn to focus on putting the end-user's needs above those of the programmer.

10.6 Integrated learning

Introducing computing to K-12 education is, for the vast majority of teachers and schools, an intimidating task. Few primary teachers have previously been exposed to CS or programming, and even fewer have formal education in these subjects. One approach that can be helpful is to use integrated learning, where computing concepts are learned in the context of other curriculum areas and vice versa.

Key concept: Integrated learning

Integrated learning is when the learning context draws on multiple areas of the curriculum (sometimes known as cross-curricular learning). In primary schools this happens naturally (e.g. working with binary numbers (from computing) naturally uses numeracy skills (from mathematics)). In computing, this is sometimes confused with e-learning, where computers are used to support other subjects; however, this would only be integrated learning if the students were learning about computing at the same time (such as writing a computer program to simulate a social studies scenario).

Integrated (cross-curricular) learning can appear in many forms in computing classes. Investigating early cryptographic methods can open enquiry relevant to social studies around the use of codes in wartime; and writing programs to play music can exercise both topics at the same time (Engelman et al., 2017; Aaron and Blackwell, 2013). Lee, Martin and Apone (2014) integrate computing lessons with storytelling, science investigations and analysing locational data, while Smith and Burrow (2016) use computing in the context of story writing.

There are several benefits of using integrated learning. One is that lessons are using partially familiar ideas (e.g. teaching programming in the context of music for a teacher who is confident with music means that just the programming is the new knowledge domain for the teacher). In contrast, having students write a program to convert binary numbers could have both the teacher and students working with two new knowledge domains.

This explains why beginner programming languages tend to be spatially orientated, using 'turtle' graphics with commands like 'forward', 'left' and 'right'. For younger students, these are concepts that they will be becoming familiar with anyway, so they are writing programs that give them experience in a familiar domain, rather than introducing something completely new.

Another advantage of integrated learning is that it means that the new subject of computing is having a positive effect on the existing curriculum rather than squeezing the time available. For example, teaching geometrical ideas such as distance and angles through a language like Scratch can be motivating for students because the system helps them visualize what is happening; at the same time, they are learning to sequence and possibly iterate commands (Duncan and Bell, 2015). The use of computational tools like this is analogous to using reading in other subjects; young students need to learn reading skills specifically, but exercising them in other subjects reinforces their understanding, and helps them to understand the value.

10.7 Case study two: Programming – what are the main concepts?

A lot of the improvements in curriculum focus on learning programming (or 'coding'), so we provide a second case study here to unpack the real concepts at play.

Example: Kidbots

In the 'Kidbot' activity, a large grid (typically an 8 by 8 grid of 30 cm squares) is used so that students can step out simple instructions like 'Forward', 'Turn left' and 'Turn right' (see Figure 10.3). Three students play the roles of 'Bot', 'Programmer' and 'Tester' respectively. The 'Bot' stands on a square in the grid and another square is identified that they need to get to. The programmer writes a series of instructions using the commands and then gives their 'program' to the tester to read them to the bot. Once the tester gets the program, it is executed without any adjustment, to simulate what happens when a program is run on a computer (this is why a tester is needed; the programmer will be very tempted to make changes on the fly!). The course can be made progressively more difficult by adding obstacles; extra challenges include finding alternative sets of instructions that achieve the same thing.

A follow-up activity is to do the same thing with a 'turtle' based system, either one with physical movement such as Bee-Bots, or an on-screen one such as Scratch Jnr.

Figure 10.3 Kidbot activity

The 'Kidbot' activity enables students to physically experience what they can later program a device to do. Although the two activities are the same at an abstract level, doing the activity away from the computer first forces the student to think through their program, rather than entering into a kind of 'programming by permutation' mode where they make small changes to a program without understanding it, in the hope that it will fix a bug that they have encountered. This can be applied at all levels; for a more sophisticated level of programming, students will often benefit from articulating how the program will work (i.e. the algorithm) before trying to write the program on a computer. Interpreted languages (such as Scratch and Python) can be useful to bridge the gap from unplugged activities to fully programmed ones, since students can try one instruction at a time (e.g. one turtle movement, or one arithmetic calculation) to see if it produces the desired effect.

Introductory programming systems such as the turtle-based approach described here, as used in languages like Scratch, Snap!, Blockly, Logo and so on, work with concrete ideas based around movement that students will be familiar with, yet can introduce fundamental ideas like sequence, selection (if statements) and iteration (loops). This is a good example of scaffolding current knowledge (movement in a 2D space) to teach some simple programming commands. For particularly young students, simplified systems like Scratch Jnr and Bee-Bot focus almost entirely on sequence and possibly iteration. While this may seem too simple to do much that is interesting, not only does it introduce some key ideas, but it is surprising how many cross-curricular concepts can be covered (e.g. at a simple level, a turtle device that goes forward five steps and back three can be used to discuss negative numbers or subtraction; or its path can be used to tell a story).

A valuable aspect of such exercises is that it is an opportunity to use technical terminology appropriately: the device is following an *algorithm* that is implemented by *programming* the device, and if *testing* shows that it doesn't work correctly then the *program* needs to be *debugged*. The importance of learning the language of the discipline is discussed further in Chapter 15.

Even these simple 'programming' exercises provide students with foundational skills for working with a 'proper' programming language. Of course, this raises the question of what a 'proper' language is. Some might argue that students should use a language used in industry, such as Java or C#, but if we focus on the big ideas in programming, writing programs is about getting a computational device to follow the steps in an algorithm, and we know that any algorithm can be programmed using just six key elements: input, output, storage, sequenced instructions, iteration (loops) and conditionals (if and case statements). These six elements make a computing system *Turing Complete* (Böhm and Jacopini, 1966; Aho, 2011); it is fully capable of computing anything that a conventional computer could compute (it's just that the input and output might look a little different, and some languages are harder to program than others for various tasks). If students learn about all six of these elements and how to combine them to achieve a desired result, then they have been exposed to the full power of computation (of course, that doesn't imply that they will then have the skill and knowledge to program effectively – programming is a skill that requires experience to develop). If the big picture is that they should be aware of the full range of what programs are and can achieve, then it is important that they gain experience with all six elements of some programming language. They will also be learning that programming isn't like a game or software with features to be learned, but more like a tool that requires skill to wield, and the process includes steps such as design and debugging.

In this light, the simple 'Kidbot' programming language introduces several important programming concepts: the use of sequence, as well as testing and debugging. It also means that if we consider a typical beginner's language like Scratch, Snap! or Logo, we can see that it contains all six elements and it is therefore suitable for teaching the full power of programming, *provided* that all those elements are exercised well. For example, Aivaloglou and Hermans (2016) found that in a sample of around 4 million Scratch programs shared online, 78.33 per cent had *no* decision points and 13.8 per cent had only one, so very few student programs were using 'if' statements or conditional loops and therefore weren't accessing the full power of a computational device.

Thinking about programming as teaching the key elements that make a system Turing complete also means that teachers should see themselves as teaching *programming*, rather than teaching a particular language. The focus should be on effective application of the six elements, and while animations or games that don't use all of these in any depth can be inspiring for students and have cross-curricula value, the teacher shouldn't lose sight of enabling students to work with the elements at an age-appropriate level. For a very young student, this might involve focusing only on sequence and possibly repetition, in the same way that in maths the preparation for algebra is to learn basic facts about numbers, in preparation for learning more powerful notation later.

The separation of algorithms from programs is also a valuable distinction. An example from everyday life would be to imagine a vending machine that gives change. Suppose the user is owed 75 cents in change (assuming a currency of 5, 10, 20 and 50 cent pieces). Students could recognize that correct change is a 50, 20 and 5 cent coin, but what is the algorithm needed to determine this and how would we avoid writing a program that gives out, say, 15 5-cent pieces? Students can practise giving out change using toy coins and at the same time try to articulate the algorithm they are using (this 'unplugged' experience before programming an algorithm is discussed further in Chapter 8). This highlights the importance of understanding the problem correctly (it was implicit that we want the minimum amount of change). For most currencies a 'greedy' algorithm is suitable, where the largest denomination is given out until it will be too much, and then the next largest denomination is considered, and so on. A student is likely to be able to articulate this algorithm if they are experienced with handling cash. Pointing out that this is the algorithm helps to show that algorithms exist without programming, although programming will be needed if a vending machine is to give out the change rather than a human. Sometimes familiar ideas like recipes or making a drink are used to illustrate what an algorithm is (e.g. Bird, Caldwell and Mayne, 2014); this can be useful, but for students that have the background, numeric examples like giving change make better use of the conventional range of computational concepts, particularly iteration and selection, and the need to keep track of a value with a variable.

Focusing first on algorithms and then the program as an *example* of how the algorithm could be implemented also emphasizes that there can be many correct answers to a programming problem. It also dispels the myth that computing is changing so fast that knowledge will be out-of-date too quickly; on the contrary, the fundamental elements of modern programming languages that are used to program the latest devices would be recognized by Alan Turing, and are no more powerful computationally than the nature of computation that he articulated in the 1930s (Turing, 1937).

Viewing programming through the lens of CT helps to articulate that there's something different about computation. CT relates to this Turing-completeness of language: the computational model (whether von Neumann machines, Turing machines, functional programming or some other paradigm for programming) provides an expressive power that requires a new way of thinking (Aho, 2010). This is epitomized in being able to set up a loop that terminates at the right time (such as giving change in the example above, stopping when nothing more is owed) compared with a mechanism that always runs the same course. However it is approached, CT is a level of reasoning that is different from getting a single correct answer to a problem. Software, once released, must work in every imaginable situation that it will be deployed in, with every possible input that the user might come up with. Even the simplest interface, such as setting the time on a microwave oven, must anticipate every possible sequence of keys that might be pressed. This kind of thinking involves understanding the process (program) that one is creating, and not just solving one-off problems.

Because the focus is on CT and not programming, students will be learning generally applicable skills (such as giving clear and unambiguous instructions) as well as realizing that computers do only what a program says to and not necessarily what the programmer intends. Another key idea is that most programs will need debugging and the act of programming has to include this. It is appropriate at primary level to be getting familiar with these ideas as general skills and to appreciate what a program is. This is not with a view to every child having a career in programming, but simply making sure that students have the opportunity to understand the world they are growing up in, where digital systems are increasingly a part of nearly everything we do.

10.8 Summary: The purpose of teaching computing in primary schools

Now that we have both a big picture of what computing is about and some detailed examples that relate to this, the purpose of teaching these topics in primary schools comes into focus. A key purpose of education is to prepare students for their future, and enable them to contribute positively to society. The particular programming language that they learn at six or eight years old is unlikely to be one that they use later in life (if they program at all in their careers) but the principles that they exercise by exploring computational thinking *will* be used later. Ideas that they could pick up from the ideas discussed above include:

- programming involves combine a few key elements to create powerful applications;
- digital systems should be designed with the user in mind, and programs should be written with the next programmer in mind;
- there are many ways to represent data using two symbols, but the precision of the representation will be a trade-off between the physical cost of high accuracy against the human costs of insufficient accuracy, such as low quality images or a limited range of text characters that can't express their language properly;
- computation is an interaction between algorithms and data, and that this can be made to happen by writing programs.

These are just some (important) examples of the general ideas that students can get to grips with as they engage in learning based around computational thinking. At the same time they will be gaining a familiarity with jargon (such as 'algorithm' and 'binary') by using it in practice. Students will also have the opportunity to see why numeracy and literacy are important by exploring these in a computational context, so that they don't abandon learning these in favour of 'coding'.

Despite the value of introducing computational thinking at primary school, there are also challenges in the process. Any kind of change in an educational system is difficult, and these changes involve a considerable amount of learning for teachers, and making space in the curriculum can mean a change in priorities that not all education systems are ready for (Brown et al., 2014).

To make the transition more achievable, we need to bear in mind that the main objective is to give an understanding of the topic and unlock students' passion for it, not to push students as far as possible with concepts. Most importantly, we need to be clear on the objective of introducing computing into a curriculum and remain focused on the big picture of lasting concepts, particularly when teaching the details of topics.

Key points

- Focusing on the big ideas and goals of teaching computing can avoid it turning into a disjoint collection of topics that need to be taught.
- The key point of teaching binary numbers is not to become expert at converting from decimal to binary, but to appreciate the power and limitations of binary representation.
- Digital systems are designed for humans, and computing education needs to bring students back to thinking about how each sub-topic studied affects humans.
- Computational thinking can be exercised by teaching skills and knowledge in computing
- There are several reasons for introducing computing to primary aged students; many of these mean that their learning should ignite their interest rather than overwhelm them with information.
- Integrated learning can help to reinforce the applicability of computing, give teachers more confidence with the subject and avoid displacing other subjects in the school day.
- Learning programming should be seen as gaining a broad understanding of what computing is, rather than a specific skill in a particular language.
- Bringing in a new subject to the curriculum is challenging; it is important to keep in mind the main purposes for teaching the new topics.

Further reflection

- How could topics from computing be used to enhance other subjects in the curriculum with integrated (cross-curricular) learning?
- What would different interest groups (parents, teachers, industry, government) see as the main reasons for introducing computing in primary schools?

References

Aaron, S, and AF Blackwell (2013). 'From Sonic Pi to Overtone' in *Proceedings of the First ACM SIGPLAN Workshop on Functional Art, Music, Modeling & Design* – FARM '13 (p. 35).(New York, NY, ACM Press).

Aho, AV (2010). *What is Computation?* Ubiquity Symposium, January.

Bird, J, H Caldwell and P Mayne (eds), (2014). *Lessons in Teaching Computing in Primary Schools.* Learning Matters.

Bell, T (2016). 'Demystifying Coding for Schools – What are We Actually Trying to Teach?' *Bulletin of the European Association for Computer Science (BEATS)*, (October), 126–134.

Bell, T, C Duncan, and J Atlas (2016). 'Teacher Feedback on Delivering Computational Thinking in Primary School' in *Proceedings of the 11th Workshop in Primary and Secondary Computing Education*, 100–101.

Böhm, C and G Jacopini (1966). 'Flow Diagrams, Turing Machines and Languages with only Two Formation Rules' 9(5) *Communications of the ACM* 366–371, May.

Brown, NCC, S Sentance, T Crick and S Humphreys (2014). 'Restart: The Resurgence of Computer Science in UK Schools' 14(2) *Trans Comput Educ* 9:1–9:22.

Duncan, C and T Bell (2015). 'A Pilot Computer Science and Programming Course for Primary School Students' in *Proceedings of the Workshop in Primary and Secondary Computing Education* (WiPSCE '15) (New York, NY, ACM).

Duncan, C, T Bell and J Atlas (2017). 'What Do the Teachers Think? Introducing Computational Thinking in the Primary School Curriculum' in *Proceedings of the Nineteenth Australasian Computing Education Conference*, 65–74.

Duncan, C, T Bell and S Tanimoto (2014). 'Should Your 8-year-old Learn Coding?' in *Proceedings of the 9th Workshop in Primary and Secondary Computing Education* (WiPSCE '14) (New York, NY, ACM Press) 60–69.

Engelman, S, B Magerko, T McKlin, M Miller, D Edwards and J Freeman (2017). 'Creativity in Authentic STEAM Education with EarSketch' in *Proceedings of the 2017 ACM SIGCSE Technical Symposium on Computer Science Education* (SIGCSE '17) (New York, NY, ACM) 183–188.

Falkner, K, R Vivian and N Falkner (2014). 'The Australian Digital Technologies Curriculum: Challenge and Opportunity' in *Proc. Sixteenth Australasian Computing Education Conference* (ACE 2014) Auckland, NZ 3–12.

Lee, I, F Martin and K Apone (2014). 'Integrating Computational Thinking across the K-8 Curriculum'. 5 *ACM Inroads* 4 (December 2014) 64–71.

Schulte, C, M Hornung and S Sentance (2012). 'Computer Science at School/CS Teacher Education: Koli Working-group Report on CS at School' in *Koli Calling '12 Conference on Computing Education Research* 29–38.

Siegmund, J, C Kästner, S Apel, C Parnin, A Bethmann, T Leich, . . . A Brechmann (n.d.). Understanding Source Code with Functional Magnetic Resonance Imaging, 378–389.

Smith, S and LE Burrow (2016). 'Programming Multimedia Stories in Scratch to Integrate Computational Thinking and Writing with Elementary Students' 9(2) *Journal of Mathematics Education* 119–131.

Tedre, M and PJ Denning (2016). 'The Long Quest for Computational Thinking' in *Proceedings of the 16th Koli Calling Conference on Computing Education Research* 120–129.

Turing, AM (1937). 'On Computable Numbers, with an Application to the Entscheidungsproblem' 2(1) *Proceedings of the London Mathematical Society* 230–265.

Wing, J (2014). 'Computational Thinking Benefits Society' in *Social Issues in Computing*. Available at: http://socialissues.cs.toronto.edu/index.html%3Fp=279.html

11

Assessment in the Computing Classroom

Sue Sentance, Cynthia Selby and Maria Kallia

Chapter outline

Chapter synopsis

This chapter gives a general introduction to assessment for learning and applies this to the teaching of computing in school, with reference to recent research studies in this area. A variety of methods that can be used for assessment are discussed including self and peer assessment, automated tools, rubrics, concept maps and multiple-choice questions. Ways of assessing programming projects are discussed and evaluated.

11.1 Assessment overview

In this chapter, we will address the practical aspects of assessment in the computer science classroom. Assessment is critical to education both for accreditation and to support learning. Key aspects of formative assessment are questioning, dialogue and developing students' abilities to self-assess (Black and Wiliam, 1998) and in order to learn more, students need feedback on their progress. Students can use teacher feedback to work harder on their areas of weakness; this puts the responsibility and power into the hands of the student. Students should be able to use self-assessment to identify their own weaknesses and apply themselves to overcome these.

In this chapter, we focus primarily on formative assessment or assessment for learning, which includes feedback, questioning, self-assessment opportunities, peer assessment and a range of other strategies in the context of computing. While assessment opportunities such as projects or tests may be used formatively or summatively, in this chapter we primarily discuss these in terms of their contribution to formative assessment, drawing on existing research in the field.

Formative and summative assessment

A key feature of assessment is that it concerns making judgements. This enables an assessment *of* learning to be made, known as *summative assessment*. With this type of assessment, students are graded at the end of a course or module. This can be for certification purposes, or also for diagnostic purposes.

Another type of assessment is assessment *for* learning, known as *formative assessment*, which is used to identify what students know, what they still need to learn, and how to get there. There are many methods that can be used to formatively assess students, some of which are discussed in this chapter.

Formative assessment taking place at school has the intention of promoting further learning for the student, whereas summative assessment revolves around key points where a student's achievement is measured, giving data that can be used not only by the student but a number of other stakeholders, including the school and employers.

It is necessary to make a distinction between the assessment opportunity and the assessment activity; in this chapter we discuss both. The assessment opportunity is a task that may be set with the intention of using it for assessment. The assessment activity is the provision of feedback, dialogue, student discussion, generated as a result of the task, that provides an opportunity for learning by the student. For some tasks, feedback is inherent but in others, it happens later. Thus, it is possible to provide an assessment opportunity that does not provide much assessment for learning.

11.2 Assessment methods

Grover makes the case for the need for a range of different assessment types (Grover, 2017) and describes how the FACT curriculum, developed in the USA, has achieved this. In this section we look at some of the different methods individually and unpick their respective strengths. In particular we focus on:

- Self and peer assessment
- Automated tools

- Parson puzzles
- Rubrics
- Concept maps
- Response systems and MCQs.

Self and peer assessment

Peer and self-assessment are effective methods of formative assessment, both useful in the classroom. Boud and Falchikov (2007) define peer assessment as a process of providing feedback on peers' work based on success criteria that the students may have established previously. Self-assessment can be defined as formative assessment evaluating the extent to which oneself or one's work meets requirements or success criteria. Peer review or assessment has been used as a learning process to improve the quality of computer programs for at least thirty years (Luxton-Reilly, 2009).

Example activity: Using peer assessment in the classroom

Ask students to write an algorithm to control a red, amber and green traffic light. Writing the algorithm is the assessment *opportunity*. Using peer assessment, the students can then share their algorithms, either on paper or by presenting them in small groups. You should decide on some criteria to assess the algorithms such as 'functionality', 'notation' and 'improvements'. The writing and giving of feedback is the assessment *activity*. At the end of the peer assessment, students should understand their strengths and where they need to improve, possibly with recommendations on how to do so. The more often you carry out peer assessment the more familiar students become with it, and they will be able to give increasingly constructive feedback to their peers, as well as having a growing understanding of what the criteria mean.

Advantages

By engaging with peer assessment, students move from mere observers in the classroom to more active participants, engaging with the learning process. In addition, the levels of collaboration and sense of community are increased by the use of peer assessment (Clark, 2004). Topping (2009) suggests that peer assessment helps students really understand the aims and objectives of a course. This leads to students developing a better understanding of the assessment criteria against which they themselves will be judged. Students, assessing the work of others, benefit by developing skills to identify errors in their own work (Sitthiworachart and Joy, 2003). Self-assessment can also help them to identify errors and to further develop the ability to accurately measure their performance against requirements, which is important for creating effective learners (Boud, et al., 2013).

How reliable are self and peer assessment?

A small-scale study, examining students' ability to self-assess their programming skills that used a survey aligned to Bloom's Taxonomy, found that students self-assessment was accurate in relation to their summative assessment (exam) scores (Alaoutinen and Smolander, 2010). A study by Chinn (2005) showed a high correlation between students' quality of peer assessment and general performance on an algorithms course. In a large-scale study of 1,500 students, feedback on each other's programs was found to be as good as or better than tutor feedback (Hamer et al., 2009). In a high-school environment, teachers' and students' assessment scores were highly correlated (Tseng and Tsai, 2007). However, there are other studies showing that students demonstrate a tendency to be more generous with self-assessment marks (Sajjadi, et al., 2016) and with peer assessment of their friends (Sitthiworachart and Joy, 2003). Weaker students appear less accurate when self-assessing (Murphy and Tenenberg, 2005).

Conclusion

The benefits of self and peer assessment include increasing levels of engagement and collaboration in the classroom, increasing understanding of assessment criteria, and identification of strengths and weaknesses in a student's work. Although several studies report parity of assessment by peers and tutors, not all studies are as positive. However, as assessment activities, both self and peer assessment are suitable for the computer science classroom. The value of these may be increased by the addition of rubrics. This approach is discussed further below.

Automated tools

There have been many tools designed to automate the problem of assessing programs. Mostly these relate to higher education courses; many are even specific to an institution. An example tool suitable for use in school is Dr Scratch (Moreno-León and Robles, 2015), which gives feedback on the complexity of a Scratch program. Although the terminology used by the tool may be quite difficult for children to understand, this would be a useful tool for teachers to support them in the assessment of their learners' projects, alongside their own rubric.

Parson's puzzles

Parson's puzzles are drag-and-drop tasks which present fragments of code that students need to put in the correct order to solve a problem. Parson's puzzles are supported by tools like Hot Potatoes, Ville, and JSParson (Ihantola and Karavirta, 2011). Table 11.1 presents an example in the Ville environment. Students regard this type of task as easier than writing code, and more creative and objective than other assessment tasks (Denny et al., 2008). The tools also provide feedback to students. Teachers can use these puzzles as an alternative to open-ended code writing questions and identify students' difficulties and misconceptions.

Table 11.1 Example of Parson's puzzles adapted from Ville example (Ihantola and Karavirta, 2011)

Program	Exercise description

def main():
    a = 1
    b = −1
    `a = 1`
    `tmp = a`
    `b = tmp`
	Order the lines of code so that the function swaps the contents of variables a and b

Rubrics

Rubrics are used in teaching to describe expectations for an assignment. They provide a way of offering more consistent assessment of student performance. They are used to define detailed criteria that describe what students should achieve (Becker, 2003) and they have two shared characteristics. The first is a list of criteria that is necessary for the particular task; the second is the degree of quality (Andrade, 2000). These features make rubrics proper tools to reliably evaluate students' performance, but they can also help students to understand their progress (Black and Wiliam, 2009). Popham (1997) refers to rubrics as instructional illuminators.

Rubrics have been used to assess computer programming assignments from the early 1980s (Miller and Peterson, 1980; Hamm et al., 1983) to the current day (Becker, 2003; Barney et al., 2012; Mustapha et al., 2016). An example of a rubric is shown in Table 11.2.

Rubrics are regarded as fair and reliable tools with which students can better understand what is expected of them (Barney et al., 2012) and the amount of effort needed to reach a specific level of performance (Mustaph et al., 2016). Additionally, rubrics are useful in peer and self-assessment and can help students to evaluate their performance or that of their peers. Alternatively, students can be involved in developing the rubrics, so they feel more engaged with the whole process.

Table 11.2 An example of a rubric for a solution in a programming task (adapted from Eugene, et al. (2016))

	Weak 0–3	Emerging 4–6	Good 7–8	Excellent 9–10
Solution for 1 b)	An incomplete solution is implemented. It does not compile and/or run	Runs but has logical errors. *Apply Emerging if program does not use 2D array or has incorrect results*	A complete solution is tested and runs but does not meet all the specifications and/or work for all test data. *Apply good if program misses one data entry line*	A completed solution runs without errors. It meets all the specifications and works for all test data.

Concept maps

A concept map is a schematic representation of concepts and the relationships they form and can be used by students to represent their knowledge of a subject (see Chapter 8). Figure 11.1 shows an example of a concept map.

As an assessment tool, it can be used to measure students' quality of understanding and the structure of their knowledge (Borda et al., 2009). Markham et al. (1994) suggested a detailed scoring system (Table 11.3) to help teachers evaluate students' concept maps.

By employing concept maps, teachers can monitor students' levels of learning and organization of knowledge, which leads to teachers identifying students' misconceptions and misunderstandings (Moen, 2009; Wei and Yue, 2016). In a study conducted at university level, students reported that concept maps are more entertaining than other assessment methods (Freeman and Urbaczewski, 2001).

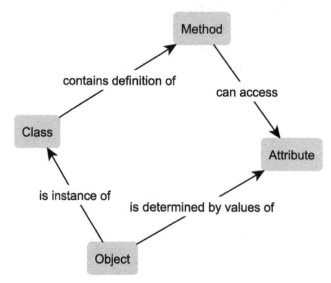

Figure 11.1 Example of a concept map (Mühling, 2016)

Table 11.3 Concept map scoring system (Markham et al., 1994)

Component	Description	Score
Concepts	No of concepts	1 point for each concept
Concepts Relationships	No of valid relationships	1 point for each valid relationship
Branching	Scores for branching varied according to the amount of elaboration	1 point for each branching 3 points for each successive branching
Hierarchies	No of hierarchies	5 points for each level of hierarchy
Cross-links	No of cross-links	10 points for each cross-link
Examples	No of examples	1 point for each example

Response systems and multiple-choice questions

Audience response systems, informally known as 'clickers', allow the teacher to display a multiple-choice question (MCQ) with optional responses. Learners respond to the question by pressing a button on an electronic device. A receiver picks up the signals from the clickers, sends the responses to software and the software interprets and displays the results (Ribbens and National Science Teachers Association, 2007). The teacher can see the results and can choose to share them with the class.

Online versions of the 'clicker' provide more accessible use of technology in the classroom. These online systems include Kahoot!,[1] Socrative,[2] Poll Everywhere[3] and Diagnostic Questions.[4] The facilities offered by each are slightly different, but they all incorporate a mechanism for hosting a live interactive quiz made up of multiple-choice questions. These particular systems require each student to have a device connected to the Internet.

The use of response systems has several advantages for learners. Thirty-six of thirty-eight papers reviewed found that students have positive views about the technology systems (Kay and LeSage, 2009). In the classroom, a natural competitiveness among learners exists to answer the questions quickly and accurately (Cutri et al., 2016). Learners' self-confidence improves because of the opportunities for interaction with their peers (Coca and Slisko, 2013; Fotaris et al., 2016). There is some support for suggesting that the use of response systems leads to improved academic performance (Kay and LeSage, 2009), but this is contradicted by a more recent study (Wang et al., 2016). Therefore, while improvement in academic performance may not be guaranteed by the use of response systems, students perceive the systems as a positive addition to the classroom.

The online systems have advantages for the teacher. Not only do students get immediate feedback about the correct response, but the teacher gets immediate feedback about what the students know and do not know, thereby making it ideal for formative assessment (Kay and LeSage, 2009). Collecting and analysing data about individuals or groups of students is possible with the online systems. Some provide analytics that can help teachers identify gaps in knowledge by groups and individuals and feature the ability to allow comparisons to all other users of the system.

The use of response systems and online quizzes is not without disadvantages, however. Although students view the systems as engaging and motivating, an abundance of enthusiasm could lead to challenging classroom management situations. In schools, the challenge lies in acquiring the skills to use the tool as part of the learning process, rather than just as an engaging and motivating game. Students may need to be trained in how to use the online quizzes as part of the learning process and not view them just as a game.

Regardless of the delivery method, developing the MCQs is a difficult challenge (Dell and Wantuch, 2017; Kay and LeSage, 2009). Writing multiple-choice questions may seem an easy task, but writing questions to allow identification of real confusion or misconceptions is challenging (Dell and Wantuch, 2017). However, the online systems allow the sharing of questions and quizzes between all users, thereby reducing the time for resource creation.

---

[1] See https://getkahoot.com
[2] See https://socrative.com/
[3] See www.polleverywhere.com/
[4] See https://diagnosticquestions.com/.b = tmp

> ### Example: Crowd-sourcing assessment with Project Quantum
>
>
>
> Project Quantum helps computing teachers check their students' understanding, and support their progress, by providing free access to an online assessment system. The assessments are formative, automatically marked, of high quality and support teaching by guiding content, measuring progress and identifying misconceptions. Students are asked to justify their answers to each question and this information is available to their teachers. Teachers can contribute their own questions and see how other students elsewhere have performed on the questions available.

Research indicates that students find the use of MCQs, via clickers or online systems both motivating and engaging. From the teacher's perspective, the most powerful motivation for using these systems is their contribution to formative assessment. While the challenges of using these systems in the school environment will be different to those in Higher Education, the rewards, especially in affording formative assessment, may be just as abundant.

11.3 Assessing programming projects

The challenge of assessing programming skill is present at all levels of education, from primary to university. In university, large cohorts and the necessity to reduce marking time have led to many innovative approaches to machine marking of computer programs. However, at primary and secondary level, the programming tasks are not as complex and the number of students at most institutions is not as large. In common with other laboratory settings, there is also a need to assess the process of artefact creation. Perhaps we can consider four potential solutions to the problem of assessing programming projects:

- Assess the process
- Assess the product/artefact
- Assess by interview
- Assess the design.

Assess the process

Computer science is not the first subject challenged with assessing a process as opposed to an artefact. In Israel, design-based learning (Doppelt, 2009) was an attempt to assess the thinking processes of high-school students in a course combining mechanics, electrical engineering and programming. Students documented both the process of producing their group projects and the thinking skills employed during the process. The thinking and problem-solving skills were not as well documented as the system development (Doppelt, 2009). The approach of documenting the creation process, incorporating reflection and evaluation, is seen in some computing classrooms, by the use of learning journals, portfolios or coursework submissions.

Observation is another approach to assessing process in a laboratory setting. In the science laboratory (Hofstein and Lunetta, 2004) students are observed as they engage in practical activities. An observer summatively assesses students according to planning, design, performance and analysis. This same approach may be used in the computing classroom. Observation of real-time programming was carried out using the Scratch environment (Brennan and Resnick, 2012). Most often, however, observational assessment in computing is formative rather than summative.

Assess the product/artefact

The most obvious method of assessing skills in programming is to assess the artefact, the program code created (Insa and Silva, 2015; Lobb and Harlow, 2016). The artefact only approach is also used with students of other ages.

The Alice visual programming language was used by 325 middle school children (Werner, Campe, and Denner, 2012) in a twenty-hour course. The children followed a self-paced study programme and then designed and created their own games. About one-third of the artefacts used variables and one-half used built-in functions. Only a single student created a custom function.

Using games in assessing computer science was also explored with fifty-nine middle school girls in a fourteen-week programme (Denner et al., 2012). The software of choice for this study was Stagecast Creator. No requirements were set for the games. On inspection of the artefacts, 18 per cent did not include interaction, only 1 per cent included an 'and if' type test, and very few changed rule names from the default of 'untitled'.

A group of fourth grade students completed a set of challenges using Scratch, a visual programming language for elementary students. The SOLO taxonomy was used to assess understanding of the problem domain (i.e. the requirements, based on the artefact alone (Seiter, 2015)). She used specific characteristics of Scratch (synchronization, broadcast) to assess correctness of the code produced. The majority of students gave relational level (one from the top) rather than extended abstract (top) responses in their code.

The Scratch group (Brennan and Resnick, 2012) attempted to assess computational thinking through examination of the artefacts uploaded to the Scratch community website. They mapped Scratch blocks to computational thinking concepts. The scripts were analysed to determine the number and distribution of the different types of blocks. They concluded that knowing the type and count of blocks used was not sufficient to evidence computational thinking.

In some way, all of these studies were uncontrolled. Some (Denner et al., 2012) lack specifications for the artefacts that may allow students to evidence their learning. Others (Brennan and Resnick, 2012; Seiter, 2015; Werner et al., 2012) provide no information about the process of producing the artefacts. Based on these studies, it seems unlikely that students will spontaneously produce evidence of learning in their artefacts.

Assess by interview

Adding another assessment instrument may strengthen the artefact-based judgements. Several researchers (Brennan and Resnick, 2012; Portelance and Bers, 2015) have used interviews to fulfil this purpose.

Scratch artefacts formed the basis of interviews with programmers from the Scratch community (Brennan and Resnick, 2012). In interviews lasting from sixty to 120 minutes, Scratch programmers were asked a series of questions about the production of their projects. The responses to these questions allowed the researchers to form detailed descriptions of the development process (Brennan and Resnick, 2012).

Artefact-based interviews were also employed with a group of second graders in the USA (Portelance and Bers, 2015) who used ScratchJr to create programs. This study is innovative because it uses both peer interviewers and video interviews. However, the questions were designed by researchers to elicit the information needed to make informed judgements about what was being learned.

Moving up the age scale, App Inventor artefacts were used as assessment for non-CS majors at university (Honig, 2013). Each level of Bloom's Taxonomy was mapped to a statement about the project. Students self-assessed their projects; instructors also assessed the projects. Instructors assessed higher than the students did, but the instructors also had access to exam marks and had seen student presentations. These presentations could be viewed as similar to an interview because they are a mechanism for revealing the understanding of the programmer.

An advantage of using the artefact and interview approach is that formative feedback can be freely used throughout the coding process to aid understanding and acquisition of skills. However, the addition of an interview requires more of an assessor's time. This may prove impractical when scaled to secondary school cohorts.

Assess the design

One approach that forgoes employing a student-created artefact is described as design scenarios (Brennan and Resnick, 2012). In this approach, three sets of two Scratch projects each were created by an educator. The sets were designed to increase in difficulty and aesthetically appeal to different groups. The Scratch user was asked to explain what the project did, describe an extension to the project, fix a bug in the project, and remix the project to add a feature (Brennan and Resnick, 2012). This process can be observed in real time, which allows understanding to be tracked. This approach still requires a significant amount of the assessor's time. It also has the disadvantage that the programming stages of fixing a bug and remixing may be subject to unacknowledged influences, in much the same way as the artefact-only approach.

Conclusion

None of the approaches to assess programming skills and computational thinking discussed above is without disadvantages. However, there does seem to be an acknowledgement that the very popular approach of assessing code artefacts alone has shortcomings. The addition of another assessment format is needed to validate the artefact assessment. This additional method could be an interview, observation or a test. Although coding scenarios appear promising, their use would require significant remodelling of classroom activities.

11.4 Assessment in practice: Case studies

In a study of how teachers assess computer science in school, Yadav et al. (2015) conducted interviews with teachers about their assessment practices. Teachers reported that they employ a number of techniques to measure students' learning. They use multiple-choice assessment, open-ended assessment and rubrics summatively. They use quizzes, and set program writing tasks formatively. This study gives a useful perspective on what teachers actually do. Here we build on this by presenting two case studies of teachers and their impressions of useful assessment. One of these teachers, Eliza, teaches students aged 11 to 18; the other teaches students aged 4 to 11 as a specialist computing teacher in a primary school. The data was gathered during interviews that took place as part of a study described by Barendsen et al. (2015).

Case Study 1: David

David is a primary teacher in England specializing in the teaching of computing. He studied computer science at school to the age of eighteen, and has a degree in politics and a teaching qualification. He has moved from being the subject leader of ICT to being coordinator and in this role, supports other teachers in his school through a team-teaching model. He also provides professional development outside his school to other teachers. Table 11.4 shows the range of assessment strategies described by David and Eliza.

David is keen to record evidence of pupil work so that he can look at it later, including the process of creating the work. He tries to include students by talking about what they have done and

Table 11.4 Assessment strategies described by David and Eliza

David's assessment strategies	Eliza's assessment strategies
Observation – including documentation of observations	Setting **multiple-choice questions**
	Monitoring **group programming tasks**
Questioning – with prompt questions about problem-solving processes	Asking students to **debug** programs/algorithms
	Asking students to **explain** an algorithm
Dialogue with children about their understanding	**Tests**
Photographic and physical **evidence of work**	Programming tasks marked with **own rubric**
Recording childrens' talk	**Observation** of student work
Tests and online **quizzes**	**Self-assessment** through progress checks
Primary (elementary) school	**Secondary (middle/high) school**

recording them talking about their work for the school website: this can be part of an assessment process.

In fact, David is keen to emphasize that this means that you don't lose the evidence of students' work when it is over and this means you can prepare for summative assessment by being careful to record students' work at appropriate times. David is aware that the product itself is not necessarily the evidence of understanding and the challenge of capturing the lightbulb moment, when a child grasped a new concept or idea:

> It's when a child gets that lightbulb moment – that's when the real power comes – being able to capture those, in assessment terms. It's a challenge, but it's also well worth it.

He emphasizes the importance of dialogue as a way of enabling children to articulate what works and doesn't work about their program and frequently uses this in his teaching. Another strategy he uses is to give students incorrect or less than perfect examples of work to put right.

Case Study 2: Eliza

Eliza is a secondary computing teacher in England with twelve years' experience. She had eight years' experience in industry before moving into teaching. As well as teaching in her own school, she has developed teaching materials for other teachers, has examined for national awarding bodies and has run professional development for other teachers. The strategies she uses are highlighted in Table 11.4.

Eliza teaches students from ages 11 to 18 so covers a range of different levels. She describes assessment as identifying gaps in students' knowledge using a range of different strategies:

> The thing is it's somehow like an ice-field with crevices in and you're trying to find the crevices. You are trying to find the gaps in their knowledge and you are trying to give them all sorts of different exercises to find out where the crevices are.

In some ways Eliza demonstrates similar strategies to those used by David with younger children by asking students to fix programs with errors in and also to modify partly completed programs. However, she also makes more use of tests throughout her teaching, which is to be expected as students at this age will be preparing for national examinations. She has also developed her own rubrics which she has created herself to assess the students' programs. She uses a range of self-assessment methods with her students, particularly some progress sheets that she has developed including confidence indicators, which she uses to enable students to rate their confidence on various topics. However, Eliza discusses how her formative assessment in computing is more focused on programming than assessing algorithmic thinking, and reflects that she could develop her assessment in this area.

11.5 Summary

The value of both peer and self-assessment, part of formative assessment, is supported in the research (Liu et al., 2001; Boud et al., 2013). Not only do learners receive valuable formative feedback, but it also gives them an opportunity to understand better the requirements or objectives of the task they are undertaking. The one concern to acknowledge is that the assessment by peers may not always be congrous with assessment by teachers. Peers may have a tendency to be generous with marks (Sajjadi et al., 2016).

In the computer science classroom, because much time is devoted to programming, it is tempting to assess the outcome of that task (Insa and Silva, 2015; Lobb and Harlow, 2016). However, assessing the artefact produced by the task of programming has been shown to be less reliable than methods that assess the process of producing the artefact (Brennan and Resnick, 2012; Portelance and Bers, 2015).

An assessment opportunity is a task that may be set with the intention of using it for assessment. These may include a programming environment with the ability to generate feedback for the learner or the teacher. Automated tools are used extensively in higher education, but few exist for the school environment. Rubrics are a fair and reliable (Barney et al., 2012) assessment tool, where learners can reflect on their own performance and judge how to reach a higher level (Mustapha et al., 2016). When learners produce concept maps they reveal how they organize their knowledge and understanding. Teachers can interpret the maps to reveal students' misconceptions (Wei and Yue, 2016). Multiple-choice questions can be used, as formative assessment tools, in several different ways in the classroom. Clicker technologies (Ribbens and National Science Teachers Association, 2007) and online systems bring a competitive environment to the activity of assessment while allowing the teacher to collect immediate feedback and respond immediately to misunderstandings and misconceptions (Kay and LeSage, 2009). However, to reap the most benefit from these systems, the students and teachers must use them as a tool, rather than just an engaging activity. Contests and competitions, sponsored by many organizations, are found to be motivating for some students: the resources produced for use in these competitions are often publicly available and can be useful as classroom resources. Using the challenges in the classroom allows teachers to identify the development of computational thinking skills.

Much of the research in computer science education has been conducted in higher education. It has yet to be tested in schools with younger learners. Areas of particular interest include developing an understanding for how classroom dialogue be leveraged to formatively computational thinking skills and understanding if peer and self-assessment in schools reflects the bias shown in higher education. Reproducing and testing these studies in a new context will lead to more effective teaching and learning.

Key points

- Many assessment methods can be used in conjunction to effectively formatively assess students in computing.
- Self and peer assessment enable students to become familiar with the criteria used to assess them and thus become more aware of what they need to do to progress.
- Concepts maps are useful to examine students' understanding of the relationship between key concepts and ideas.

- In the computer science classroom, it is tempting to assess the outcome of that task. However, assessing the artefact produced by the task of programming has been shown to be less reliable than methods that assess the process of producing the artefact.
- Multiple-choice questions and response systems using technology can give both teacher and student instant feedback about their progress and stimulate discussion about right and wrong answers to questions.

Further reflection

- For each of the assessment *approaches* listed in this chapter, make a list of example topics that would benefit from this type of assessment, and devise some assessment *opportunities*.
- Focusing on a topic in computing that students might find difficult, reflect on the type of assessment that would enable a teacher to have a good understanding of what the student understood and any persistent misconceptions.

References

Alaoutinen, S, K Smolander (2010). 'Student Self-assessment in a Programming Course using Bloom's Revised Taxonomy' in *Proceedings of the Fifteenth Annual Conference on Innovation and Technology in Computer Science Education*, 155–159. ACM.

Barendsen, E, L Mannila, B Demo, N Grgurina, C Izu, C Mirolo, S Sentance, A Settle and G Stupuriene (2015). 'Concepts in K–9 Computer Science Education' in *Proceedings of the 2015 ITiCSE on Working Group Reports*, 85–116. ACM.

Becker, K (2003). 'Grading Programming Assignments Using Rubrics' 35(3) *ACM SIGCSE Bulletin* 253.

Black, P and D Wiliam. (1998). *Inside the Black Box: Raising Standards through Classroom Assessment* (London, GL Assessment).

Boud, D and N Falchikov (2007). *Rethinking Assessment in Higher Education* (London, Kogan Page).

Brennan, K and M Resnick (2012). 'New Frameworks for Studying and Assessing the Development of Computational Thinking' in *Proceedings of the 2012 Annual Meeting of the American Educational Research Association*, Vancouver Canada. AERA.

Clark, N (2004). 'Peer Testing in Software Engineering Projects' in *Proceedings of the Sixth Australasian Conference on Computing Education*, 41–48. Australian Computer Society, Inc.

Coca, D and J Slisko (2013). 'Software Socrative and Smartphones as Tools For Implementation of Basic Processes of Active Physics Learning in Classroom: An Initial Feasibility Study With Prospective Teachers' 4(22) *European Journal of Physics Education* 8.

Cutri, R, LR Marim, JR Cordeiro, HAC Gil and CCT Guerald (2016). 'Kahoot, a New and Cheap Way to get Classroom-Response instead of Using Clickers'. Available at: https://peer.asee.org/25512

Dell, KA and GA Wantuch (2017). 'How-to Guide for Writing Multiple Choice Questions for the Pharmacy Instructor' 9(1) *Currents in Pharmacy Teaching and Learning* 137–144.

Denner, J, L Werner and E Ortiz (2012). 'Computer Games Created by Middle School Girls: Can They Be Used to Measure Understanding of Computer Science Concepts?' 58(1) *Computer Education* 240–249.

Doppelt, Y (2009). 'Assessing Creative Thinking in Design-Based Learning' 19(1) *International Journal of Technology and Design Education* 55–65.

Fotaris, P, R Leinfellner, T Mastoras and Y Rosunally (2016). 'Climbing up the Leaderboard: An Empirical Study of Applying Gamification Techniques to a Computer Programming Class' 14(2) *Electronic Journal of e-Learning* 94–110.

Grover, S (2017). 'Assessing Algorithmic and Computational Thinking in K-12: Lessons from a Middle-School Classroom' in P Rich and C Hodges *Emerging Research, Practice and Policy on Computational Thinking* (Cham, Springer International Publishing).

Hofstein, A and VN Lunetta (2004). 'The Laboratory in Science Education: Foundations for the Twenty-first Century' 88(1) *Science Education* 28–54.

Honig, WL (2013). 'Teaching and Assessing Programming Fundamentals for Non-Majors with Visual Programming' in *Proceedings of the 18th ACM Conference on Innovation and Technology in Computer Science Education*, Canterbury, England. ACM.

Insa, D and J Silva (2015). 'Semi-Automatic Assessment of Unrestrained Java Code: A Library, a DSL, and a Workbench to Assess Exams and Exercises' in *Proceedings of the 2015 ACM Conference on Innovation and Technology in Computer Science Education*, Vilnius, Lithuania. ACM.

Kay, R H and A LeSage (2009). 'Examining the Benefits and Challenges of Using Audience Response Systems: A Review of the Literature' 53(3) *Computers & Education* 819–827.

Lin, SSJ, EZF Liu and SM Yuan (2001). 'Web-based Peer Assessment: Feedback for Students with Various Thinking-Styles' 17 *Journal of Computer Assisted Learning* 420–432.

Liu, EZF, SS Lin, CH Chiu and SM Yuan (2001). 'Web-based Peer Review: The Learner as Both Adapter and Reviewer. 44(3) *IEEE Transactions on Education* 246–251.

Lobb, R and J Harlow (2016). 'Coderunner: A Tool for Assessing Computer Programming Skills' 7(1) *ACM Inroads* 47–51.

Loughran, J, P Mulhall and A Berry. (2004). 'In Search of Pedagogical Content Knowledge in Science: Developing Ways of Articulating and Documenting Professional Practice' 41(4) *Journal of Research in Science Teaching* 370.

Luxton-Reilly, A (2009). 'A Systematic Review of Tools that Support Peer Assessment' 19(4) *Computer Science Education* 209–232.

Luxton-Reilly, A and P Denny (2010). 'Constructive Evaluation: A Pedagogy of Student-contributed Assessment' 20(2) *Computer Science Education* 145–167.

Markham, KM, JJ Mintzes. and MG Jones (1994). 'The Concept Map as a Research and Evaluation Tool: Further Evidence of Validity' 31(1) *Journal of Research in Science Teaching* 91–101.

Moreno-León, J and G Robles (2015). 'Dr. Scratch: A Web tool to Automatically Evaluate Scratch Projects' in *Proceedings of the Workshop in Primary and Secondary Computing Education* 132–133. ACM.

Mühling, A (2016) 'Aggregating Concept Map Data to Investigate the Knowledge of Beginning CS students' 26(2–3) *Computer Science Education* 176–191.

Murphy, L and J Tenenberg (2005) 'Knowing What I Know: An Investigation of Undergraduate Knowledge and Self-knowledge of Data Structures' 15(4) *Computer Science Education* 297–315.

Portelance, D J and MU Bers (2015). 'Code and Tell: Assessing Young Children's Learning of Computational Thinking Using Peer Video Interviews with Scratch Jr'. In *Proceedings of the 14th International Conference on Interaction Design and Children, Boston, Massachusetts*. ACM.

Porter, L, D Bouvier Q Cutts, S Grissom, C Lee, R McCartney, B Simon (2016). 'A Multi-institutional Study of Peer Instruction in Introductory Computing' in *Proceedings of the 47th ACM Technical Symposium on Computing Science Education*, Memphis, Tennessee. ACM.

Ribbens, E and National Science Teachers Association, AVA (2007). 'Why I Like Clicker Personal Response Systems' 37(2) *Journal of College Science Teaching*, 60–62.

Sajjadi, MS, M Alamgir and U von Luxburg (2016). 'Peer Grading in a Course on Algorithms and Data Structures: Machine Learning Algorithms Do Not Improve over Simple Baselines' in *Proceedings of the Third (2016) ACM Conference on Learning@ Scale* 369–378. ACM.

Seiter, L (2015). 'Using SOLO to Classify the Programming Responses of Primary Grade Students' in *Proceedings of the 46th ACM Technical Symposium on Computer Science Education*, Kansas City, Missouri 540–545. ACM.

Sitthiworachart, J and M Joy (2003). 'Web-based Peer Assessment in Learning Computer Programming' in *Proceedings of the Third ICEE International Conference* on *Advanced Technologies*, Athens, Greece, 180–184. IEEE.

Teague, D, C Fidge and Y Xu (2016). 'Combining Unsupervised and Invigilated Assessment Of Introductory Programming' in *Proceedings of the Australasian Computer Science Week Multiconference*, Canberra, Australia. ACM.

Topping, KJ (2009). 'Peer Assessment' 48(1) *Theory into Practice'* 20–27.

Tseng, SC, CC Tsai (2007). 'Online Peer Assessment and the Role of Peer Feedback: A Study of High School Computer Courses' 49 *Computer & Education*, 1161–1174.

Wang, AI, M Zhu and R Sætre (2016) 'The Effect of Digitizing and Gamifying Quizzing in Classrooms' in *Proceedings of the 10th European Conference on Games Based Learning*. ECGBL.

Werner, L, S Campe and J Denner (2012). 'Children Learning Computer Science Concepts via Alice Game-Programming' in *Proceedings of the 43rd ACM Technical Symposium on Computer Science Education*, Raleigh, North Carolina, USA. ACM.

Part 3

Delving Deeper: Research-led Teaching of Computer Science

12

Introduction to Part 3
Delving Deeper: Research-led Teaching of Computer Science

Carsten Schulte

According to the Hattie study there are many good teachers out there, but only some very good teachers (Hattie (2012): Chapter 3) – and these very good teachers are markedly better than those who are already good. Based on his work summarising meta-studies it seems hard to give concrete advice, but Hattie concludes that for teachers the most important advice would be not to simply stick to the most effective teaching methods, but 'to become evaluators of their own teaching'. By constantly monitoring and testing what works in one's own classroom, a teacher can adapt her teaching portfolio to the most effective approaches in her specific local situation and context. Thus the most important task for teachers is to develop a mind frame in which they are foremost evaluators of their own impact on students learning (Hattie (2012): Chapter 3).

So, how can one dig deeper to become not only a good, but a very good teacher? It is about knowing the students, it is about being able to communicate successfully, it is about knowing where to set the goals – and it's about a reflective teaching practice, a research-based view so that each year of additional experiences really adds to the professional teaching competence.

This research-led teaching is a belief in good teaching, a way to frame one's own identity and self-view as a teacher.

Specific areas we think can be a start to delve deeper and work on such research-led teaching in computer science classroom are discussed in the following chapters:

(a) *Misconceptions of students*. Students do not enter the classroom as blank slates, ready to be filled with concepts from computer science – instead they understand the content based on their prior knowledge, interests and so on. Thus knowing misconceptions and knowing how to uncover them are vital. Chapter 13 gives an overview on typical misconceptions in the computing classroom, and gives some advice for misconception-sensitive teaching.

(b) *Students are different*: Understanding is also based on interests and motivation, and the feel of belonging, based in internal variables. Especially in a subject like computer science which is about objectivation, about analysing, and rationality it is easy to forget this and to focus on the neutral content – but it isn't neutral with regard to students. Most likely some ways of representation resonate more closely with some types of students, and not with others. So knowing and respecting equity and inclusion is important. Chapter 14 addresses the problem of minorities and underrepresented groups in computer science classes, especially when students can choose whether to participate or not. Based on research in equity and inclusion some strategies for teaching computer science are suggested to broaden participation and engagement of a broader variety of CS students.

(c) The language being used in the classroom. Chapter 15 outlines the differences between everyday and scientific language and the need to reflect on the differences in meaning between computing terminology and everyday language (e.g. terms such as code, memory, saving, etc).

(d) The success of teaching needs to be measured. The choice of instruments and measurements depends on the goals of teaching. These goals are more and more research led and summarized as taxonomies and competence models. In order to understand these, some background knowledge is needed, presented in Chapter 16. The chapter introduces approaches to ensure that evaluation does indeed measure those aspects of learning that are intended to be measured.

Reference

Hattie, J (2012). *Visible Learning for Teachers: Maximizing Impact on Learning* (London, Routledge).

13

Misconceptions and the Beginner Programmer

Juha Sorva

Chapter outline

Chapter synopsis

In this chapter, we will review the literature on misconceptions about programming: the underdeveloped or flawed ideas that beginners have about specific programming constructs or about the way programs work in general. We will spend much of the chapter looking at examples of common misconceptions and exploring the factors that give rise to them. We will then briefly view misconceptions from the perspective of educational theory before concluding with suggestions on how to address student misconceptions in teaching.

13.1 Introduction

Here are two examples of what we will call *misconceptions* in this chapter.

> **M1** A variable can store multiple values; it may store the 'history' of values assigned to it.
>
> **M2** Two objects with the same value for a `name` or `id` attribute are the same object.

Since the computer does not negotiate the syntax or semantics of a programming language, misconceptions about programming constructs will result in practical problems: a student with a misconception will produce programs that do not work. When a misconception persists, it can leave the student frustrated and unable to make progress. Moreover, the student may find it hard to appreciate further instruction and learn from it, unless that instruction is sensitive to misconceptions.

Research in physics education suggests that knowledge of misconceptions is an important component of teachers' pedagogical content knowledge. In a study of hundreds of physics teachers, Sadler et al. (2013) found that those teachers who could identify their students' most common misconceptions were more effective in fostering student learning than those who could not. In computing education, misconceptions research is not yet as well established as in physics education. Nevertheless, there is a substantial and growing body of work that documents misconceptions and demonstrates that some of them occur across individuals and teaching contexts. Much of this work has focused on introductory-level programming, but researchers have also studied misconceptions of data structures and algorithms (e.g. Vahrenhold and Paul, 2014; Gal-Ezer and Zur, 2004), program correctness (e.g. Kolikant and Mussai, 2008), theory of computation (e.g. Gal-Ezer and Trakhtenbrot, 2016), and digital logic (e.g. Herman et al., 2008).

Like most studies to date, we will primarily consider text-based programming. Blocks-based programming (e.g. Scratch) has been researched less, but there is some evidence that similar misconceptions arise in both types of programming and that the frequency of particular misconceptions may depend on the chosen type (Weintrop and Wilensky, 2015; Grover and Basu, 2017).

Many misconceptions arise due to a combination of factors that involve the targeted content, students' prior knowledge, and instructional design. Let us begin by reviewing some of these factors; we will see more examples of specific misconceptions as we go.

The examples in this chapter, such as **M1** and **M2** above, have been selected and paraphrased from the hundreds of misconceptions reported in the literature (see Clancy, 2004; Sorva, 2012 and references therein).

13.2 Sources of misconceptions about programming

Mathematics

In many programming languages, dividing the integer 99 by 100 produces zero. This often surprises students but is ultimately just a detail. It is, however, an example of a more general pattern: students bring their mathematics knowledge to the programming class, but many of the concepts, notations and terms of programming are subtly different from those that students are familiar with from school mathematics.

The variables and assignment statements of (typical imperative) programming look deceptively familiar. Many of the most commonly reported misconceptions are associated with these constructs.

> **M3** A variable is merely a pairing of a name (symbol) with a value. It is not stored within the computer, apart from the program code.
>
> **M4** An assignment statement such as a = b + 1 stores an equation in memory or stores an unresolved expression b + 1 in variable a.

It is well documented that beginner programmers struggle with sequencing statements; a simple three-line swap of variable values is hard for many students (Lister, 2016). It is highly likely that prior knowledge and notations influence some of these difficulties: even though a sequence of assignment statements is a step-by-step mechanism for manipulating state, it looks much like a set of declarations that hold simultaneously.

> **M5** A program, especially one with assignment statements, is essentially a group of equations.
>
> **M6** Several lines of a (simple non-concurrent) program can be simultaneously active.

Pea (1986) notes that many students find it quite reasonable to sequence a piece of (imperative) code so that the lines that read user inputs into variables follow the line that uses the input data to compute a result. Jimoyiannis (2011) illustrates how some students attempt to 'solve' programs much as one would a group of equations, substituting variable names with the right-hand sides of other assignment statements (see also Kohn, 2017).

Equations are symmetric, as is the notation a = b, but assignment statements are not. It is possible that prior knowledge of mathematics also plays a role in the formation of misconceptions such as the following.

> **M7** Assignment statements such as a = b work both directions: they swap the values of two variables.

We have now seen that students sometimes interpret code through the lens of mathematics. Whether they do so or not can depend on whether a piece of code looks familiar from maths class.

> **M8** A variable name needs to be a single letter; longer identifiers are interpreted as (parts of) commands.

Grover and Basu (2017) document an instance of **M8** in which students failed to recognize a variable called NumberOfTimes as a variable because its name was so long. Instead, the students came up with different speculative meanings for the statement in which the identifier appeared.

Vocabulary

Some misconceptions arise from the natural-language semantics of words that have particular meanings in programming languages. For instance, some programming languages use the word 'then' exclusively in selection statements: IF a **THEN** b **ELSE** c, but in English the word also — and usually — implies a sequence: 'first a, then b'. Another well-known example is the while keyword, which appears in many imperative programming languages. There is evidence from multiple studies over the past few decades that many students assume the word implies a continuous check

> **M9** A while loop's condition is evaluated constantly. The instant it becomes false, the loop exits.

Students may attribute a similar quality to if statements. The English expression 'If you need any help, call me' does not suggest an immediate, one-time check; it means that the listener ought to call the speaker in the event that they need help later.

> **M10** An if statement triggers whenever its condition becomes true.

What is missing from this conception is the notion of control passing from one instruction to the next (much as in **M6** above). Pea (1986) cites a student who explains: '[The computer] looks at the program all at once because it is so fast.'

Analogies

Teachers often employ analogies between programming concepts and more familiar concepts; students also come up with their own analogies and may share them with their peers. Analogies can be a useful element of teaching and reasoning, but they can also be a source of misconceptions: since any analogy is a mapping between things that are similar, but not identical, there is the risk that learners overextend the analogy.

The classic example from introductory programming is the analogy of a variable being like a box. A variable does indeed have some box-like characteristics, but the analogy may still lead to misconceptions. **M1**, above, is one example: a box can hold multiple objects at the same time, but a variable only has one. Here are two more examples:

M11 Assignment statements such as a = b move values from one variable to another. The source variable is emptied in the process.

M12 Variables are initially empty containers and do not need to be initialized.

Purpose vs structure

Consider the statement a = a + 1. Here is how a student, teacher or textbook might describe it: 'It increments the variable a by one.' This is a summary of the *purpose* of the line of code: it says what the line accomplishes for the programmer. What was left unsaid is the *structure* of the code: it is an assignment statement, which involves evaluating the composite expression a + 1 and assigning its value to the variable a. That is how the programming environment handles it. Students, however, may simply memorize the 'statement type for incrementing counters' and fail to discern its constituent components (especially if they view assignment statements as equations as in **M4** above, since a = a + 1 does not fit that interpretation.)

M13 Incrementing a variable is an indivisible operation; no conception of evaluation and assignment.

A piece of code is a causal mechanism that consists of many components. Research on mental models suggests that it is important to be able to reason about a causal system in terms of its individual components without mixing them up with the purpose of the whole (de Kleer and Brown, 1983): it is such an understanding that allows one to debug unexpected behaviour and to combine components in novel ways. While **M13** is viable for many purposes, it is not felicitous for building a general understanding of program components — expressions and statements.

Programs tend to have a conspicuous line-based format. It can be tempting for students (and teachers) to treat lines as the main constituents of programs and gloss over their internal structure. Often, the concepts of expression and evaluation receive little attention. Here is another example:

```
test = List("An array", "that", "contains", "four strings")
```

The overall purpose of the line might be summarized as: 'Stores four strings in test.' An experienced programmer will not take this too literally. They will perceive that this, too, is an assignment statement, which evaluates the right-hand side and stores the resulting reference in a variable; they will realize that test is not really the name of a list object but of a variable. A beginner may well have more trouble.

> **M14** Conflation of referring variable with object; the name of the variable is a part of the object. Assignment statements change the names of objects.
>
> **M15** An object can only be referenced by one variable.
>
> **M16** Declaring a variable also creates an object of the appropriate type.

Let us consider another facet of our example. The description 'Stores four strings in test.' is *metonymous*: it refers to an entity, the list of strings, via a structurally associated entity, the name of a variable. Metonymy is pervasive in human communication: we can say things like 'she likes to read Kafka' and it will be obvious we refer to the literary works associated with an author. However, the computer system takes instructions literally and requires us to spell out our purpose in terms of the structural components the system can manipulate. Beginners may expect the computer to work out what their metonymous instructions mean, which is a potential source of many errors such as confusing array elements with their indices or attempting to use the values of attributes to reference objects (Miller, 2014).

> **M17** A field that has distinct values for each object, such as name or id, works as an identifier for objects.

Metonymy is an example of a still broader source of student difficulties, discussed next.

Expectations of interpretive intelligence

Miller (1981) and Pane et al. (2001) studied how non-programmers describe procedures and structure instructions in natural language. Among other things, they found that many aspects that are commonly explicit in programs were implicit or entirely absent in people's natural descriptions: the details of looping, variable declarations, parameter passing, else clauses, and so on.

In the light of those studies, it is no surprise that beginner programmers are so often taken aback by the level of detail that is required in programming. Beginners frequently assume that what they write says more between the lines than it actually does.

M18 Programs are interpreted more or less like sentences in natural conversation. The computer or programming environment is, for practical purposes, able to deduce the intention of the programmer. It may, for instance, fill in 'obvious' missing information without being told.

M19 The computer/environment does not allow operations that are unreasonable or pointless.

Pea (1986) identified what he termed the *superbug* behind many beginner mistakes: students behave as if 'there is a hidden mind somewhere in the programming language that has intelligent, interpretive powers'. This is not to say that students believe that there is a homunculus running the machine or that computers reason in the same way human brains do. However, when beginner programmers are unsure what to do, they commonly fall back on analogies with familiar forms of language use and introduce elements of human conversation into their programs. Typically they overestimate the reasoning capabilities of the system. Many scholars have reported on student behaviour consistent with the superbug.

Students sometimes expect the system to find meaning in identifiers. For example:

M20 The natural-language semantics of variable names affects which value gets assigned to which variable. E.g. `smallest` will surely not store a number greater than the one in `largest`.

Analogies with natural conversation may also influence students' difficulties with specific programming constructs. As one example, `else` clauses are conspicuously rare in non-programmers' process descriptions, as people often forget about alternative branches and may consider them too obvious to merit consideration. This may be part of the reason why some students have difficulties with `else`, including the following misconceptions.

M21 Using `else` is optional: the code that follows an `if` statement is the `else` branch (in case one is necessary).

M22 Both `then` and `else` branches are always executed.

Intangible concepts beneath program code

Some aspects of programming are more visible than others. In particular, program code – the *static* aspect of programs – is very tangible. It is natural to think about programs in terms of the code that the programmer directly manipulates. However, some of the concepts and processes that explain the runtime behaviour of code – the *dynamic* aspect of programs – are not explicit in code but nevertheless impact on what the programmer should do. Common examples of the latter group include references, transfer of control between statements, expression evaluation and memory allocation.

Consider functions. The program code that defines and calls them is tangible, but function activations at runtime are not. Students commonly find it hard to understand parameter passing, local scope, the lifetime of variables and return values. Some of these difficulties may persist even as students advance in their studies (Fisler et al., 2017). Here are just a few of the reported misconceptions:

> **M23** Variable names must be different in the calling code and in the function signature.
>
> **M24** Parameter passing forms direct links between variable names in the call and the signature.
>
> **M25** The local variables of methods are members of the object whose method was called. Or vice versa: object members are initialized anew at each method invocation.
>
> **M26** Any recursive function is essentially a loop within a single activation of the function.

References, too, are only implicitly present in program code. Students who are unfamiliar with the concept often form misconceptions such as the following (see also **M14–M17** above).

> **M27** Assigning an object to a variable (always) stores the data of the object in the variable.
>
> **M28** Assignment statements copy properties from a source object to a target object.
>
> **M29** Two objects with identical states are the same object.

Another example is the relationship between a class and its instances. In many programming languages, classes are tangible, essentially static definitions, whereas object creation happens dynamically at runtime. This is a notoriously difficult idea in introductory object-oriented programming, as are the related concepts of the constructor and the `this` (or `self`) reference (see, e.g. Holland et al., 1997; Ragonis and Ben-Ari, 2005; Ragonis and Shmallo, 2017).

> **M30** An object is essentially just a piece of code, difficult to distinguish from a class.
>
> **M31** A class is a collection of — or container for — objects.
>
> **M32** Instantiation involves only the execution of the constructor body, not the allocation of memory.
>
> **M33** Providing a constructor definition is sufficient for object creation to happen.
>
> **M34** `this` is the class in which a method is implemented.

Implicit notional machines

Many or even most of the misconceptions that we have discussed so far illustrate a common point: students commonly lack a viable model of program execution. In other words, they fail to understand the notional machine that they are learning to control (du Boulay, 1986; Sorva, 2013).

Key concept: Notional machine

A *notional machine* is not a physical computer but an abstraction of computer software and hardware; it is the set of capabilities that a particular programming language or environment affords to the programmer. Understanding a notional machine enables a programmer to answer questions such as: What can this programming system do for me? What are the things it can't or won't do? What is the division of labour between myself and the computer system (i.e. between the human instructor and the mechanistic instructee)? What changes in the system does each of my instructions bring about as my program is run? How do I reason about what my program does?

Different programming languages and paradigms call for different notional machines. For instance, a notional machine for Python may involve concepts such as memory allocation, flow of control, references and call stack. A notional machine for pure functional programming may be simpler. Even programs in a single language can be viewed in terms of different notional machines.

Often, notional machines are not explicitly discussed by textbooks, teachers or students. Even so, they are implicit in the programming languages used.

Limited variation in programs

Students commonly cite concrete experiences with programs as their main source of programming knowledge (e.g. Fleury, 2000). Whether from given examples or programs they write themselves, students infer implicit 'rules' from the programs they encounter. Limited exposure to different programs can lead to under- or overgeneralized 'rules' that limit students' ability to make use of programming constructs. Here are some examples of misconceptions that unnecessarily restrict the programmer:

M35 Object attributes must be numbers or similarly primitive data.

M36 Function arguments must be literals or constants.

M37 Comparisons must appear within a conditional expression and not, e.g. in return or assignment statements. Booleans are perceived as a part of control structures, not as values in the same sense as numbers.

M38 Only one instance can be created for each class.

> **M39** A method can be invoked only once (on each object, or in total).
>
> **M40** A class can have only one method. / A class can have only one member variable.

Misconceptions such as **M8, M17** and **M20**, from earlier in this chapter, indicate that some students find it difficult to understand how the programming environment handles identifiers. Indeed, students may have difficulty telling the difference between an identifier chosen by the programmer and a construct of the programming language; it is known that some learners search the Internet for variable names and other program-specific identifiers as they attempt to find help for programming problems (Dorn, 2010). Limited variation in programs can exacerbate these difficulties. For instance, if all or most objects have a `name` or `id` attribute, students are more likely to think of the identifier as part of the language, as in **M17**. Another example, from personal experience: in a course that frequently used `another` as the parameter name in methods that compare the target object with the given object, numerous students ended up thinking `another` was a reserved word akin to `this`.

Limited exposure to programs may also lead to more general difficulties with the notional machine. Beginners sometimes find it hard to distinguish between a program text and the program's textual output. Du Boulay (1986) observes that typical introductory programs, which contain merely print statements, may add to this confusion. Such difficulties may lie behind some of students' misconceptions concerning control flow, such as this widely reported one:

> **M41** Subprograms are executed in the order they are defined in the program text.

Teachers

As noted at the beginning of this chapter, teachers' knowledge of students' likely misconceptions makes a difference to student learning. In addition, the same study by Sadler et al. (2013) shows that teachers' own subject-matter knowledge is a necessary (but insufficient) precondition of knowledge of misconceptions. In other words, teachers who 'know their stuff' are less likely to encourage misconceptions in their students, especially if the teacher additionally knows how 'the stuff' challenges learners.

Other aspects of teachers' ability and instructional design also matter, of course. For instance, excessively complex or unmotivating tasks will result in poorer learning and may contribute to misconceptions.

13.3 Some theoretical perspectives on misconceptions

Misconceptions have long been of interest to researchers of *conceptual change* (Vosniadou, 2008). Theories of conceptual change seek to characterize the nature of people's conceptual structures and how those structures change as we learn.

Classical conceptual change theory posits that conceptual structures are 'theory-like' in that even intuitive knowledge is relatively organized and structurally coherent. Moreover, people are generally averse to disturbing this relatively harmonious state, which explains the resilience of existing conceptions. In the classical view, misconceptions are usually seen as obstacles that either need to be avoided or confronted; learning results from cognitive conflict between an existing conception and the demands of a novel situation, leading to the rejection of the existing conception and its replacement with a new one. By designing situations that engender cognitive conflict, teachers can help students overcome their flawed conceptions.

Knowledge-in-pieces theories of conceptual change reject the classical view: their proponents argue that intuitive knowledge has no coherent overall organization and consists of largely isolated, highly context-dependent elements. Since people apply different elements in different situations, it is possible and common for a person to have multiple apparently contradictory understandings of a phenomenon, each particular to a different context. A programming student, for example, might draw on distinct conceptual structures for:

- assignment statements that involve objects vs assignment statements that involve primitive values (Sorva, 2008)
- scalar variables vs array variables (Lister, 2016), or
- assignment statements that increment a variable (**M13**) vs other assignment statements (**M4** and **M5**).

It is the fragmented nature of knowledge that makes misconceptions resilient: a learner can add a parallel understanding rather than supplanting an existing one.

Knowledge-in-pieces theories encourage an emphasis on the productive parts of learners' existing conceptions. Learning is not seen as being about confronting flawed conceptions but about connecting and organizing intuitive ideas and discovering to what extent they are viable and how they can be developed. Elements of intuitive knowledge – so-called misconceptions included – are raw materials for learning that evolve into more general, theory-like structures.

The neo-Piagetian perspective of Lister (2016) complements knowledge-in-pieces theories of conceptual change. Lister describes how it is normal for many beginner programmers to initially exhibit a low level of commitment to their conceptions about programming, to routinely swap between conceptions, and to develop error-prone *ad hoc* tracing strategies for different programs.

13.4 Summary: Implications for pedagogy

A notional machine as a learning objective

One of the foremost recommendations from the misconceptions literature is that teachers need to help students form a model of program execution that is appropriate for the targeted programming language and environment. That model does not need to be a low-level hardware model; program execution can be viewed in terms of an abstract notional machine that operates just beneath the level of program code that students manipulate.

This means that students may need to learn concepts which are not directly visible in program code but which help explain the behaviour of programs, such as expression evaluation, memory allocation, references or the call stack. These concepts can be introduced alongside new programming constructs, gradually extending a simple initial notional machine. Sorva and Seppälä (2014) have described one example of a university course that makes program dynamics an explicit area of focus.

This is not a call to add more content to already crowded curricula. It is a call to acknowledge content that is already in but often neglected. Any programming language implies a notional machine that students will need to cope with. Without help, students are forced to rely on guess-work, fragile analogies and mistaken assumptions, which can prohibit productive programming and effective learning.

Advice for misconception-sensitive teaching

Try to learn to see programming concepts and language constructs from your students' perspectives. Discussions, observation and collecting feedback can all help in this, but you may need to probe deep: 'It was not until we did the tedious work of having students walk through every command in a program, thinking aloud and explaining how the computer would interpret it, that we became aware of the prevalence of these [conceptual] bugs. After that, we saw them everywhere' (Pea, 1986).

Expect students to conceptualize code constructs in unexpected ways. Expect conceptions that are fragmented and tied to particular contexts and that may appear to be inconsistent with each other. Reflect on your own assumptions; do not assume that students share them. Draw on the research literature to prepare for common misconceptions that your students may develop. Where possible, consider using concept inventories and similar instruments (Taylor et al., 2014; Parker and Guzdial, 2016; Grover and Basu, 2017) to assess students' prior knowledge and the effectiveness of your teaching.

Find the valuable aspects of students' conceptions and build on them. When you encounter a misconception, remember to consider the situations for which the conception is viable. Guide students to explore the viability of their knowledge for different kinds of programs.

One does not learn to program without program-writing practice, but don't take that to mean that the most effective way to learn is *only* to write programs; to learn to write code, students also need to learn to *read* code (Lister, 2016). Design code-reading activities that improve students' understandings of the targeted notional machine. Use worked-out examples and case studies of programs (Skudder and Luxton-Reilly, 2014; Linn and Clancy, 1992). Have students fix or extend given programs; this motivates careful study of the given code and lets them work on more interesting applications than they could write from scratch.

Encourage students to explain program behaviour in detail to themselves and to others. Arrange for students to receive feedback on their explanations. Consider peer instruction (Porter et al., 2013) as a way to explore and address misconceptions. Design classroom discussions around apparent or expected student misconceptions (Ginat and Shmallo, 2013).

Teach students self-explanation skills (Fonseca and Chi, 2011) so that they can focus on underlying principles rather than the surface features of a particular program. Be aware that learning to trace programs may require repeated practice; present general principles as feedback for tracing attempts that embody those principles (Lister, 2016).

Teach students to explain both the overall purpose of a piece of code (the forest) and its individual constituents (the trees). Watch out for explanations that mix purpose with structure, both in what you say and in what students say. Highlight that lines of code are not atomic; acknowledge expressions and evaluation as significant concepts.

In popular constructionist pedagogies, students use tools such as Scratch to build and share fun creations but may fail to learn foundational concepts; complement constructionism with other approaches that target conceptual understanding (Grover and Basu, 2017; Passey, 2016).

The example programs that students encounter are a major source of their programming knowledge; strive for exemplary examples. Use lists of known misconceptions as inspiration for the design of examples and related activities. Try to make sure that students encounter sufficiently rich variation in programs to prevent particular misconceptions: Did my example class have just one instance or just one method (**M38, M40**)? How have I highlighted to my students that the execution order of statements makes a difference (**M5**)? Have I used multiple variables referencing a single object and a single variable referencing a succession of objects (**M14, M15**)? Have the students had to deal with multiple identical but distinct objects (**M29**)? Do my examples of `while` discourage the 'continuous evaluation of condition' interpretation (**M9**)? Do I have an example that shows how changing the value of a variable does not impact on the values of other variables, even those initialized using it (**M4**)? Have I included an example of multiple variables with the same name in different scopes? What about nested function calls and other complex function arguments (**M36**)? And so on.

Pay particular attention to examples that introduce a concept. Note that using the simplest imaginable example may give a misleading first impression (e.g. the first variable students see is assigned an integer literal). Do not only use code that works; make use of erroneous programs as well. Use combinations of examples with minimal differences to separate aspects and highlight contrasts (Guo et al., 2012).

Have students view, draw or manipulate visualisations of hidden processes, or role-play the processes. Consider using program visualisation software designed for education (Sorva et al., 2013). Recognize that reading a visualisation is itself a skill that needs to be learned and that struggling beginner programmers may struggle to decipher the visualisations, too.

Analogies and metaphors can provide viable alternatives to technical terms; look for consistent analogies that can help explain a broad part of a notional machine (e.g. Gries, 2008). Reflect on the borders of any analogies you use and deliberately explore those with your students. Watch out for known issues with common analogies (e.g. variable as box).

Consider the similarities and differences between natural language conversation and programming. Explore natural-language phenomena such as metonymy in an age-appropriate manner and discuss their applicability to programming. Consider what other prior knowledge the students have that might be leveraged or otherwise taken into account (see, e.g. Simon et al., 2008).

Be on the lookout for subtle ways in which deceptively familiar notations and terms from mathematics may impact on student understandings. Explicitly point out some of the most common pitfalls.

Don't forget about program-writing practice either.

Key points

- It is common for beginner programmers to harbour misconceptions about specific programming constructs and about programs more generally.
- Some of the factors that contribute to student misconceptions, often in combination, are: limited exposure to different programs, intangible concepts and an implicit notional machine, students' prior knowledge of mathematics and natural language, and the analogies employed in teaching.
- To teach most effectively, teachers should be familiar both with the programming concepts and with how students commonly view the concepts.
- Teachers can build their pedagogical content knowledge of programming by eliciting their students' conceptions and studying the literature.
- Teachers can help students construct increasingly productive knowledge of programming by providing ample practice with reading and tracing code, involving students with a rich variety of programs, designing examples to target common misconceptions, bringing the intangible aspects of programming into focus, and probing the borders of analogies and metaphors.

Further reflection

- Review a programming textbook or the materials you use for teaching. Consider whether the text, examples and activities are likely to prevent – or encourage – the misconceptions listed in this chapter.
- Reflect on the notional machine that is embodied in the programming language and environment that your students use. What capabilities of the environment are invoked by the commands in the language? What do the students need to know about those capabilities in order to reason reliably about program behaviour?

References

Clancy, MJ (2004). 'Misconceptions and Attitudes that Interfere with Learning to Program' in S. Fincher and M. Petre (eds), *Computer Science Education Research* (Abingdon, Routledge) 85–100.

de Kleer, J and JS Brown (1983). 'Assumptions and Ambiguities in Mechanistic Mental Models' in D Gentner and AL Stevens (eds), *Mental Models* (New Jersey, Lawrence Erlbaum) 155–190.

Dorn, B (2010). *A Case-Based Approach for Supporting the Informal Computing Education of End-User Programmers*. Doctoral dissertation, School of Interactive Computing, Georgia Institute of Technology.

du Boulay, B (1986). 'Some Difficulties of Learning to Program' 2(1) *Journal of Educational Computing Research* 57–73.

Fisler, K, S Krishnamurthi and P Tunnell Wilson (2017). 'Assessing and Teaching Scope, Mutation, and Aliasing in Upper-level Undergraduates' in *Proceedings of the 2017 ACM SIGCSE Technical Symposium on Computer Science Education*, SIGCSE '17, 213–218.

Fleury, AE (2000). 'Programming in Java: Student-constructed Rules' 32(1) *SIGCSE Bulletin* 197–201.

Fonseca, BA and MTH Chi (2011). 'Instruction Based on Self-explanation' in RE Mayer and PA Alexander (eds), *Handbook of Research on Learning and Instruction* (Abingdon, Routledge) 296–321.

Gal-Ezer, J and M Trakhtenbrot (2016). 'Identification and Addressing Reduction-related Misconceptions' 26(2–3) *Computer Science Education* 89–103.

Gal-Ezer, J and E Zur (2004). 'The Efficiency of Algorithms – Misconceptions' 42(3) *Computers and Education* 215–226.

Ginat, D and R Shmallo (2013). 'Constructive Use of Errors in Teaching CS1' in *Proceedings of the 44th ACM Technical Symposium on Computer Science Education*, SIGCSE '13, 353–358.

Gries, D (2008). 'A Principled Approach to Teaching OO First' 40(1) *SIGCSE Bulletin* 31–35.

Grover, S and S Basu (2017). 'Measuring Student Learning in Introductory Block-Based Programming: Examining Misconceptions of Loops, Variables, and Boolean Logic' in *Proceedings of the 2017 ACM SIGCSE Technical Symposium on Computer Science Education*, SIGCSE '17, 267–272.

Guo, JP, MF Pang, LY Yang and Y Ding (2012). 'Learning from Comparing Multiple Examples: On the Dilemma of "Similar" or "Different"' 24(2) *Educational Psychology Review* 251–269.

Herman, GL, LC Kaczmarczyk, MC Loui and C Zilles (2008). 'Proof by Incomplete Enumeration and Other Logical Misconceptions' in *Proceeding of the Fourth International Workshop on Computing Education Research*, ICER '08, 59–70.

Holland, S, R Griffiths and M Woodman (1997). 'Avoiding Object Misconceptions' 29(1) *SIGCSE Bulletin* 131–134.

Jimoyiannis, A (2011). 'Using SOLO Taxonomy to Explore Students' Mental Models of the Programming Variable and the Assignment Statement' 4(2) *Themes in Science and Technology Education* 53–74.

Kohn, T (2017). 'Variable Evaluation: An Exploration of Novice Programmers' Understanding and Common Misconceptions' in *Proceedings of the 2017 ACM SIGCSE Technical Symposium on Computer Science Education*, SIGCSE '17, 345–350.

Kolikant, YB-D and M Mussai (2008). 'So my Program Doesn't Run!' Definition, Origins, and Practical Expressions of Students' (Mis)conceptions of Correctness 18(2) *Computer Science Education* 135–151.

Linn, MC and MJ Clancy (1992). 'The Case for Case Studies of Programming Problems' 35(3) *Communications of the ACM* 121–132.

Lister, R (2016). 'Toward a Developmental Epistemology of Computer Programming' in *Proceedings of the 11th Workshop in Primary and Secondary Computing Education*, WiPSCE '16 5–16.

Miller, CS (2014). 'Metonymy and Reference-point Errors in Novice Programming' 24(2–3) *Computer Science Education* 123–152.

Miller, LA (1981). 'Natural Language Programming: Styles, Strategies, and Contrasts' 20(2) *IBM Systems Journal* 184–215.

Pane, JF, CA Ratanamahatana and BA Myers (2001). 'Studying the Language and Structure in Non-programmers' Solutions to Programming Problems' 54(2) *International Journal of Human–Computer Studies* 237–264.

Parker, MC and M Guzdial (2016). 'Replication, Validation, and Use of a Language Independent CS1 Knowledge Assessment' in *Proceedings of the 12th International Computing Education Research Conference*, ICER '16, 93–101.

Passey, D (2016). 'Computer Science (CS) in the Compulsory Education Curriculum: Implications for Future Research' 22(2) *Education and Information Technologies* 1–23.

Pea, RD (1986). 'Language-independent Conceptual "Bugs" in Novice Programming' 2(1) *Journal of Educational Computing Research* 25–36.

Porter, L, C Bailey-Lee and B Simon (2013). 'Halving Fail Rates Using Peer Instruction: A Study of Four Computer Science Courses' in *Proceedings of the 44th ACM Technical Symposium on Computer Science Education*, SIGCSE '13, 177–182.

Ragonis, N and M Ben-Ari (2005). 'A Long-term Investigation of the Comprehension of OOP Concepts by Novices' 15(3) *Computer Science Education* 203–221.

Ragonis, N and R Shmallo (2017). 'On the (Mis)understanding of the "this" Reference' in *Proceedings of the 2017 ACM SIGCSE Technical Symposium on Computer Science Education*, SIGCSE '17, 489–494.

Sadler, PM, G Sonnert, HP Coyle, N Cook-Smith and JL Miller (2013). 'The Influence of Teachers' Knowledge on Student Learning in Middle School Physical Science Classrooms' 50(5) *American Educational Research Journal* 1020–1049.

Simon, B, DJ Bouvier, T-Y Chen, G Lewandowski, R McCartney and K Sanders, (2008). 'Common Sense Computing (Episode 4): Debugging' 18(2) *Computer Science Education* 117–133.

Skudder, B and A Luxton-Reilly (2014). 'Worked Examples in Computer Science' in J Whalley and D D'Souza (eds), *Proceedings of the 16th Australasian Conference on Computing Education (ACE '14)*, vol 148 of *CRPIT*, 59–64.

Sorva, J. (2008). 'The Same but Different – Students' Understandings of Primitive and Object Variables' in A Pears and L Malmi (eds), *The 8th Koli Calling International Conference on Computing Education Research*, Koli Calling '08, 5–15.

Sorva, J (2012). 'Misconception Catalogue' in *Visual Program Simulation in Introductory Programming Education*, 358–368. Doctoral dissertation. Department of Computer Science and Engineering, Aalto University.

Sorva, J (2013). 'Notional Machines and Introductory Programming Education' 13(2) *ACM Transactions on Computing Education* 1–31.

Sorva, J and O Seppälä (2014). 'Research-based Design of the First Weeks of CS1' in *Proceedings of the 14th Koli Calling International Conference on Computing Education Research*, Koli Calling '14, 71–80.

Sorva, J, V Karavirta and L Malmi (2013). 'A Review of Generic Program Visualisation Systems for Introductory Programming Education' 13(4) *ACM Transactions on Computing Education* 1–64.

Taylor, C, D Zingaro, L Porter, K Webb, C Lee and M Clancy (2014). 'Computer Science Concept Inventories: Past and Future' 24(4) *Computer Science Education* 253–276.

Vahrenhold, J and W Paul (2014). 'Developing and Validating Test Items for First-year Computer Science Courses' 24(4) *Computer Science Education* 304–333.

Vosniadou, S (ed) (2008). *International Handbook of Research on Conceptual Change* (Abingdon, Routledge).

Weintrop, D and U Wilensky (2015). 'Using Commutative Assessments to Compare Conceptual Understanding in Block-based and Text-based Programs' in *Proceedings of the Eleventh Annual Conference on International Computing Education Research*, ICER '15, 101–110.

14

Equity and Inclusion in Computer Science Education

Jill Denner and Shannon Campe

Chapter outline

Chapter synopsis

This chapter provides an introduction to research on equity and inclusion in computer science education. Topics include why it is important to intentionally address equity and inclusion in computer science education, the challenges to increasing diversity according to theoretical perspectives and empirical research and five different types of strategies that teachers can use to support equity and inclusion in computer science classes.

14.1 Introduction: Setting the stage

Teaching computer science effectively in schools requires attention to equity and inclusion. Despite the growing enthusiasm worldwide for making computer science a regular part of a student's education experience, there has not been a corresponding level of attention paid to the under-representation of certain groups in computer science, including girls, racial/ethnic minorities and persons with learning differences/disabilities. This chapter focuses on strategies to improve the teaching of computer science in countries where representation gaps continue.

Globally, when conversations turn to equity and inclusion in computer science education, the focus is usually on gender, because in all countries but one, men outnumber women in computing fields. Only in Columbia do women outnumber men – 70 per cent of all bachelor's degrees in computer science were awarded to women – in most countries women earned 20 per cent or less of these degrees (OECD, 2011). One result of these discrepancies is that there are not enough people to fill open jobs. For example, by 2024 there will be almost 4.6 million high-wage jobs in computer science and related fields in the US alone (Bureau of Labor Statistics, 2015) but not enough people to fill these positions, with the greatest shortfall among women and certain ethnic minority groups. Among the bachelor's degrees awarded in computer and information science in 2013–2014 in the US, only 18 per cent were awarded to women (National Center for Education Statistics, 2106) down from 23 per cent in 2004 (National Student Clearinghouse Research Center, 2015). The UK has also seen a decline in interest among students in information and communication technologies subjects, particularly among girls (Ofsted, 2011); only 7.5 per cent of those who took the computing A-level entry course were girls (The Royal Society, 2012). The problem is similar in many other countries, including India (Raman, Venkatasubramanian, Achuthan and Nedungadi, 2015) and Australia (Craig, 2014).

Data on the participation of students from racial and ethnic minority groups is less available outside of North America. In the US, among the bachelor's degrees awarded in computer and information science in 2013–2014, only 11 per cent were received by Black students and 9 per cent by Hispanic students (National Center for Education Statistics, 2016). Among secondary students in the US, Black students were less likely to have dedicated computer science (CS) classes in school than White students and Black and Latino students were less likely than White students to use a computer at home at least most days of the week (Google, Inc and Gallup, Inc, 2016). The low numbers are of great concern because recent research suggests that girls, boys and students from racial/ethnic minority groups have positive views of computing classes and careers. In a US survey of college-bound Latino high school students, 30 per cent (49 per cent of boys and 13 per cent of girls) said that being a computer scientist/software designer would be a very good profession for them or someone like them (Association for Computing Machinery, 2009). Similarly, a US study found that a computer/technology career was among the top interest of four out of ten Hispanic and African American teens; 31 per cent were definitely interested in a career in information technology and another 39 per cent said they may be interested (Versta Research, 2014).

Although no data exists on their representation in computing fields, it is widely believed that not enough effort is being made to accommodate students with disabilities and learning differences. According to Ladner and Israel (2016), 15 per cent of students in K-12 grade in the US have a disability; the most common are in areas of learning, speech and language, health impairments, developmental delay and emotional disturbance. Approximately 5.7 million children in the US are served by the Individuals with Disabilities Education Act, which includes both learning disabilities and attention deficit disorders (Cortiella and Horowitz, 2014). Many with learning disabiliites do not have any intellectual disability; because of their differences, these students contribute a unique perspective on the world and an ability to approach and solve complex problems in innovative ways that may be particularly beneficial for learning computer science (Wille, Century and Pike, 2017). Although grouped under the umbrella of disabilities and learning differences, these students bring a range of needs and strengths that are just beginning to be addressed in K-12 computer science classes.

Public support for integrating CS education into the schools is mixed. In countries like Russia, there has been a system for teaching computer science in schools since 1985 (Khenner and Semakin, 2014). In the UK, government officials have begun to publicly support CS education efforts (Brown, Sentance, Crick and Humphreys, 2014). However, there are examples across many different countries of a reluctance to make computer science education a core academic subject. For example, a nationwide effort to integrate CS into the schools in New Zealand required public media campaigns to address concerns about what it was replacing (Bell, Andreae and Robins, 2014). In India, while the majority of students feel that computer science should be a compulsory subject, over half of the teachers do not agree (Raman et al., 2015). This reluctance is also found in higher education; a recent survey in Australia found that many members of the CS community do not support K-12 efforts because they believe that not everybody can learn to code (Vivian, Falkner and Szabo, 2014). While most parents in the US want their children's schools to offer computer science (Google, Inc and Gallup, Inc, 2015) and most Americans believe that it is as important to learn computer science as it is to learn reading, writing and mathematics (Horizon Media, 2015), integration across states and school districts varies greatly.

In addition to the country-wide differences in integration and accessibility, the variation in computer science enrollment and diversity across countries is due in part to stereotyped belief systems and structural inequalities. Countries like Malaysia do not have a gender discrepancy and this is attributed to the cultural norm that computing is NOT viewed by young people as a masculine field (Othman and Latih, 2006) and to girls being encouraged and given access at an early age (Sien, Mui, Tee and Singh, 2014). And in Israel, extensive CS education in high school has led to more equal numbers of women and men taking the CS exam (Armoni and Gal-Ezer, 2014). The story is different in countries like the US, where 27 per cent of girls in middle school report an interest in a tech career, but that drops to 18 per cent in high school (Lang, 2016). Studies show that female US students are less likely than male students to be told by a parent or teachers that they would be good at CS (Google, Inc and Gallup, Inc, 2016). These findings suggest that across cultures, low expectations plus a lack of access prevent many students from developing an interest and a sense of confidence with computing.

A lack of diversity in CS has implications not just for the people who are left out, but for society as a whole. Creating more opportunities and supports in K-12 can lead to more diverse CS classes, majors and ultimately the workforce. As teachers play a powerful role in determining who becomes engaged and persists in computer science, this chapter provides a resource for teachers who want to try new ways to increase equity and inclusion in primary and secondary computer science education. The focus is on how to create learning experiences and institutions that provide opportunities for all youth to have access to a range of technologies as well as the support that students need to gain both the skills and motivation to influence how technologies are used and ultimately to influence the kind and range of technologies that are produced.

Diversity refers to the representation of different kinds of individuals in computer science, across languages, learning styles and other differences, as well as a range of social or cultural groups (across race, ethnicity, class, gender, sexual orientation, dis/ability status, etc.).
Inclusion involves an active and intentional engagement with diversity such that a range of individuals are able to fully participate in computer science education.
Equity requires the creation of opportunities for historically underrepresented populations to have equal access to and participation in computer science education; it requires an understanding of why disparities exist.

14.2 Reasons for the lack of equity and inclusion: The challenges

Theoretical frameworks

Several theoretical frameworks form the basis of research on equity and inclusion in computing. They describe a range of factors that influence peoples' decisions to pursue computing opportunities and to persist with them over time. These factors are at the individual, relational and institutional levels and are influenced by systems of power that cut across the levels (Denner, Martinez and Thiry, 2016). The expectancy-value theory has long been used by researchers to identify the specific factors that influence educational and career pathways. This theory views individuals as goal-oriented and suggests that their behaviour toward a goal is a function of the expectations they have for success as well as the extent to which they value that goal (Eccles, Wigfield and Schiefele, 1997). The expectancy-value theory also shows how achievement goals are influenced by culturally based gender-role beliefs and the costs that students associate with spending time on one activity versus another, as well as by expectations by teachers and other influential adults (Eccles, 2007). Many studies have shown how positive reinforcement and encouragement from family, peers and other adults can have a powerful influence on girls' decisions to pursue CS (Hong, Wang, Ravitz, and Fong, 2015).

Social cognitive career theory (SCCT) has also been widely used to understand why students do or do not pursue a computing career. SCCT suggests that persistence in computing fields is influenced by self-efficacy beliefs, outcome expectations, interests, social supports and barriers and goals (Lent, Lopez, Lopez and Sheu, 2008). Self-efficacy is similar to the expectations for success described in the expectancy-value theory; it refers to an individual's beliefs about her/his ability to perform or succeed in particular domains. Outcome expectations are beliefs about the consequences of a particular choice or behaviour; thus an activity is more likely to be performed when a student believes it will lead to approval, rewards or other benefits (Lent et al., 2008). When students experience success or failure in reaching their goals, they consider this to be feedback on their interests, self-efficacy beliefs and outcome expectations. Thus, the SCCT suggests that people are more likely to become interested in, choose to pursue and perform better in computing when they have strong self-efficacy beliefs, as long as they also have positive experiences and the support they need to pursue these activities. Self-efficacy can be increased by creating opportunities for personal accomplishments, vicarious experiences (observing similar others succeed), social persuasion and positive emotional states (Bandura, 1999).

Self-theories suggest that having a growth Mindset (the belief that intelligence is not fixed and can be developed) is positively associated with academic achievement and persistence in the face of challenges (Dweck and Master, 2008). Studies across the globe support this theory; a recent study in Chile found that a growth Mindset can temper the negative effects of poverty on academic achievement (Claro, Paunesku and Dweck, 2016). Although these theories have not been applied to the field of K-12 computer science education, they suggest that efforts to engage a range of students in CS must include the message that success is the result of hard work. However, when students decide that they are not good at CS and believe that CS abilities are fixed, they will choose other pathways.

Other theories of equity and inclusion suggest that building students' understanding and capacity to respond to the broader systems that influence their opportunities and experiences is a key part of promoting inequity and inclusion in computer science education. For example, theories of intersectionality suggest that students have overlapping or intersecting social identities; as a result of those identities they may experience systems of oppression, domination or discrimination (Kvasny, Trauth and Morgan, 2009). These social identities may include race/ethnicity, as well as gender, social class, and dis/ability as they apply to a given individual or group, and they create overlapping and interdependent systems of discrimination or disadvantage (Charleston, Adserias, Lang and Jackson, 2014). Thus, knowing a person's race or ethnicity is not enough. Indeed, cultural-historical activity theory suggests that assumptions about homogeneity within racial and ethnic groups can perpetuate inequities and stereotypes when there are similarities and variance in how members of a community participate in social practices (Gutierrez and Arzubiaga, 2012). Thus, if efforts to engage youth do not consider the role of cultural practices and how they vary within groups, and if they do not help students navigate institutionalized discrimination, they will not speak to the experiences of, or engage, a range of youth.

These theoretical perspectives suggest that efforts to engage young people in CS must recognize that students bring multiple and overlapping social identities and that they negotiate them within a range of contexts that vary in the extent to which they support, acknowledge or undermine these different identities. These different theories have formed the basis of some research on equity and inclusion in education and have great potential to inform research on computer science education.

Research on factors that cause and perpetuate the problem

Empirical studies provide some support for the theories described above, including how psychological, relational and institutional factors cause or perpetuate inequity in computer science. The majority of this research focuses on the students' belief systems. For example, confidence is a strong determinant for some, and students' decisions about whether or not to pursue computing are based partially on their perceptions of their mathematics and problem-solving abilities (Hong et al., 2015) and the extent to which they believe their performance can be improved by hard work. Another important determinant of who pursues and persists in CS is the extent to which someone is interested in or values it. Studies show that girls' decisions to pursue computer science are influenced by their interest in mathematics and problem solving, as well as the extent to which they think positively about CS and related careers and see their potential for social impact (Hong et al., 2015). Girls' interest in computing is also influenced by their curiosity about how technology works (Denner, 2011) and their interest in problem solving, creativity and design (Cooper and Heaverlo, 2013). While interest can initially motivate students to seek out opportunities to learn computing, relational and institutional structures and supports are needed to sustain that interest.

There are several ways in which relationships and social networks can serve as both supports and challenges in students' decisions to pursue and persist in computing fields. Disinterest in computing fields is often due to negative stereotypes about students' potential success in technology perpetuated by parents (Frome and Eccles, 1998; Furnham, Reeves and Budhani, 2002) as well as by teachers and administrators (Google Inc and Gallup Inc, 2015; Margolis et al., 2010). Similarly, Ladner and Israel (2016) describe how individual education plans can hold back students with certain disabilities when they are based on the educator's belief that a student is intellectually limited. These stereotype-based messages sent by adults are often small, subtle and cumulative in nature; they result in lower self-concept and expectations for success in computing fields (Else-Quest, Mineo and Higgins, 2013).

Relationships can also serve an important supportive role. One study of middle school students in the US found that perceived support from school peers and teachers predicts girls' interest in computing classes and careers (Denner, 2011). And women in Science, Technology, Engineering and Mathematics (STEM) classes in college are more likely to persist when they have a sense of belonging among their peers (Dasgupta, Scircle and Hunsinger, 2015). Thus, for some, persistence is connected to fitting in and having relationships with other students. However, other studies show that women's reasons for persistence in computer science vary, and that some thrive on feeling different and are motivated to prove that the stereotypes about women are wrong (Denner, Lyon and Werner, 2015; Lewis, Anderson and Yasuhara, 2016).

There is less research on the role of institutional or organizational factors in who pursues a computing field, but studies reveal inequity in access to computer science curriculum in countries where there is no national or statewide mandate. Although an increasing number of K-12 classes in the US use computers, schools in the US that serve low income African American and Latino/a students rarely offer advanced topics or engage students in CS content (Google, Inc and Gallup, Inc, 2015; Margolis et al., 2010). This includes less access to these classes both within their schools, as well as to out of school opportunities. Even when classes are provided, they are not always staffed by teachers who know how to engage all students, such as how to scaffold students with learning differences, and do not always use tools that are made to be accessible, such as screen readers for visually impaired students (Ladner and Israel, 2016). In addition, the physical environment of a classroom can limit students' interest in computing – women report less interest in computer science when the classroom walls are decorated with posters that reinforce stereotyped beliefs about who should be in computer science (i.e. not them), because that reduces their sense of belonging in computing (Master, Cheryan and Meltzoff, 2016). Similarly, the media can either promote or undermine interest in computing fields. Exposing girls to non-traditional STEM professionals can positively impact their identification with STEM professions (Steinke et al., 2009), but in a study when girls saw highly feminine STEM role models, they had lower STEM interest and confidence, compared to when they saw gender-neutral models (Betz and Sekaquaptewa, 2012).

In summary, whether or not a person chooses to pursue and persist in a computing field is influenced by a multitude of factors that include personal beliefs, early experiences with computer science activities, messages from other people and the environment about whether it is a field that includes people 'like' her or him, and the extent to which the learning environment provides the necessary tools and scaffolds that a student needs to succeed both in and beyond the classroom.

14.3 Opportunities for change

In this section we describe some different types of strategies that can be used to address the individual, relational and institutional factors that perpetuate a lack of diversity in computer science education. These strategies are organized within the structure suggested by Liben and Coyle (2014), who identified five change mechanisms based on theories and research on gender development. Their five goal types have been used to describe interventions for addressing the gender gap in STEM fields, but they also provide a useful organizational framework for summarising efforts to increase the participation and persistence of women, minorities and persons with learning and physical disabilities in computer science. Table 14.1 describes these change mechanisms; the terms used by Liben and Coyle were adapted to fit with a computer science focus. The following sections describe them in more detail.

Table 14.1 Five intervention goals for increasing equity and inclusion in computer science

Goal types	Definition
Remediate	Fix personal qualities that are considered important for success in CS (e.g. increase confidence, boost skills)
Revise	Modify CS pedagogy and tools so they better fit a diverse audience
Refocus	Highlight compatibilities between what it takes to succeed in CS and what different groups have to offer
Recategorize	Shift thinking about certain identities (e.g. feminine) being incompatible with CS
Resist	Work to challenge stereotypes, biases and discriminatory practices

Remediate

Strategies in this area focus on changing students' skills or their beliefs about their abilities. This includes building students' knowledge or understanding of computing concepts, problem-solving abilities and computational thinking. Nationwide curriculum have been developed to address specific learning outcomes starting in elementary school, such as one in Russia that includes algorithmic thinking, systems thinking and information security (Khenner and Semakin, 2014). Specific strategies, such as teaching children to program computer games, have been used to increase their understanding of programming concepts and their problem-solving capacities; the results have been replicated in countries as diverse as Turkey, Taiwan and the US (Akcaoglu, 2013; Al-Bow et al., 2009; Wang and Chen, 2011).

Strategies which target individual belief systems include helping them develop attributions for performance that focus on factors that they can change. For example, a study of South African high school girls shows the importance of a growth Mindset and grit for learning programming (Kench, Hazelhurst and Otulaja, 2016). Teaching Scottish college students about Mindset and giving them feedback resulted in an increase in their belief about a growth Mindset and higher test scores (Cutts, Cutts, Draper, O'Donnell and Saffrey, 2010). However, similar interventions in the US have not been as successful in shifting Mindset beliefs (Simon et al., 2008). In addition, some preliminary research on software engineering students in the UK suggests that promoting a growth Mindset about general intelligence is not enough; interventions must target Mindsets that are domain specific, such as their beliefs about whether programming aptitude is fixed or malleable (Scott and Ghinea, 2014). While efforts to 'remediate' individuals without regard to the contexts of learning have fallen out of favour, changes in students' beliefs and skills remain the most popular measure of success.

Revise

Strategies that aim to revise the learning environment focus on identifying inclusive pedagogies and tools. Shah et al. (2013) describe equitable CS classrooms as those that include access to rich course content, quality instruction with ongoing assessment, strategic collaboration with peers and opportunities to build a CS identity. A review of research suggests that students from under-represented groups are more likely to be engaged when the curriculum is relevant to their lives, the peer environment is welcoming, collaborative work is encouraged and role models challenge stereotypes about who is good in tech (Ashcraft, Eger and Friend, 2012). For example, pair programming (where two students work side-by-side at one computer) is often used as a strategy to engage students from under-represented groups. When the right supports and scaffolds are in place, pair programming can be an effective strategy for promoting equity and learning in CS classrooms (Campe, Denner and Werner, 2013; Lewis, 2011). Pairs are most successful and engaged when they develop a shared mode of communication that allows them to try new things, problem solve and build on each other's knowledge. While working with a partner does not appeal to all students, this approach can have particular benefits for those with less experience or confidence when the teacher strategically pairs students and provides scaffolds for their communication.

The Universal Design for Learning (UDL) approach aims to accommodate a range of learning differences, including students who have physical and cognitive disabilities, conditions such as attention deficit hyperactivity disorder (ADHD), or are learning English as a second language. There are increasing efforts to use UDL to increase the engagement and success of students with disabilities and learning differences in computing classes (Burgstahler, 2011). Pedagogical strategies include increasing font size and darkness for visually impaired students, providing tools such as outlines and graphical organizers to scaffold student learning, making software accessible using tools such as a screen reader, ensuring that terms are developmentally and culturally familiar and also providing scaffolding and encouragement to students who are usually not expected to succeed (Hansen, Hansen, Dwyer, Harlow and Franklin, 2016; Ladner and Israel, 2016; Snodgrass, Israel and Reese, 2016). For example, students with dyslexia can learn programming when they are provided with sequential assessments, multi-modal approaches to learning, assistive learning technologies and tutoring support designed to meet their specific needs (Stienen-Durand and George, 2014). A study in Italy found that blind and visually impaired adults can solve computer science problems almost as quickly as sighted adults when they are taught with inclusive pedagogical techniques that include being activity-orientated and using multiple senses to learn (Capovilla and Hubwieser, 2013).

Wille, Century and Pike's (2016) work with high school students builds off the UDL approach by adding testing accommodations for subgroups of learners in the classroom. To inform modifications, they developed guidelines to identify possible underlying psychological processes associated with learning and attention disorders, propose strategies organized within lesson adjustment categories (presentation, response, timing, setting, social interactions) and provide examples of strategies within whole class discussions (e.g. rephrasing, providing examples of how to give feedback), partner/group (e.g. modelling) and individual activities (e.g. reading aloud, students using voice-to-text software). In the US, several programs have been developed to increase the participation of people with disabilities in computing fields at centres such as Access Computing and AccessCS10K. These efforts have shown that students with disabilities can learn and persist in computing fields, when they have the right tools and supports.

Example activity: Using pair programming to promote equity and inclusion

Working with a partner while learning to program a computer can increase students' engagement and learning when it is managed effectively. Start by asking students to choose two to three people they are willing to work with and use that information to match them to a partner with similar prior experience and confidence. Build the pair's communication and rapport through non-computer-based activities such as 'Draw what I say'. Demonstrate what both effective and ineffective communication looks like through videos and role plays. Reinforce effective communication with public acknowledgments, such as 'Pair of the Week'.

Refocus

This set of strategies aims to challenge the stereotype that only a limited type of skills or interests (i.e. programming) are compatible with a career in computing. Many young people lack accurate information about career options in computing fields and do not recognize that an interest in creativity and design are a good foundation for someone to succeed in computing. For example, digital storytelling, media computation and computer game design and programming provide opportunities for design to intersect with computing. Digital storytelling is often used as a mechanism for the designer to interpret and share the world around them and to highlight voices which may not be heard otherwise. Workshops such as Skins incorporate digital design, animation and game programming to modify digital games based on the traditional stories of their Native American community (Lameman and Lewis, 2011). Digital storytelling has also been found to increase learning, motivation and critical thinking among Taiwanese students learning English as a second language (Yang and Wu, 2012). In the US, media computation has been used to introduce computing to undergraduates via manipulating multimedia, but can also be applied pre-college (Guzdial, 2013). It builds on young people's interest in sound, photography and video, while introducing them to computing concepts and skills. However, while media computation succeeds in changing how much students value computing and retains more students than traditional computing classes, it does not increase long-term participation in computing because it does not address the relational or systematic factors (Guzdial, 2013).

Recategorize

The majority of strategies in this category aim to challenge stereotypes about who is good at (and who should pursue) computer science. For example, Craig (2014) describes an intervention in Australia where the media and local speakers challenge stereotypes that CS is not for girls, raise awareness among teachers about CS careers, and where girls have opportunities to shadow CS college students and attend a 'Girls in Computing' day. In the US, programs that connect girls with same-sex role models and near-peer mentors challenge negative stereotypes about computer science careers and increase interest and an intention to pursue these types of careers among female and Latino students (Denner, Martinez and Thiry, 2016; Lang et al., 2010; Stout, Dasgupta, Hunsinger and McManus, 2011). As identities are still fluid in adolescence and remain open to external feedback, studies show the importance of sending the message that a range of identities are compatible with an identity as someone who is good with technology (Denner and Martinez, 2010; Scott and White, 2013).

A smaller number of programs send the message that computing is compatible with a range of cultures and identities. These strategies include integrating knowledge that is relevant to students' identities and communities within activities that are designed to promote computational learning. For example, Scott, Sheridan and Clark (2014) describe a culturally responsive approach to engaging students from racial/ethnic minority groups in computing fields by including activities and approaches that build on their interests and incorporate familiar cultural practices. Other programs describe the history of Black computer scientists and also show the connection to more current cultural references (Eglash, Gilbert, Taylor and Geier, 2013). These approaches have been found to increase learning achievement in computing among African American and Latino high school students in the US (Eglash, Gilbert and Foster, 2013). A culturally responsive computing approach can also provide opportunities for students to explore their multiple and intersecting identities by creating spaces to build a computing identity that does not detract from, or conflict with other important identities (e.g. friend, daughter) (Denner and Martinez, 2010). Finally, a culturally responsive computing approach builds critical consciousness and provides opportunities for youth to take on leadership roles (Scott, Aist and Zhang, 2014). Part of this process involves helping young people to develop a critical eye so they can identify instances of educational inequity and use technology to build potential solutions (Denner, Martinez, Thiry and Adams, 2015).

Resist

Fewer strategies are focused on helping students develop a critical consciousness about how institutionalized systems of power, bias, and oppression perpetuate inequity in CS. Jenkins et al.'s (2009) analysis of participatory culture in digital media provides a framework for how to help students understand the ways that technology influences them and who controls the production of technology. Using this framework, Jenson, Dahya and Fisher (2014) describe how a media production class created opportunities for middle school students to experience and critically examine the ways that the institutional structure of the school constrains who participates and how they participate. The CompuGirls program also fosters conversations about social justice, race and how to use technology for social change; girls select a social justice issue that is relevant to them and they conduct research and create technology solutions to address it (Scott and White, 2013). In the Apps for Social Justice class, participants receive mentoring to create apps that address local community needs; through that experience they learn computer science concepts and develop a critical consciousness about the structural issues that affect their community and limit the opportunities for its youth (Vakil, 2014). Similarly, Computing for the Social Good is a curriculum that teaches fifth-grade students how to program games that explore social justice at their school (Denner et al., 2015). Exploring Computer Science (ECS) is a program that can be embedded in the regular school day in a way that is responsive to both the values of the students and their communities, as well as the culture and climate of the schools (Margolis, Goode and Chapman, 2015). ECS goes beyond just a curriculum to also include strategies that transform the school and community climate, such as teacher professional development (Ryoo et al., 2013).

14.4 Summary

In summary, efforts to increase access to quality computer science education have been hampered both by a lack of focus on equity and inclusion and a lack of research on the most disadvantaged students. While an increasing number of studies have aimed to understand when and why students choose not to study CS, the focus has been largely on the gender gap in the US. A recent global snapshot of CS education shows that one challenge to looking at equity and inclusion is the wide variation in the terms used and the learning outcomes targeted across countries (Hubwieser, Armoni and Giannakos, 2015). However, there remains a need for studies of racial/ethnic minority groups in countries besides the US, as well as studies of other marginalized groups such as immigrants and English language learners.

Liben and Coyle's (2014) intervention types provide a useful framework for teachers to be intentional in how they support equity and inclusion in their computer science classes and programs. While it is not possible to address all five goals at one time, it is important to be clear about which are being targeted and why a particular goal should be a priority for a given group of students. By organizing our efforts using the framework, it will become more clear which strategies are not yet being addressed. Ultimately, it is important to develop and test strategies for all five change mechanisms if the field is going to make the needed progress on increasing diversity.

14.5 Recommendations

Teachers can use the framework in several ways to evaluate whether their strategies are inclusive starting by looking at their students and assessing which parts of the framework are in need of more immediate attention and which parts they are already succeeding in addressing with their current curriculum and strategies. Most large-scale efforts begin by working to incorporate computer science into the schools with a focus on building individual skills and competencies. In this chapter we advocate for incorporating the other goals early on in the process. To this end, teachers can advocate for sufficient training including learning pedagogies and having access to tools that are inclusive of different types of learners. They can coordinate with extracurricular programs to build off the excitement that they generate, and provide access to role models that represent a range of types of people who are in computer science. They can also reflect on their own biases and assumptions and how they influence their interactions with their students.

Key points

- A focus on equity and inclusion is an important part of quality computer science education.
- The challenges to fostering an equitable and inclusive learning environment exist at the institutional, relational and individual levels.
- A range of different types of strategies are being used to address the lack of diversity in computer science.
- The most common strategies focus on remediating individuals or revising the pedagogy or tools.
- The least common strategy is helping students develop a critical consciousness to transform the structural issues that perpetuate the disparities.

Further reflection

- For each of the five strategies described in this chapter, list two to three activities that would fit within each approach.
- Considering the challenges to equity and inclusion in computer science education, reflect on which will be the most amenable to change in your own classroom.

References

Akcaoglu, M (2013). Cognitive and motivational impacts of learning game design on middle school children. Michigan State University.

Al-Bow, M, et al. (2009). 'Using Game Creation for Teaching Computer Programming to High School Students and Teachers' 41(3) ACM *SIGCSE Bulletin* 104–108.

Armoni, M and J Gal-Ezer (2014). 'Early Computing Education: Why? What? When? Who?' 5(4) *ACM Inroads* 54–59.

Ashcraft, C, E Eger and M Friend (2012). *Girls in IT: The Facts* (Boulder CO, National Center for Women and Information Technology) 1–79.

Association for Computing Machinery (2009). 'New Image for Computing' Available at: http://cahsi. cs.utep.edu/Portals/0/about/New_Image_Computing.pdf

Bandura, A (1999). 'Moral Disengagement in the Perpetration of Inhumanities' 3(3) *Personality and Social Psychology Review* 193–209.

Bell, T, P Andreae and A Robins (2014). 'A Case Study of the Introduction of Computer Science in NZ Schools' 14(2) *ACM Transactions on Computing Education* (TOCE) 10.

Betz, DE and D Sekaquaptewa (2012). 'My Fair Physicist? Feminine Math and Science Role Models Demotivate Young Girls' 3(6) *Social Psychological and Personality Science* 738–746.

Brown, NC, S Sentance, T Crick and S Humphreys (2014). 'Restart: The Resurgence of Computer Science in UK Schools' 14(2) *ACM Transactions on Computing Education* 9.

Bureau of Labor Statistics. (2015). Employment by major occupational group, 2014 and projected 2024 (Table 4). Available at: www.bls.gov/news.release/ecopro.t04.htm

Burgstahler, S (2011). Universal Design: Implications for Computing Education. 11(3) *ACM Transactions on Computing Education* 19.

Campe, S, J Denner and L Werner (2013). 'Intentional Computing: Getting the Results you Want from Game Programming Classes' *Journal for Computing Teachers*. Available at: www.iste.org/store/product?ID=2850

Capovilla, D and P Hubwieser (2013). 'Teaching Spreadsheets to Visually Impaired Students in an Environment Similar to a Mainstream Class' in *Proceedings of the 18th ACM Conference on Innovation and Technology in Computer Science Education* 99–104.

Charleston, L, RP Adserias, NM Lang, and J Jackson (2014). 'Intersectionality and STEM: The Role of Race and Gender in the Academic Pursuits of African American Women in STEM' 2(3) *Journal of Progressive Policy and Practice* 273–293.

Claro, S, D Paunesku and CS Dweck (2016). 'Growth Mindset Tempers the Effects of Poverty on Academic Achievement' 113(31) *Proceedings of the National Academy of Sciences* 8664–8668.

Cooper, R and C Heaverlo (2013). 'Problem Solving and Creativity and Design: What Influence do they have on Girls' Interest in STEM Subject Areas?' 4(1) *American Journal of Engineering Education* 27.

Cortiella, C and SH Horowitz (2014). *The State of Learning Disabilities: Facts, Trends and Emerging Issues*, 3rd edn. (New York, NY, National Center for Learning Disabilities).

Craig, A (2014). 'Australian Interventions for Women in Computing: Are We Evaluating?' 18(2) *Australasian Journal of Information Systems* 91–110.

Cutts, Q, E Cutts, S Draper, P O'Donnell and P Saffrey (2010). 'Manipulating Mindset to Positively Influence Introductory Programming Performance' in *Proceedings of the 41st ACM Technical Symposium on Computer Science Education* 431–435.

Dasgupta, N, MM Scircle and M Hunsinger (2015). 'Female Peers in Small Work Groups Enhance Women's Motivation, Verbal Participation, and Career Aspirations in Engineering' 112(16) *Proceedings of the National Academy of Sciences* 4988–4993.

Denner, J (2011). 'What Predicts Middle School Girls' Interest in IT? 3(1) *International Journal of Gender in Science, Engineering, and Technology*. Available at: http://genderandset.open.ac.uk/index.php/genderandset/article/view/106/245

Denner, J and J Martinez (2010). 'Whyville versus MySpace: How Girls Negotiate Identities Online' 2 *Girl Wide Web* 203–222.

Denner, J, J Martinez and H Thiry (2016). 'Strategies for Engaging Hispanic/Latino Youth in the US in Computer Science' in YA Rankin and JO Thomas (eds), *Moving Students of Color from Consumers to Producers of Technology* (Hershey, PA, IGI Global).

Denner, J, J Martinez, H Thiry and J Adams (2015). 'Computer Science and Fairness: Integrating a Social Justice Perspective into an After School Program' 6(2) *Science Education and Civic Engagement: An International Journal* 41–54.

Dweck, CS and A Master (2008). 'Self-theories Motivate Self-regulated Learning. Motivation and Self-regulated Learning: Theory, Research, and Applications' 31–51.

Eccles, JS, A Wigfield and U Schiefele (1997). 'Motivation to Succeed' in W Damon and N Eisenberg (eds), *Handbook of Child Psychology* (Vol. 3) (New York, NY, John Wiley and Sons, Inc).

Eccles, L (2007). 'Gender Differences in Teacher-Student Interactions, Attitudes and Achievement in Middle School Science' (Doctoral Thesis). Western Australia: Science and Mathematics Education Centre, Curtin University of Technology.

Eglash, R, JE Gilbert and E Foster (2013). Toward Culturally Responsive Computing Education' 56(7) *Communications of the ACM* 33–36.

Eglash, R, JE Gilbert, V Taylor and SR Geier (2013). 'Culturally Responsive Computing in Urban, After-school Contexts: Two Approaches' 48(5) *Urban Education* 629–656.

Else-Quest, NM, CC Mineo and A Higgins (2013). 'Math and Science Attitudes and Achievement at the Intersection of Gender and Ethnicity' 37(3) *Psychology of Women Quarterly* 293–309.

Frome, PM and JS Eccles (1998). 'Parents' Influence on Children's Achievement-Related Perceptions' 74(2) *Journal of Personality and Social Psychology* 435.

Furnham, A, E Reeves and S Budhani (2002). 'Parents Think their Sons are Brighter than their Daughters: Sex Differences in Parental Self-Estimations and Estimations of their Children's Multiple Intelligences' 163(1) *The Journal of Genetic Psychology*, 24–39.

Google, Inc and Gallup, Inc (2015). Images of Computer Science: Perceptions among Students, Parents, and Educators in the US. Available at: https://goo.gl/F3SSWH

Google Inc and Gallup Inc (2016). Diversity Gaps in Computer Science: Exploring the Under-representation of Girls, Blacks and Hispanics. Available at: http://goo.gl/PG34aH

Gutiérrez, KD and A Arzubiaga (2012). 'An Ecological and Activity Theoretic Approach to Studying Diasporic and Nondominant Communities'. *Research on Schools, Neighborhoods, and Communities: Toward Civic Responsibility*, 203–216.

Guzdial, M (2013). 'Exploring Hypotheses about Media Computation' in *Proceedings of the Ninth Annual International ACM Conference on International Computing Education Research* 19–26.

Hansen, AK, ER Hansen, HA Dwyer, DB Harlow and D Franklin (2016). '*Differentiating for Diversity: Using Universal Design for Learning in Computer Science Education*'. Proceedings of SIGCSE.

Hong, H, J Wang, J Ravitz and ML Fong (2015). 'Gender Differences in High School Students' Decisions to Study Computer Science and Related Fields' in *Proceedings of the 46th ACM Technical Symposium on Computer Science Education*.

Horizon Media, Inc (2015). Horizon Media Study Reveals Americans Prioritize STEM Subjects over the Arts; Science is 'Cool'. Available at: www.horizonmedia.com/press?pressRelease=2481

Hubwieser, P, M Armoni and MN Giannakos. (2015). 'How to Implement Rigorous Computer Science Education in K-12 schools? Some Answers and Many Questions'. 15(2) *ACM Transactions on Computing Education* 5.

Jenkins, H, R Purushotma, M Weigel, K Clinton and AJ Robison (2009). *Confronting the Challenges of Participatory Culture: Media Education for the 21st Century*. (Cambridge, MA, MIT Press).

Jenson, J, N Dahya and S Fisher (2014). Valuing Production Values: A 'Do It Yourself' Media Production Club 39(2) *Learning, Media and Technology* 215–228.

Kench, D, S Hazelhurst and F Otulaja (2016). 'Grit and Growth Mindset among High School Students in a Computer Programming Project: A Mixed Methods Study'. in *Annual Conference of the Southern African Computer Lecturers' Association* (Cape Town, Springer International Publishing) 187–194.

Khenner, E and I Semakin (2014). 'School Subject Informatics (Computer Science) in Russia: Educational Relevant Areas' 14(2) *ACM Transactions on Computing Education* 14.

Kvasny, L, EM Trauth and AJ Morgan (2009). 'Power Relations in IT Education and Work: The Intersectionality of Gender, Race, and Class' 7(2/3) *Journal of Information, Communication and Ethics in Society* 96–118.

Ladner, R and M Israel. (2016). 'Broadening Participation "For All" in "Computer Science for All"' 59(9) *Communications of the ACM* 26–28.

Lameman, B and J Lewis (2011). 'Skins: Designing Games with First Nations Youth' 1 *Journal of Game Design and Development Education* 54–63.

Lang, M (2016). 'Gender Gap in Tech Starts Younger Than You Think: Study'. Available at: www.thestar.com.my/tech/tech-news/2016/10/24/gender-gap-in-tech-starts-younger-than-you-think-study/

Lent, RW, AM Lopez, FG Lopez and HB Sheu. (2008). 'Social Cognitive Career Theory and the Prediction of Interests and Choice Goals in the Computing Disciplines 73(1) *Journal of Vocational Behavior* 52–62.

Lewis, CM (2011). 'Is Pair Programming More Effective than Other Forms of Collaboration for Young Students?' 21(2) *Computer Science Education* 105–134.

Lewis, CM, RE Anderson and K Yasuhara (2016). 'I Don't Code All Day: Fitting in Computer Science when the Stereotypes Don't Fit' in *Proceedings of the 2016 ACM Conference on International Computing Education Research* 23–32.

Liben, LS and EF Coyle (2014). 'Chapter Three: Developmental Interventions to Address the STEM Gender Gap: Exploring Intended and Unintended Consequences' 47 *Advances in Child Development and Behavior* 77–115.

Margolis, J, J Goode and G Chapman (2015). 'An Equity Lens for Scaling: A Critical Juncture for Exploring Computer Science' 6(3) *ACM Inroads* 58–66.

Margolis, J, R Estrella, J Goode, JJ Holme and K Nao (2010). *Stuck in the Shallow End: Education, Race, and Computing* (Cambridge MA, MIT Press).

Master, A, S Cheryan and AN Meltzoff (2016). 'Computing Whether She Belongs: Stereotypes Undermine Girls' Interest and Sense of Belonging in Computer Science' 108(3) *Journal of Educational Psychology* 424.

National Center for Education Statistics (2016). Digest of education statistics 2014, 50th edition. Available at: https://nces.ed.gov/pubs2016/2016006.pdf

National Student Clearinghouse Research Center. (2015). Snapshot Report, Degree Attainment. Available at: https://nscresearchcenter.org/wp-content/uploads/SnapshotReport15-DegreeAttainment.pdf

OECD (2011). 'Share of Women Graduates by Field of Education'. Available at: www.oecd.org/gender/data/shareofwomengraduatesbyfieldofeducation.htm

Ofsted (2011). ICT in schools: 2008–2011. Available at: www.gov.uk/government/uploads/system/uploads/attachment_data/file/181223/110134.pdf

Othman, M and R Latih (2006). 'Women in Computer Science: No Shortage Here!' 49(3) *Communications of the ACM* 111–114.

Raman, R, S Venkatasubramanian, K Achuthan and P Nedungadi (2015). 'Computer Science (CS) Education in Indian Schools: Situation Analysis using Darmstadt Model' 15(2) *ACM Transactions on Computing Education* 7.

Royal Society (2012). 'Shut Down or Restart? The Way Forward for Computing in UK Schools'. Available at: https://royalsociety.org/~/media/education/computing-in-schools/2012-01-12-computing-in-schools.pdf

Ryoo, JJ, J Margolis, CH Lee, CD Sandoval and J Goode (2013). 'Democratizing Computer Science Knowledge: Transforming the Face of Computer Science through Public High School Education' 38(2) *Learning, Media and Technology* 161–181.

Scott, KA and MA White (2013). 'COMPUGIRLS' Standpoint Culturally Responsive Computing and its Effect on Girls of Color' 48(5) *Urban Education* 657–681.

Scott, K, G Aist and X Zhang (2014). 'Designing a Culturally Responsive Computing Curriculum for Girls' 6(2) *International Journal of Gender, Science and Technology*, 264–276.

Scott, KA, K Sheridan and K Clark (2014). Culturally Responsive Computing: A Theory Revisited 40(4) *Learning, Media and Technology* 412–436.

Scott, MJ and G Ghinea (2014). 'On the Domain-specificity of Mindsets: The Relationship between Aptitude Beliefs and Programming Practice' 57(3) *IEEE Transactions on Education* 169–174.

Shah, N, CM Lewis, R Caires, N Khan, A Qureshi, D Ehsanjpour and N Gupta (2013). *Building Equitable Computer Science Classrooms: Elements of a Teaching Approach* (Denver CO, SIGCSE).

Sien, VY, GY Mui, EYJ Tee and D Singh (2014). 'Perceptions of Malaysian Female School Children towards Higher Education in Information Technology' in *Proceedings of the 52nd ACM Conference on Computers and People Research* 97–104.

Simon, B, B Hanks, L Murphy, S Fitzgerald, R McCauley, L Thomas and C Zander (2008). 'Saying Isn't Necessarily Believing: Influencing Self-theories in Computing' in *Proceedings of the Fourth international Workshop on Computing Education Research* 173–184.

Snodgrass, MR, M Israel and GC Reese (2016). 'Instructional Supports for Students with Disabilities in K-5 Computing: Findings from a Cross-case Analysis' 100 *Computers and Education* 1–17.

Snyder, T, C de Brey and S Dillow (eds), (2016). *Digest of Educational Statistics 2014*, 50th edn (Washington, DC, Department of Education, Institute of Education Sciences, National Center for Education Statistics). Available at: https://nces.ed.gov/pubs2016/2016006.pdf

Steinke, J, M Lapinski, M Long, C Van Der Maas, L Ryan and B Applegate (2009). 'Seeing Oneself as a Scientist: Media Influences and Adolescent Girls' Science Career Possible Selves' 15(4) *Journal of Women and Minorities in Science and Engineering* 279–301.

Stienen-Durand, S and J George (2014). 'Supporting Dyslexia in the Programming Classroom 27 *Procedia Computer Science*, 419–430.

Stout, JG, N Dasgupta, M Hunsinger and MA McManus (2011). 'STEMing the Tide: Using Ingroup Experts to Inoculate Women's Self-Concept in Science, Technology, Engineering, and Mathematics (STEM) 100(2) *Journal of Personality and Social Psychology* 255.

Vakil, S (2014). 'A Critical Pedagogy Approach for Engaging Urban Youth in Mobile App Development in an After-School Program' 47(1) *Equity and Excellence in Education* 31–45.

Versta Research (2014). 'Teens' Views on Tech Careers. Creating IT Futures Foundation'. Available at: www.creatingitfutures.org/researching-solutions/teen-views-on-tech-careers

Vivian, R, K Falkner and C Szabo (2014). 'Can Everybody Learn to Code?: Computer Science Community Perceptions about Learning the Fundamentals of Programming' in *Proceedings of the 14th Koli Calling International Conference on Computing Education Research* 41–50.

Wang, L-C and MP Chen (2011). 'The Relationships of Social Economic Status and Learners' Motivation and Performance in Learning from a Game-design Project'. Paper presented at the *11th IEEE International Conference on Advanced Learning Technologies* (ICALT), Rome, Italy.

Wille, S, J Century and M Pike (2016). 'Computer Science Principles (CSP) and Students with Learning Differences: Expanding Opportunities for a Hidden Underrepresented Group in *Research on Equity and Sustained Participation in Engineering, Computing, and Technology* (RESPECT) 2016, 1–8.

Wille, S, J Century and M Pike (2017). 'Exploratory Research to Expand Opportunities in Computer Science for Students with Learning Differences' 19(3) *Computing in Science and Engineering* 40–50.

Yang, YC and WI Wu (2012). 'Digital Storytelling for Enhancing Student Academic Achievement, Critical Thinking, and Learning Motivation: A Year-long Experimental Study' 59 *Computers and Education* 339–352.

15

Language and Computing

Ira Diethelm, Juliana Goschler and Timo Lampe

Chapter outline

Chapter synopsis

Spoken and written language and computer science (CS) terminology can cause difficulty in the computer science classroom. In addition, students who are weak in literacy may face difficulties with programming tasks. This chapter will primarily focus on instructional language in the computer science classroom and also address other aspects of language and literacy development through computer science. We introduce some aspects of theory related to this problem domain to start a meta-discourse on spoken language for teaching CS. We will also give hints and pedagogical suggestions for teachers how to support CS understanding and learning, as well as supporting literacy development in students.

15.1 Introduction

It is a well-established and widely accepted truth that we are living in a world that, over the last years, has undergone massive changes in the way we live our lives and experience the world around us. Computers accompany us in every situation of our lives, smartphones are always there to take a quick look at, digital media is beginning to replace classic media such as newspapers and so on. In order to participate in this modern world, a certain skill set is necessary. Amongst many other skills, one has 'to be able to discern the accuracy and integrity of [...] data. [...] People need to be aware of privacy and security issues (Leahy and Dolan, 2010: 214). Talking and writing about Computing in schools is no longer restricted to programming.

15.2 Digital literacy

Digital literacy is an important skill in the technological world in which we live. It ecompasses many aspects and not one but several definitions that try to describe its different facets. The British Computer Society (BCS, 2016) tries to narrow down a definition while also acknowledging the individual. For them, digital literacy involves

> [t]hose capabilities that mean an individual is fit for living, learning and working in a digital society. Digital Literacy is about being able to make use of technologies to participate in and contribute to modern social, cultural, philosophical and economic life (BCS, 2016).

The Digital Competence Framework for Citizens (DigComp) was introduced by the European Commission in 2013, with the aim of being a tool 'to improve citizens' digital competence, to help policy-makers to formulate policies that support digital competence building, and to plan education and training initiatives to improve digital competence of specific target groups' (Vuorikari et al., 2016: 5), while also providing a set of terminology to 'describe the key areas of digital competence [and therefore of Digital Literacy] and thus [offer] a common reference at European level' (ibid.).

Digital literacy also encompasses the aspect of communication. In this case, communication not only means communicating with support from digital media, but it also includes talking about digital media. If one wants to communicate successfully about digital media certain skills are required. A learner needs to know about the terminology of the subject of interest. It is important not only to know the terminology, but also how to use it in a given context. Certain words may have context-specific meanings that change depending on the subject at hand. Certain fields may have a higher number of metaphors. Or there may be numerous words from a field that have found their way into the subject vernacular, but with slightly changed meanings. These specifics need to be known to communicate successfully about them and to exchange and expand knowledge. Our focus will therefore be on language, communication and terminology in computer science education.

15.3 Language in education

So far, we have argued that successful communication about digital media, computers and computer science requires certain linguistic skills. Thus, learning about digital media and computers is closely connected to the ability both to understand and produce appropriate descriptions and explanations of the subject matter (Diethelm and Goschler, 2014). Linguistic competence, therefore, is key to the successful acquisition of knowledge and learning of skills, especially in schools, where most instruction is delivered using oral explanations by the teacher and written textbooks.

Key concept: Educational language

The variety of language used in school – in the German context often described as 'Bildungssprache' ('educational language') – differs considerably from that used in everyday communication. It is usually less dialogic, more abstract, it uses more complex constructions and in general is more orientated towards written discourse rather than spoken discourse (even in if it is delivered verbally). To master this communication, one needs more and other linguistic and communicative skills than are necessary for everyday interaction outside of educational contexts.

These different skills have been described in the context of the Northern American educational situation of bilinguals as Basic Interpersonal Communication Skills (BICS) versus Cognitive Academic Language Proficiency (CALP) (Cummins, 1979, 2008). BICS are sufficient to manage simple 'conversational' language used in everyday communication outside professional or educational contexts. This typically consists of small talk, simple orders and requests, simple narrations and the like. CALP, in contrast, is necessary to master educational and academic language. This language used in schools, universities or in professional contexts includes different text types such as news, reports, scientific papers, talks or more complex narrative texts like novels. Cognitive Academic Language Proficiency therefore requires – among a lot of pragmatic knowledge – a larger lexicon with more abstract terminology as well as the mastery of certain complex grammatical constructions like sentences in the passive voice, complex noun phrases, complex sentences often including multiple embedding and, in languages such as German, other inflectional forms (like past forms of verbs).

Not all pupils are sufficiently equipped with this linguistic knowledge. Many pupils have not had enough input in the required variety because they do not talk much about topics outside of everyday interest in their family and their peer groups, because they do not read much and/or because they do not engage in activities that make complex and abstract language necessary. The situation can be even worse for children and young people growing up with more than one language: for many of them, even a large part of everyday communication takes place in another language than in the one they have to use in school, so that their input in the language used in school is even more diminished. But even if bi- or multilingual pupils have a lot of input in academic and educational varieties, using their second language often means a higher cognitive load and requires greater concentration on the processing and production of language.

The problem described above is present in all school subjects and in most educational contexts, but every specific subject has its own, additional, variety of language, consisting of a specific terminology, specific frequent syntactic constructions, specific semantic conventions and specific communicative routines. This is also the case for computer science and computer science education. We will discuss these specific features in turn in the following section.

15.4 Language in computing education

It is clear that every subject comes with a specific terminology that has to be learned alongside the concepts connected to them. If the terminology consists of words that are only used in connection with the subject, then most of the time teachers are aware that these words have to be part of their explicit teaching. In computer science, words like byte, integer, compiler, recursion and acronyms like RAM/ROM or CAD/CAM have to be specifically taught.

Example activity

Ask students to write down scientific terms and words that are connected to the present topic of your course and collect them all. Then let your students create a glossary of the twenty or thirty most important of these words: each student should provide a description for one term in his or her own words. Then two other students should review and adjust each description. Repeat this for each new topic of your course at the beginning of a unit or for preparing for a test.

Other words are more difficult to be detected as possible challenges by the teachers. This is often the case with words that have a specific meaning within the computer science community, but a slightly or sometimes completely different meaning in everyday discourse (e.g. nouns like code, memory, address, folder, loop, bug, value or verbs to save, to code, to retrieve, to submit). Very often teachers are not aware of the fact that these differing meanings have to be taught and learned just like completely new words. If this explicit teaching/learning does not take place, pupils try to make sense of the words and the contexts they occur in with their knowledge from everyday communication. This can lead to unhelpful misunderstandings and misconceptions. Even teachers' questions, which aim to ensure that everything is understood (in a text or a talk) often fail to yield appropriate responses from pupils, because they think they 'understand' all the words that were used, because they 'know' them – albeit with a different meaning.

In the context of German schools, the fact that a lot of computer science terminology consists of English words makes the situation different from English speaking countries: On the one hand, having to learn and use a variety of words in another language than the one the subject is taught in could be an additional difficulty for pupils. On the other hand, it makes terminology more distinct (with a different meaning than the same word in everyday discourse). In cases where there are German words, however, the problem of different usage in different discourses and communities remains (e.g. terms like programmieren ('to program'/'to code') or ein Programm schreiben ('write code'/'write a program')).

This terminology is not used on its own. The terms appear in sentences, whose construction differs from those in the vernacular. Most scientific communities and the texts produced within these communities use very specific linguistic constructions that can be rare in everyday discourse or – just like terminology – come with subtly different meanings. Sometimes these differences are rather obvious and easy to figure out: If a teacher orders his or her pupils to 'tell' the computer something, in most cases the pupils would understand that they are meant to type something in, not to say something. However, in some cases it might be less obvious and more likely to produce a misunderstanding: If a teacher wants his or her students to print a sentence, they might assume that they have to use the printer. In programming, printing a sentence usually refers to displaying a sentence on screen.

In other cases, the use of highly specific constructions could mean that not everything is understood by the pupils (e.g. 'please create two derived classes that inherit the properties of the base class and override two inherited methods, but also remember to regulate access through access control attributes').

15.5 Metaphors of information technology and computer science

Complex sentences like the one above can be even more confusing for pupils when metaphors whose meanings are not made clear are incorporated into the sentence. What are metaphors? They are not just fancy additions to our language – more often than not, they reflect certain conceptions and help us to understand abstract things by transferring our knowledge about more concrete things to abstract domains. This is also the case for computers and things connected to them. It is not unusual to describe computers as containers, sometimes specifically buildings, where things on the inside are moved around, for example in expressions like:

- The data is transferred.
- I will move the file to another folder.

More typical words reflecting this metaphor are identified in the study by Izwaini: architecture, library, sign in/log in, sign out/log out, platform, port, window (Izwaini, 2003: 3).

The metaphorical description of the computer or parts of it as a living being or even a person is also frequent:

- The computer memorizes previous activities.
- The computer fell asleep/woke up.
- The compiler looks into the memory address.

Izwaini identifies more words used in talking about computers that imply that it is a living being: 'client, conflict, dialogue (conversation between the computer and the user), generation, language, memory, protocol, syntax, widow/orphan, and virus and bug (it can get ill)' (Izwaini, 2003: 2).

Other metaphors suggest that the computer is a workshop or a manufacturer (equipment, hardware, install, load, template, tools) or an office (desktop, directory, document, file, folder, mail, trash, can, wastebasket) (ibid.).

It has become clear that complex and subtle knowledge about the specific use of language within a scientific or educational community is necessary to properly understand what is said in the classroom or written in textbooks. It has also become clear that one cannot expect pupils to come readily equipped with all that knowledge, but that teaching specific linguistic knowledge and skills is, in fact, part of education – thus, subject teaching and language teaching, as well as subject learning and language learning, are inseparable.

15.6 From everyday language to scientific language

In the previous sections, we have presented different linguistic aspects (e.g. terminology or specific language constructions or metaphors of computing education). These special constructions and frequently occurring concepts lead to a variety of different situations that require special attention when teaching computer science. This chapter will focus on these situations and raise questions that teachers want to consider when they prepare their lessons.

So far, we have seen how metaphors are used when talking about computer science and quickly touched upon the importance of avoiding misconceptions. One of the problems that arises when teaching computer science is ambiguity. In general, computer science uses a variety of 'dead metaphors'. These metaphors are not only used, they are 'lived by' (Lakoff and Johnson, 2003). Words like 'packet', 'string', 'protocol', 'cloud', 'stack', 'program', 'model' and many more are no longer used metaphorically. These ambiguous terms have found their way into the general terminology of the field and are now considered scientific terms (Diethelm and Goschler, 2014: 3). Their meanings shift depending on who uses them and in which context they are used. In computer science lessons, there are also, as we have seen in the previous chapter, anthropomorphized metaphors. These are metaphors where comparisons with the human body are made. A computer works like a brain, it can break down, can get a virus and needs care (Steffen, 2006: 42), processes can be killed and there is inheritance in programming.

Key concept: Metaphors

Metaphors can help pupils and teachers to conceptualize very abstract things and make them cognitively more manageable. However, it always has to be clear that these are, in fact, metaphors, not factual descriptions of the parts and actions of the computer.

Some metaphors can be helpful in some respects and on certain levels of description (e.g. the distinction between programs and folders) but they can be misleading in other respects and on other levels (e.g. if one wants to explain the basic nature of 'information' the computer uses). To avoid long-lasting misconceptions, which can result in resistance to learning new conceptualizations, teachers have to be aware of the metaphors used in classroom language, to avoid them or use alternatives if a specific metaphor blocks the understanding of a certain concept. We also suggest that teachers should explain carefully rather than penalize the usage of anthropomorphized metaphors. After all, even professionals tend to use them (Anton, 2010: 68). Using metaphors leads to discourse about them, thus students engage more in topics and incentives to talk and use language to express thoughts are established.

In his PhD thesis, Busch researched the usage of metaphors in computer science (Busch, 1998). This allows for a first detailed look at the way metaphors are used in computer science in general and the way they are used in teaching in particular (Diethelm and Goschler, 2014). Busch provides a three-step-system, which can help teachers if they want to use metaphors:

1 Clarification of meaning of the term in other non-CS contexts.
2 Speculation about possible meanings of that term in CS, and also about what it would certainly not mean
3 Development of the CS-related meaning of the term (Busch, 1998: 125).

These three steps can be used by teachers to make sure that the origin as well as the meaning of a metaphor are made clear to the students, that the way the metaphor is used by the students is correct and that the students can distinguish between metaphors for everyday language and those used in technical contexts.

Teachers can also make these distinctions by clarifying the level of language that is used in classroom settings. Essentially, there are two different levels of language: the everyday (or common) language and scientific language. There is also a third language which blurs the lines between these two levels. The shaping of a language takes a lot of time, as a study conducted by Rincke shows (Rincke, 2010: 56–59). It is a long process and needs constant attention. Teachers must ensure that there is time to talk about (scientific) language and its benefit in the classroom.

To introduce new scientific language to the classroom, Martin Wagenschein suggests three phases (Wagenschein, 1980: 130–138). The first phase aims to cause surprise. Students are encouraged to express their feelings and thoughts in their own words. Every utterance is valuable to the discourse. The teacher needs to take a step back and only guide the discussion using non-scientific language. The second phase aims to preserve these thoughts by embedding them into everyday language in a way 'that it could be explained to oneself or others in a way that it could be understood later on, e.g. in a year' (ibid.). So far, only common language is used. This changes in the third phase. This uses the preserved text and transforms it into a scientific text. Wagenschein suggests that scientific language should not be taught explicitly. We, on the other hand, suggest that the transformation in phase three should be taught explicitly to make sure that students understand that the terminology used is different from everyday language. This way, inaccuracies and misconceptions can be avoided and clearer lines can be drawn between the different levels of language. A way for teachers to introduce new language explicitly in phase three is to incorporate a meta-discourse in their lessons.

Key concept: Meta-discourse

The meta-discourse's aim is 'to engage students in a discussion about language including syntactic and semantic features of informal everyday talk and of formal scientific use' (Rincke, 2011). Teachers can single out the settings in which scientific words or phrases occur, make distinctions between the ways they are used in common language and scientific language and make cross-disciplinary comparisons to show how words and sentences surrounding the word in question shape meaning.

Using a meta-discourse allows students not only to understand where a word or a phrase comes from and what it means, but it also allows students to assign to it a level of language. It is then easier for students to distinguish between the levels of language. In his book, Lemke suggests that the ability to talk about science also leads to the ability to do science 'in terms of reasoning, observing, analysing and writing' (Diethelm and Goschler, 2014: 3). Lemke also recommends that students 'should be required to be able saying anything in science in more than one way, and taught how to do so. [...] Saying the meaning without the same set of words' (Lemke, 1990: 170).

15.7 Structuring lessons

When structuring their lessons, teachers need to be aware of possible difficulties when introducing new language. A common model used to structure student-orientated lessons is Educational Reconstruction. This model can also be applied to plan a language-orientated lesson including a meta-discourse. The model places a phenomenon caused by CS at its centre and surrounds it with five aspects that all interact with and influence each other (see Figure 15.1). Each of these components can be used for student- and language-orientated lessons.

The first aspect is the analysis of social demands. This aims to explain why a certain concept or phenomenon needs to be taught. What makes it important? Why should students be able to talk about this concept? We have already talked about digital literacy and have established that it is important to be literate in CS in order to be able to fulfil the requirements of today's society.

When a phenomenon is being chosen as the topic for a lesson, it is not only important to choose a topic that the students experience outside of their classrooms, but the teacher also needs to ask questions regarding the origin of the phenomenon. What is its name and where does it come from? Is it necessary or helpful for the students that they get this information as well? Essentially, the teacher needs to decide if the phenomenon itself needs a linguistic analysis in class or not. Even if the phenomenon does not need explicit linguistic coverage, its parts just might. The Science Content Structure 'describes how the phenomenon could be explained scientifically and which subject domain knowledge is required to understand the phenomenon' (Diethelm and Goschler, 2014). Kattmann et al. list several questions for this step, one of which is especially important for a language-orientated lesson: 'Which terms are used in scientific publications and textbooks and

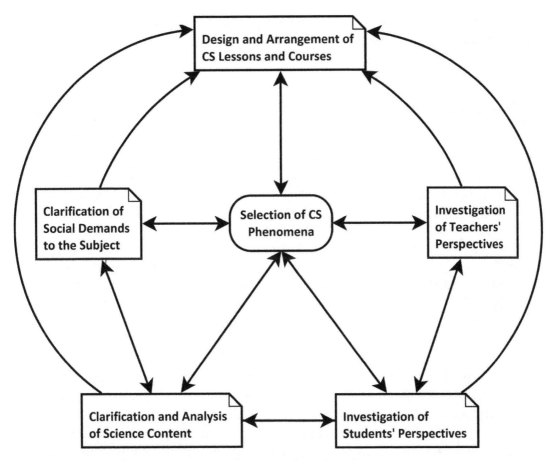

Figure 15.1 Educational reconstruction for computing education

which of them could hinder or support learning due to the narrow meaning of the word or parts of it?' (cited in Diethelm and Goschler, 2014). It is the teacher's task to choose which terms are important for the lesson, which need to be addressed linguistically and how these terms are defined. Teachers need to make sure that new scientific terms are not defined by other scientific terms unless this is unavoidable. In addition, definitions should be phrased in a way that they can be extended once a deeper understanding of the topic is achieved.

While analysing the content structure, it is also important to consider the perspectives of both students and teachers.

When considering the students' perspectives it is important for teachers to understand that these matter just as much as the content structure. It is important to understand, that students' conceptions are not synonymous with misconceptions, because the 'term "mis" already suggests that the students' conceptions would be wrong or not worthwhile and thus have to be replaced in their minds by something that is more "correct" in any respect' (Diethelm, Hubwieser and Klaus, 2012). It is important to understand the terms students use and why they use them, because they provide insight into the students' life, enable connections to be established and expand their knowledge. Teachers need to ask themselves where their students' conceptions derive from, if they derive from linguistic phenomena and also if a meta-discourse can help to create awareness.

Example

A study by Diethelm and Zumbrägel has shown what some pupils think about the way streaming a video works. In their study, 26 per cent of students thought that the video they stream is actually played online and they just watch it, similar to watching a movie in the cinema or on television (cf. Diethelm and Zumbrägel, 2010). While planning a lesson, teachers can then make time to analyse the word 'streaming' together with the children, so that they understand that data is actually transported to their computers, much like water in a stream. Of course, depending on the grade one is teaching, the explanation can be more or less detailed. It can also be used to introduce a new topic: the internet, packaging or protocols. Understanding the students' perspectives shapes the way the content structure is presented. Adjustments can be made so that these perspectives are incorporated, problematized and expended in the lesson.

Teachers' perspectives can, just like those of the students, be very different from one another. Due to their different backgrounds, like a general computer science degree (MA) or a specific degree for teaching (MEd) and because computer science doesn't have a long tradition in schools, approaches to lesson planning and to the importance of different aspects are likely very different (cf. Diethelm and Goschler, 2014). Teachers will use different methods, have different pedagogical knowledge, different content knowledge, different psychological knowledge and so on (cf. Diethelm, Hubwieser and Klaus, 2012). Therefore, teachers need to ask themselves which terms are known to them and how they would explain these terms to their students. This question will also reveal if there are uncertainties around a certain topic. They have to ask themselves which terms are known to them through their work or studies and if there are limits to their own knowledge and where they need to catch up to be able to properly explain concepts to their students. At the same time, CS teachers should also talk to their colleagues or CS teachers from other schools. That way, they can compare definitions for terms amongst each other. If one supposes that a class has several teachers throughout their years at a school, one can also suppose that the students will encounter teachers who use different definitions for the same terms. By comparing terms, teachers can create a common understanding and use the same terms in the same way, so that the students can continue to use the terms they learned without any misunderstandings. One way to make this common ground available for present as well as future teachers is through the implementation of a wiki. Our work with teachers has shown us that, given a specific concept, different teachers come up with different definitions. These definitions aim to explain the same concept using different terms, which in turn leads to lively discussions. Through these discussions, teachers experience different points of view and in the end find similar definitions.

All of these aspects influence the design and arrangement of lessons and courses. 'If we focus on "CS classroom language", this means that they all have an influence on the terms that occur in class during different phases of the lessons, used by different participants' (Diethelm and Goschler, 2014). Through iterative execution of the analysis of these aspects, lessons can be planned that are student- as well as language-orientated and which create an awareness for the language and terminology that is used throughout the lessons.

15.8 Recommendations

As a result of our thoughts presented so far, and based on the works of Lemke (1990) and Wagenschein (1980), we can summarize with the following recommendations:

1 Give students more practice talking (computer) science, encourage students to talk about CS to one another and to talk in everyday language. This way, they will get used to using the terminology presented in class.

2 Teach students how to describe phenomena and CS concepts in everyday language (e.g. on the phone to somebody). Students will then be able not only to communicate with other computer scientists, but will also be able to mediate and explain to other learners.

3 Require your students to be able to say anything in more than one way and always in full sentences to make sure about the meaning. This allows the teacher to check for understanding and to see where there are still problems that need to be addressed.

4 You as well should prepare and provide different explanations in everyday language and in scientific language for the same concept and make it explicit when you use each (e.g. do I make a difference in the use of 'programming' and 'coding'? Where is this difference and how can I explain it to my students in everyday language?)

5 Teach the meta-discourse, discuss the different meanings of terms, their usage and their origins and metaphors. For example, show different definitions from textbooks and negotiate on a set of central terms for that course and their meanings and write down a common glossary. A glossary can help students in class, when doing homework, to get used to terminology and also when they prepare for tests.

6 Practice with your students to translate from everyday language into scientific language and back again and grade this activity.

7 Become familiar with the everyday language used by those of your students with different cultural backgrounds, from a different gender, the non-native speakers and students with special needs.

8 Emphasize the human side of CS (e.g. in modelling processes) or about information technology as an everyday phenomenon and CS as one way of describing the world etc.

9 Involve your students in decision processes on the contexts and on examples for the concepts you'd like to teach. This way, the students' connection to CS will be strengthened and your lessons will have more meaning to them. That way, they might talk more about CS with their peer groups.

10   Allow room for a discussion about the nature of computer science. Teach your students about different viewpoints on our discipline, the different scientific methods we use and on their benefits for different application domains.

Key points

- Digital literacy requires talking about digital artefacts and processes with scientific terms in different contexts.
- The scientific language of CS consists of many metaphors that might cause misunderstandings.
- Both students and teachers, need to talk about CS to negotiate meanings of terms and to avoid misunderstandings.
- Everyday language, educational language and scientific language have to be considered by teachers to support learning.
- When introducing a new term students and teachers should reflect on other meanings in non-CS-contexts before using it scientifically.
- The framework of educational reconstruction helps planning lessons from different perspectives.
- The meta-discourse about CS terms and their usage supports learning and connecting CS terms and knowledge to everyday life.

Further reflection

- Try the meta-discourse within a workshop with your colleagues: Think about the terms 'coding', 'implementing', 'modelling' and 'programming'. Write down on your own one typical sentence you use for each term. Let your colleagues write down a sentence for each term also. Then compare your sentences, discuss them and agree on one definition for each term and on one exemplary sentence for each of them. Write them on a poster and place it in your classroom or another frequented wall in your school.
- Repeat this with another set of terms with 'quite the same but different' meaning.

References

Anton, MA (2010). 'Wie heißt das auf Chemisch? – Sprachebenen der Kommunikation im und nach dem Chemieunterricht' in Fenkart, Gabriele; Lembens, Anja; Erlacher-Zeitlinger, Edith (Hrsg), *Sprache, Mathematik und Naturwissenschaften*. (Innsbruck: StudienVerlag GesmbH).

British Computer Society 'BCS' (2016). BCS Digital Literacy for Life Programme. Available at: www.bcs.org/category/17853

Busch, C (1998). *Metaphern in der Informatik – Modellbildung – Formalisierung – Anwendung.* (Wiesbaden, Deutscher Universitäts-Verlag).

Cummins, J (1979). 'Linguistic Interdependence and the Educational Development of Bilingual Children' 49 *Review of Educational Research* 222–251.

Cummins, J (2008). 'BICS and CALP: Empirical and Theoretical Status of the Distinction' in *Encyclopedia of Language and Education* (Berlin, Springer) 487–499.

Diethelm, I and J Goschler (2014). 'On Human Language and Terminology Used for Teaching and Learning CS/Informatics' in *Proceedings of the 9th Workshop in Primary and Secondary Computing Education*, New York, 122–123. ACM.

Diethelm, I and S Zumbrägel (2010). 'Wie funktioniert eigentlich das Internet? – Empirische Untersuchung von Schülervorstellungen' in *Proc. Didaktik der Informatik. Möglichkeiten Empirischer Forschungsmethoden und Perspektiven der Fachdidaktik.* Bonn, 33–44.

Diethelm, I, P Hubwieser and R Klaus (2012). 'Students, Teachers and Phenomena: Educational Reconstruction for Computer Science Education' in R McCartney and M-J Laakso (eds) *12th Koli Calling Conference on Computing Education Research.* Tahko.

Gov.uk (2014). Department of Education – National Curriculum in England: Framework for Key Stages 1 to 4. Available at: www.gov.uk/government/publications/national-curriculum-in-england-framework-for-key-stages–1-to–4

Izwaini, S (2003). 'A Corpus-Based Study of Metaphor in Information Technology' in *Proceedings of the Workshop on Corpus-based Approaches to Figurative Language* Lancaster, UK 110.

Joint Information Systems Committee 'Jisc' (2014). 'Developing Digital Literacies' Available at: www.jisc.ac.uk/full-guide/developing-digital-literacies

Lakoff, G and M Johnson (2003). *Metaphors We Live By.* (Chicago, University of Chicago Press).

Leahy, D and D Dolan (2010). 'Digital Literacy: A Vital Competence for 2010?' in N Reynolds and M Turcsányi-Szabó (eds), *Key Competencies in the Knowledge Society* (Berlin/Heidelberg: Springer Verlag) 210–221.

Lemke, J (1990): *Talking Science – Language, Learning, and Values* (Westport CT: Ablex Publishing Corporation).

Norman, DA (1984). 'Worsening the Knowledge Gap – The Mystique of Computation Builds Unnecessary Barriers' in *Annals of the New York Academy of Sciences. Vol. 426* (New York, Blackwell Publishing).

Rincke, K (2010). 'Von der Alltagssprache zur Fachsprache – Bruch oder schrittweise Übergang?' in G Fenkart, A Lembens; E Erlacher-Zeitlinger (eds), *Sprache, Mathematik und Naturwissenschaften* (Innsbruck: StudienVerlag Ges.mbH).

Rincke, K (2011). 'It's Rather Like Learning a Language: Development of Talk and Conceptual Understanding in Mechanics Lessons' 33(2) *International Journal of Science Education* 229–258.

Selinker, L (1972). 'Interlanguage' 10 *International Review of Applied Linguistics*, 209–231.

Steffen, K (2006). 'Metaphern in der Informatik'. Available at: waste.informatik.hu-berlin.de/diplom/staatsexamensarbeiten/steffen.pdf

Vuorikari, R; Y Punie, S Carretero; L Van den Brande (2016). *DigComp 2.0: The Digital Competence Framework for Citizens – Update Phase 1: The Conceptual Reference Model.* (Luxembourg, Publication Office of the European Union).

Wagenschein, M (1976). *Rettet die phänomene* (Stuttgart: Klett).

Wagenschein, M (1980). *Naturphänomene sehen und verstehen* (Stuttgart: Klett).

16

Taxonomies and Competency Models

Peter Hubwieser and Sue Sentance

Chapter outline

Chapter synopsis

In this chapter, we compare two different methods used to describe the learning outcomes of students, learning objectives, including taxonomies and competencies. Traditionally, learning outcomes were described and monitored by the acquisition of certain knowledge elements or by the achievement of predefined learning objectives. During the last decade, mainly stimulated by the surprising results of the Programme for International Student Assessment (PISA) studies, the focus of the outcomes of school education has shifted – in some countries – towards target competencies. Competencies describe which 'real-world' problems or tasks students should be able to solve. Item response theory can be used in preference to classical testing approaches to assess competencies. Finally, the development of educational standards for regional or national assessment is described. To assure quality, such standards have to be based on properly defined competency models.

16.1 Introduction

In Chapter 11 we read about some techniques that an individual teacher can use to formatively assess progress in computer science. The question remains, how do we measure the learning summatively in a rigorous way? This relates not just to individual students and their progress, but to whole cohorts or even countries of students. Where we may use informal measures such as the average score on a test to measure the progress of our students, more rigorous methods can give us more accurate information. They also provide an alignment between educational goals and the instruction provided. This chapter addresses this issue by considering the current trend from learning outcomes to competencies, along with some statistical methods that are used to ensure accuracy and objectivity of this measurement.

Learning outcomes are assessed for many different purposes. For example, an individual teacher may want to assess his/her students to get feedback about the effectiveness of his/her lessons or to confer a certain qualification. Such an assessment could be performed either by a written or online test or by oral examinations. In these cases, one single teacher will examine a certain number of students that could range from one in the oral case up to hundreds in university examinations. A national school administration, several collaborating governments or even a community of many countries like the OECD[1] may want to compare the learning outcomes of their educational systems. In these cases, sometimes more than 100 people will assess a tremendous number of students, which sometimes (e.g. in the OECD PISA[2] surveys) reaches nearly 1 million. These assessment cases will differ in many respects. On the one hand, a single teacher assessing his/her students might be well informed about the learning content and teaching methods of the assessed lectures, which is unknown in large assessment projects like PISA. On the other hand, despite the very different scales of these cases, there are many common requirements. In particular, all tests and examinations should meet the basic three requirements *objectivity, reliability* and *validity*, as described by Adams nearly a century ago:

> When a test measures a function, simple or complex, as completely as possible, it is a valid measure of that function regardless of whether it measures with high or low accuracy ... Reliability ... is associated fundamentally with absence of systematic errors. ... When test and retest measure the same function twice, then the test is reliable ... Objectivity exists only when all errors of measurement are random. With the advent of correlated errors, subjectivity appears.
>
> Adams, 1936: 348–49

In this chapter, we present some general aspects and methods for assessment in computer science education (CSE) which affect particularly the *construct validity* of the assessment outcome. Construct validation identifies the constructs that account for the way students' performance in test varies (Cronbach and Meehl, 1955). In education, the constructs to be assessed in most cases are learning outcomes: certain changes in the knowledge and behaviour of students. Until the 1960s, learning outcomes were regarded predominantly as an increase of knowledge. Triggered by the modernization of education systems in the 1970s (see Robinsohn, 1967) and acknowledging

---

[1] Organisation for Economic Co-operation and Development.
[2] Programme for International Student Assessment.

that no learning progress can be observed without changes in behaviour, learning achievements were defined and measured mostly in terms of learning objectives.

During the last decade, mainly stimulated by the PISA of the OECD, the intended outcomes of learning are increasingly defined by target competencies as defined by Weinert (1999). These two paradigms rely on very different educational and psychological approaches and in consequence, show many differences. The most important might be that competencies must be very strictly based on empirical research (Klieme et al., 2004), while learning objectives tend to be set by educators according to personal beliefs or assumptions. In terms of the cognitive structure and the aspiration level of learning outcomes, learning objectives are usually organized by general, subject-independent taxonomies, while domain specific competency models are applied in the second case (Leutner, Hartig and Jude, 2008). The staistical approaches used are very different. In the case of learning objectives, the Classical Test Theory is usually applied, while competencies are measured using Item Response Theory (Hartig, Klieme and Leutner, 2008).

In CSE, many publications have focused on the suitability of learning object taxonomies (e.g. those of Anderson-Krathwohl (Anderson and Krathwohl, 2001) or Biggs (Biggs and Collis, 1982)). There have been some attempts to design specific taxonomies for CSE (Fuller et al., 2007, Meerbaum-Salant, Armoni and Ben-Ari, 2010). However, the paradigm shift from learning objectives to competencies has only just started. Only a few research projects have investigated the cognitive structure of competencies (e.g. the large German MoKoM project (Neugebauer, Magenheim, Ohrndorf, Schaper and Schubert, 2015)). Some recent progress has been made in the definition of competency models for programming (Kramer, Hubwieser and Brinda, 2016).

16.2 Learning objectives and taxonomies

The application of learning objectives in education has a long and complicated history, starting with Mager (1961). We can define a learning objective as 'a statement that tells what learners should be able to do when they have completed a segment of instruction' (Smith and Ragan, 2005: 969).

Key concept: Learning objectives

Learning objectives describe the goals that educators aim to achieve in terms of the learning progress of their students. Learning objectives may be located on very different abstraction levels. On the highest level, global objectives give the overall goals of education (e.g. the ability to act in a responsible way in the digital society). On an intermediate level, educational objectives describe the goals of some weeks or months of teaching, like 'being able to implement class diagrams in an imperative programming language'. On the most concrete level, instructional objectives detail the intended learning progress during some few lessons, e.g. 'to be able to combine different control structures to simple'. Usually, instructional objectives are formulated as combinations of a certain knowledge element and a description of observable behaviour (e.g. 'being able to implement variables'). To provide structure, learning objectives are classified by Learning Taxonomies (e.g. the Blooms Revised Taxonomy).

Bloom's taxonomy and its revision (by Anderson and Krathwohl)

The structure and hierarchy of learning objectives is described by category systems that are usually called 'taxonomies' in this context. The most famous taxonomy of learning objectives was presented by Bloom in 1956 (Bloom, 1956). Firstly, he separated three domains of objectives:

- Cognitive: mental skills (knowledge)
- Affective: growth in feelings or emotional areas (attitude or self)
- Psychomotor: manual or physical skills (skills).

Secondly, he presented a hierarchy of six levels for the cognitive domains:

1 *Knowledge*: Student recalls or recognizes information, ideas and principles in the approximate form in which they were learned.
2 *Comprehension*: Student translates, comprehends or interprets information based on prior learning.
3 *Application*: Student selects, transfers and uses data and principles to complete a problem or task with a minimum of direction.
4 *Analysis*: Student distinguishes, classifies and relates the assumptions, hypotheses, evidence or structure of a statement or question.
5 *Synthesis*: Student originates, integrates and combines ideas into a product, plan or proposal that is new to him or her.
6 *Evaluation*: Student appraises, assesses or critiques on a basis of specific standards and criteria.

Bloom's taxonomy has been widely accepted and applied in schools. Based on their experience with this taxonomy, Anderson and Krathwohl adopted it to a more outcome-focused modern education approach (Anderson and Krathwohl, 2001). They split the originally one-dimensional hierarchy into two dimensions, regarding a learning objective as a paired combination of (1) a certain type of *knowledge* and (2) an observable *behaviour* (called cognitive process). For the first dimension, the knowledge was portioned into four categories. The levels on the behaviour dimension were derived from Bloom's original taxonomy by switching from nouns to active verbs, reversing and renaming several levels. The result was the well-known 'Blooms Revised' taxonomy:

Table 16.1 The revised Bloom's taxonomy (Anderson and Krathwohl, 2001)

Knowledge	Cognitive process					
	Remember	**Understand**	**Apply**	**Analyse**	**Evaluate**	**Create**
Factual						
Conceptual						
Procedural						
Metacognitive						

Table 16.2 International comparison of key CS learning objectives (Hubwieser et al., 2015)

Global objective	Addressed by
Digital literacy (including use and handling of tools)	FI, USA, BY, KO, RUS, UK, SW, IN, IT, NRW, NZ
Computational thinking (including algorithmic and logical thinking)	FR, FI, USA, IS, RUS, UK, KO, SW, IN
Problem solving	NRW, USA, IS, KO, RUS, UK, SW, IN
Understanding of basic concepts of CS and IT	NZ, BY, IS, KO, SW, IN, FR, IT
Career preparation and choice	NRW, SW, BY, IN, FR, IT, KO
Support awareness of social, ethical, legal and privacy issues and impact of CS	NRW, KO, FR, RUS, UK, SW, NZ
General education to participate in society responsibly	NRW, BY, KO, SW, IN, RUS,
Prepare for university	NRW, KO, SW, IN

To describe the specificity of learning objectives, Anderson and Krathwohl proposed three levels (Anderson and Krathwohl, 2001):

- *global* objectives: 'complex, multifaceted learning outcomes that require substantial time and instruction to accomplish';
- *educational* objectives: 'derived from global objectives by breaking them down into more focused, delimited form';
- *instructional* objectives, 'focus teaching and testing on narrow, day-today slices of learning in fairly specific content areas'.

We will refer to this taxonomy from here on as AK. As examples of global objectives, we could take the most frequently addressed goals of CSE in K-12 according to the findings of a recent working group (Hubwieser et al., 2015). The group identified eight global objectives that were found in more than three of the analysed country reports on CSE in K-12 (see Table 16.2).

Obviously, the terms that describe educational objectives are often quite close to descriptions of potential competencies.

Example: Learning objectives and outcomes

Learning objectives may be phrased in terms of 'explain', 'program', 'design' and other 'doing' words. For example, over a period of time, you may want students to learn one or more of the following, which may be made more specific depending on the age group you are working with:

- to be able to program a type of search or sort
- to evaluate alternative models in order to choose one of them
- to write an algorithmic solution for a problem
- to explain and execute algorithms
- to exemplify how 2-D data structures can be implemented.

Taking the last example, working with 2-D data structures, a task can be designed to measure this understanding (e.g. to write a program to allow users to enter data into a one-week timetable for a school). Completing the task successfully would demonstrate that the learning objective had been achieved: breaking the task down into sub-tasks (designing the data structure, writing an algorithm to populate it, initializing the data structure, and implementing the program) would give concrete learning outcomes from the task that could indicate the level of student performance. We will see later in the chapter that specifying learning objectives in this way can be problematic.

Pre-requisites

For students to write a simple object-orientated program that simulates a traffic light they would need to meet the following learning objectives:

- Understand a class definition
- Apply a for-loop
- Be able to implement a certain mathematical formula.

However, in many cases it is impossible to achieve a set of instructional objectives in any arbitrary order, because some of them have to be learned before certain others can be reached. For example, one has to *understand* the concept of *object* (O1) before one is able to *understand* the concept of *class* (O2). This connection can be described by a *prerequisite relation* on the set of learning objectives, in this case between O1 and O2: 'O1 *is prerequisite of* O2', meaning that 'O1 has to be achieved before O2' (see Hubwieser, 2007; Hubwieser, 2008). Closer considerations show that there are (at least) two different types of prerequisite relations:

1 'Hard' pre-requisites forced by a substantial or logical dependency: in other words concept2 contained in objective O2 *is based on* concept1 contained in objective O1. This means that it is not possible to understand concept2 without having understood concept1.
2 'Soft' pre-requisites suggested by didactical deliberations: it is necessary to reach objective O1 in order to apply teaching or working methods that support didactical principles. Therefore it is not *necessary* to reach O1 before objective O2, but it is *advisable* in order to ease or to improve the learning process towards O2.

Nevertheless, in many cases it is not easy to describe lessons by instructional objectives, primarily for two reasons:

- there are huge numbers of objectives; and/or
- there are many relations between these objectives.

The SOLO taxonomy

Following a totally different approach, Biggs proposed his SOLO taxonomy (Biggs and Collis, 1982). Based on his theory of meaningful learning, he put more emphasis on the learner and the actual learning outcome, instead of the learning material. In Table 16.3, *capacity* 'refers to the

Table 16.3 The SOLO taxonomy (Biggs and Collins, 1982: 24–25)

SOLO Level	Capacity	Relating operation
Prestructural	Minimal: Cue and response confused	Denial, tautology, transduction. Bound to specifics
Unistructural	Low: Cue and one relevant datum	Can 'generalize' only in terms of one aspect
Multistructural	Medium: Cue and isolated relevant data	Can 'generalize' only in terms of a few limited and independent aspects
Relational	High: Cue and relevant data and interrelations	Induction: Can generalize within given or experienced context using related aspects
Extended Abstract	Maximal: Cue and relevant data and interrelations and hypotheses	Deduction and induction. Can generalize to situations not experienced

amount of working memory, or attention span, that the different levels of SOLO require' (Biggs and Collis, 1982: 26). The relating operation refers to 'the way in which the cue and response interrelate'. Additionally, there is an attribute of 'Consistency and closure', referring to the felt need of the learner to come to a conclusion that is consistent with the data and other possible conclusions, which increases with the levels of the taxonomy (pp. 27–28).

Taxonomies for computer science

So far, we have looked at taxonomies in general: What about for computer science?

The SOLO taxonomy was applied to programming education by Hawkins and Hedberg (1986), who proposed different programming patterns of novices that correspond to the original categories of Biggs and Collis (1982), using as an example the task of drawing simple shapes as circles or rectangles. He associated:

- Pre-structural response: Immediate mode, commands are applied by trial and error, until the result is acceptable.
- Unistructural response: Immediate mode, the commands are entered in a planned and deliberated sequence.
- Multistructural response: Programming mode, structured sequences.
- Relational response: Functions are defined and control structures are used. Code is reused.
- Extended Abstract response: Parametrized functions.

More recently, a group of researchers investigated the fit of different taxonomies (Bloom, AK and SOLO) to the specific needs of computer science (Fuller et al., 2007). The group found that some concepts and structures of these taxonomies were difficult to transfer to CS, in particular, that *understand* and *apply* have specific meaning and an unclear hierarchical position in this domain. In summary, the group recommended the use of the AK taxonomy, but proposed a change of structure. The group suggested that the cognitive process dimension be split into two sub-dimensions: *Interpreting* and *Producing*. The latter represents the more active part of the learning process (e.g. all programming activities) and contains the levels *none*, *apply* and *create*. The remaining activities of the cognitive process dimension are arranged on the *interpreting* sub-dimension.

Table 16.4 Taxonomy for computer science education (Fuller et al., 2007)

Interpreting Producing	Remember	Understand	Analyse	Evaluate
None				
Apply				
Create				

Enabled by the division in sub-dimensions, it would be possible to express different levels of applying or creating by this way. For example, a programming concept like a repetition loop could be applied without any understanding on the lowest level or by considering aspects of efficiency on the highest level *Evaluate*.

Another attempt to propose a taxonomy for computer science was published in 2010 (Meerbaum-Salant et al., 2010). Here, a combination of the SOLO and the AK taxonomies was proposed based on their evaluation of a Scratch programming course. Looking for categories that were suitable for their specific context, they merged the AK categories Remember and Understand and subdivided levels 3 and 4 of Biggs according to AK levels:

1 Multistructural – Understanding.
2 Multistructural – Applying.
3 Relational – Applying.
4 Relational – Creating.

Limitations of learning objectives

Irrespective of their usefulness for specific purposes, the use of learning objectives has fallen into disrepute during the last decades. One of the reasons might be found in the suspicion that by elaborating a sequence of fine granular objectives for their lessons, teachers might be tempted to restrict the learning process of their students to a very tightly defined sequence (see Duffy and Jonassen, 1992). It might be suggested that teachers should restrict the use of learning objectives to purposes where these are really helpful, for example:

- To identify (one or more) possible learning paths through a specific subject area that is very complicated, very broad or very difficult.
- To arrange a set of concepts sequentially forced by certain circumstances, (e.g. to write a textbook).
- To design an assessment or examination which has to take into consideration which learning progress the students have made up to its point of time.

However, despite all reservations against them, there still is a strong need for learning objectives under certain circumstances. Without these didactical tools, we would struggle to measure progress. As a compromise for the practising teacher we suggest providing only the key learning objectives for each lesson to describe, communicate and evaluate the learning processes.

Example activity: Formulating and testing instructional objectives

Describe what your students are intended to learn during the next lesson. For this purpose, pick the 2–3 concepts of computer science that are most important for this lesson and combine them with descriptions of behaviour that you expect your students to be able to perform after the lesson. Examples may be 'explain the role of the IP address for the transfer of e-mails' or 'program quick sort in Java'. Having the learning goals formulated, design a test task for each of these goals. Write an exemplary solution of these tasks and mark where the intended learning objectives are applied in this solution.

16.3 Competencies

Driven by the upsetting results of the first large-scale studies of learning outcomes such as TIMSS (Trends in International Mathematics and Science Study, see (Mullis, Martin and Loveless, 2016)) and PISA during the first years of this century, the focus of education has shifted broadly from knowledge and learning outcomes towards competencies.

Unfortunately, the terms 'competence' and 'competency' are used in a manifold of senses, ranging from the popular understanding 'something that a person is able to do' to sophisticated definitions from the field of educational psychology. Additionally, there is no consistent differentiation between the terms *competence* and *competency* (Rychen, 2003). Dörge (2010) compared the different backgrounds and use of the terms *competency, skills* and *qualification* in the German and the English language area and found considerable differences.

Here we draw on the well-known definition of Weinert (2001), who defined competencies as 'the cognitive abilities and skills possessed by or able to be learned by individuals that enable them to solve particular problems, as well as the motivational, volitional and social readiness and capacity to use the solutions successfully and responsibly in variable situations' (pp. 27–28). Furthermore, Weinert stressed that competencies may be composed of several facets: ability, knowledge, understanding, skills, action, experience and motivation. It is clear that the combination of these different elements – cognitive ability and skill, motivation and readiness, and capacity to use – make competencies much more wide-ranging and complex than learning objectives, but give us the potential to describe and assess our subject in a more comprehensive way. Thus, the development of competencies is very relevant to teachers and a competency model can ensure more effective assessment.

Competency models

The main purpose of competency research is to define intended learning outcomes of educational processes, as required by the 'customers' of these processes. Obviously, there is a strong need to measure these outcomes to evaluate the educational processes. To align learning and teaching processes and measure their success, these 'target' competencies must be defined and structured properly by suitable empirically validated competency models. For this purpose, different kinds of models are used (Klieme et al., 2004), which may focus on the structure, the different hierarchical levels or the development of the relevant competencies (Hartig, Klieme and Leutner, 2008). As regards the definition and measurement of competency models, much groundbreaking work was done in the context of the PISA studies (e.g. Seidel and Prenzel, 2008, OECD, 2013).

Klieme et al. (2004) describe three types of competency models:

- Competency *Structure* models, usually structured by dimensions (e.g. competency areas or competency characteristics) describing the cognitive dispositions that learning individuals need to solve tasks and problems in a specific content or requirement area.
- Competency *Level* models, giving information about the levels or profiles of the described competencies.
- Competency *Development* models aiming to describe, how competencies will develop over time.

Level or development models usually have to be based on structure models. As a suitable framework for the development of subject domain-specific competency models, the OECD has presented 'The Definition and Selection of Key Competencies (DeSeCo)' (Rychen, 2003).

Key concept: Competencies

Compared to learning objectives, competencies describe learning outcomes from the viewpoint of the 'customers' of educational institutions (e.g. the IT industry or universities). A competency depicts a quite complex disposal of behaviour that can be applied to solve a certain task or problem that is relevant in 'real' life (e.g. the 'ability to program a robot to move through a labyrinth').

Competencies are arranged in competency model, which come in three types as structure, level and development models.

In CSE, the development process of competency models is just beginning. As far as we know, the only serious attempt until now that could cope with the standards of PISA was the MoKoM project (see Magenheim et al., 2010; Schubert and Stechert, 2010; Neugebauer et al., 2014). The scope of MoKoM was very broad, covering the four dimensions:

- System application
- System comprehension
- System development and
- Dealing with system complexity.

The project aimed to develop an empirically-based competency model in the context of informatics in school. The work had started with a theory-driven model that was enriched through empirical data. In addition, the MoKoM-project aims to develop 'test instruments that are appropriate for competence measurement and design, and the evaluation of learning environments that have been proven to be of high quality through competence measurement' (Schubert and Stechert, 2010).

Example: A competency model for object-orientated programming

Object-orientated programming (OOP) is usually introduced in upper secondary school or senior high school. A competency model for OOP has been proposed as follows:

1 OOP knowledge and skills
1.1 Data structure (graph, tree, array)
1.2 Class and object structure (object, attribute, association)
1.3 Algorithmic structure (loops, conditional statement)
1.4 Notional machine (data, working memory, processor, statement, program, automaton)
2 Mastering representation (language defined by syntax and semantics)
3 Cognitive Process
3.1 Problem solving stage (understanding the problem, determine how to solve the problem, translating the problem into a computer language program, testing and debugging the program)
3.2 Cognitive Process Type (Interpreting, Producing).

This proposal is based on an extensive literature study on competency models of different subject areas. So far, it has been validated through several surveys among researchers, teachers, and students (Kramer, Hubwieser and Brinda, 2016).

Measuring competencies

Due to their complex structure, it is apparent that the definition and the measurement of competencies are not an easy matter. According to Klieme et al. (2004), competence can only be assessed and measured in terms of performance and can be seen as an ability to deal with a task or particular situation. This means that concrete situations need to be presented to illustrate or assess a competence. In addition, Klieme et al. stress that one performance only does not indicate a competency. They refer to a 'spectrum of performance' and require that assessment should be broad and involve a range of tests to measure competence. This also means that the assessment is not just reflecting shallow and factual knowledge.

Obviously, we need to be convinced that the range of tests or tasks do actually focus on the competency that is being measured. In classical test theory we can do this by using a measure called internal consistency; this is calculated using a statistical test called Cronbach's Alpha Coefficient (Cronbach, 1951). The common rule of thumb for internal consistency is 'excellent' for $\alpha \geq 0.9$, 'good' for ≥ 0.8 and acceptable for $\alpha \geq 0.7$. This can be used to ensure that a test is reliable when testing learning outcomes, but a different type of statistical approach is needed for competencies. This is discussed in the next section.

Item demands and abilities

To assess competencies, we need to design suitable test instruments. A test in this context is a set of tasks, which themselves comprise one or more items. For example, a typical multiple-choice question will represent one task with a textual description and several possible answers to check. Each of these answers represents a dichotomous item in this case. In other cases, for example if the result of a certain formula has to be calculated and responded as an open answer, this task represents one item only. Whether the task is open or closed, each item requires certain skills or abilities, and these are known as the 'item demands'.

The item demands correspond roughly with instructional objectives in the sense of Anderson and Krathwohl (2001). As an example, imagine a test consisting of six tasks with open response format (e.g. submitting program code) that was designed to measure the (potential) competency 'being able to manage a sequence of data by implementing linked lists and their basic operations' (see Kramer et al., 2016). One of the tasks (representing one item) could be 'define a Java class that implements a linked list'. Then, among others, this task would have the following item demands:

(a) being able to write a class definition in Java
(b) being able to define methods in a Java class definition and
(c) being able to write a constructor for Java classes.

This competency definition meets the definition of educational objectives (see Anderson and Krathwohl, 2001): '... derived from global objectives by breaking them down into more focused, delimited form', p. 15). The intended global objective could be 'being able to manage write computer programs that store and process structured information'. Obviously, the item demands could be *instructional* objectives ('focus teaching and testing on narrow, day-today slices of learning in fairly specific content areas' (Anderson and Krathwohl, 2001: 16)).

Consider an example shown in Figure 16.1. If several items (e.g. Items 1, 2 versus Item 3 in Figure 16.1) differ in their demands, two types of differences have to be decided (see Hartig, 2008):

(1) The items differ in difficulty (e.g. in the empirical solution frequencies (case 1)).
(2) The items differ in relations between responses (i.e. correlations between scores for different items (case 2)).

Figure 16.1 demonstrates how the difficulty of an item can be identified. Case 1 shows equal correlations with different difficulty level, whereas case 2 shows different correlations with equal difficulties. In case 1, all three items have equally high correlations between each other. Items 1 and 2 are equally difficult, but item 3 is more difficult. This finding could mean that the ability to master the task demand (c) highly correlates with the ability to master demands (a) and (b) and can be regarded as the 'same ability' for measurement purposes, which has to be developed to a higher degree to master task demand (c).

In case 2, items 1 and 2 have a high positive correlation. However, the correlations of item 3 with items 1 and 2 are substantially lower than the correlation between items 1 and 2. In this case, an additional ability dimension would be needed to explain the specific variation caused by the

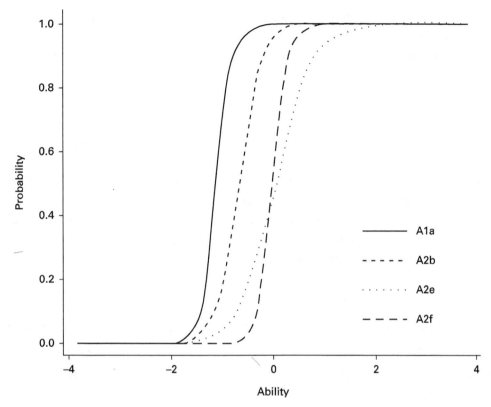

Figure 16.1 Differences in item demands

additional demand (c) of item 3. This could be regarded as a 'different ability' which is required to master item 3.

A third possibility would be that the task demand has no observable effect at all – items 1, 2 and 3 could turn out to be equally difficult and to have equal correlations among each other. In this case, the task demand would appear to be irrelevant for observable test performance.

In our linked-list example above, items 1 and 2 could require the demand (a) and (b), while only item 3 demands the implementation of a constructor (c). Then, case 1 would indicate that the implementation of a constructor is more difficult compared to (a) and (b), but nevertheless belongs to the same competency 'implementing a linked list'. In contrast, case 2 would require a separate competency dimension for implementing constructors.

Item response theory

Item Response Theory (IRT) is a way to analyse responses to tests or questionnaires with the goal of improving reliability and validity. It is a technique to ensure that the tests measure what they are supposed to measure (see Rasch, 1960). In terms of competencies, IRT is the current 'state of the art'. While in Classical Test Theory, the psychometric construct of interest (in our case a certain competency) is considered to be measured directly by item scores, IRT considers this construct as latent and not directly measurable.

Instead, the probability of correct answers on a certain item depends on the competency in a certain way:

$$P(X_{ik} = 1 \mid \theta_i, \beta_k) = f(\theta_i, \beta_k) \tag{1}$$

Here θ_i is the *ability parameter* of person i, representing his/her level of competency β_k the *difficulty parameter* of Item k, and $f(\theta_i, \beta_k)$ a certain function that is determined by the *psychometric model* (e.g. the *Rasch Model*, see below) that is assumed to fit the observations. In most cases, these parameters have to be estimated by effortful numerical calculations. Depending on the structure of the psychometric constructs that are to be measured, several different models may be applied (e.g. *unidimensional* models that cover only one single competency or, alternatively, *multidimensional* models). One of the simplest and most widely used models is the basic unidimensional *Rasch Model (RM)* with one psychometrical factor and one parameter (1F1P):

$$P(X_{ik} = 1 \mid \theta_i, \beta_k) = \frac{\exp(\theta_i - \beta_k)}{1 + \exp(\theta_i - \beta_k)} \tag{2}$$

Due to its restriction on one factor and one parameter, the application of the RM requires three preconditions that have to be met:

1 *Homogeneity* of items: This means that all items must measure the same psychometric construct. In this case, we can call this set of items *homogenous*.
2 *Local stochastic independence*: the underlying psychometric construct is the only coupling factor between items.
3 *Specific objectivity*: for all samples from the population, the item parameters are independent of the specific person sample; the same holds for all samples of items and person parameters.

Provided that this model is applicable, some very convenient simplifications can be made. For example, the sum of the scores of all individual items is a sufficient statistic, which means that the (estimated) person parameter depends only on the *total number* of correct answers given by this person. It does not matter, *which* items the person has responded to correctly.

Key concept: Item response theory

While the Classical Test Theory assumes that the constructs of interest (e.g. motivation or intelligence) can be measured more or less directly with some errors, Item Response Theory (IRT) aims to give mathematical dependencies between the personal level of the constructs of interests (e.g. the level of competency) and the probability to solve a certain item. Thus it takes both the difficulty of the item and the proficiency of the student into account.

The graph of this function looks as displayed in Figure 16.2 for four different values of β ('Ability'). These graphs are called *Item Characteristic Curves* (ICCs).

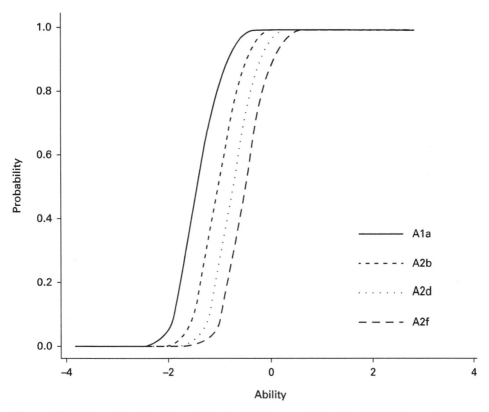

Figure 16.2 Example of an item-characteristic curve of the Rasch Model

If the difficulty (β) varies, the ICC shifts horizontally. This demonstrates a rather convenient advantage of IRT: that person and item parameters are located on the same scale. Thus, they can be directly compared to allow statements like 'the probability for a person x to solve item y is greater than 0.5 if $\theta_x > \beta_y$'.

Obviously, there might be cases where ICCs have different slopes. If so, we cannot model this situation using RM. Another model which can be used in this case is the Birnbaum Model (BM), which has an additional parameter called *Discrimination* δ_k. (Birnbaum, 1968). In the Birnbaum Model there is:

$$P(X_{ik} = 1 | \theta_i, \beta_k, \delta_k) = \frac{\exp(\delta_k(\theta_i - \beta_k))}{1 + \exp[\![(\delta)]\!]_k(\theta_i - \beta_k))} \tag{3}$$

Figure 16.3 displays the ICCs of another (real existing) item set that varies in difficulty (horizontal position) β as well as in discrimination (slope) β. As the ICCs of item A2e and A2f in Figure 16.3 demonstrate, the variation of slope can cause intersections of ICCs. This would mean that the difficulty order of the regarded items depends on the person parameter, which would violate the requirement of specific objectivity (see above). The reason for this effect might be that the answers on these items might be influenced by other factors than the construct to be measured. On the other hand, low variation of slopes and missing intersections of a certain set of items in the BM can be regarded as a good indicator that the RM is applicable on this set.

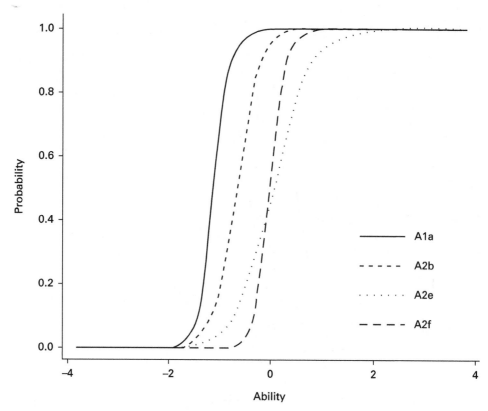

Figure 16.3 Example of an item-characteristic curve using the two-parameter Birnbaum Model

In the case that there is more than one psychometric construct to be measured, multidimensional models have to be applied. To read more about these we recommend Rost and Carstensen's original paper (Rost and Carstensen, 2002).

Factor analysis of dichotomous data

To investigate the homogeneity of a set of items, classical explorative factor analysis is applied traditionally. Yet, as the score format in competency measurement is often dichotomous (because things get much more complicated otherwise) this is not applicable. Latent trait analysis (LTA) offers a better alternative (Bartholomew, Steel, Moustaki and Galbrath, 2008).

With LTA, it is assumed that the responses of the students to a given set of items can be described by a certain psychometric model (e.g. by the *Rasch Model*). Under this assumption, one can estimate all person and item parameters based on the scoring matrix of the responses. Using the estimated values of the parameters, by calculating the probability P in equation (1) of section II.E, the expected number of occurrences $E(r)$ of all possible response patterns r (e.g. 01101 in the case of five items) can be calculated. For p dichotomous items, we have 2^p response patterns (i.e. combinations of 0s and 1s with the length p). For each pattern r, its expected frequency $E(r)$ is compared to the actually observed pattern frequency $O(r)$. For the differences, the log-likelihood test statistic G^2 and the common X^2 statistic are calculated that both describe the differences of the expected and the measured values. As both statistics are approximately X^2 distributed, we could estimate the goodness of fit of the applied Rasch Model. The precondition for this calculation is a sufficient number of datasets, which assures that the frequency of each pattern has an expectation value of at least 5 (Bartholomew et al., 2008).

Rasch Model tests

In addition to LTA, a set of standard tests for the fit of the chosen psychometric model (e.g. the Rasch Model) are often applied. These standard tests for specific objectivity (remember that objectivity is one of the goals in improving summative assessment) are used to check that the model would produce the same results for different groups of participants. They use the idea of a splitting criteria to split participants into groups and test that the results fit for each group. Examples of three tests that can be used are as follows:

- *Likelihood-Ratio-Test* (Andersen, 1973) with the splitting criteria *median* (respectively *mean)*, values of *combination score* and *gender* on the level of the total item set.
- *Martin-Löf-Test* (Martin-Löf, 1974) with the splitting criterion *median* (respectively *mean)* on the level of the total item set.
- *Wald-Test* (Wald, 1943) with the splitting criteria *median* (respectively *mean)* and gender on the level of single items.

These tests can be carried out using a statistical package such as R; we do not have space to explore these any further here.

16.4 Educational standards

Educational standards are sets of competencies depicted in detail that were decided by educational authorities to be the minimal or average learning outcomes of educational institutions (e.g. some algebraic competencies that should be achieved by all Year 9s of regional grammar schools). In an influential paper on the development of national educational standards, Klieme et al. state:

> Educational standards, as conceived of in this report, draw on general educational goals. They specify the competencies that schools must impart to their students in order to achieve certain key educational goals, and the competencies that children or teenagers are expected to have acquired by a particular grade. These competencies are described in such specific terms that they can be translated into particular tasks and, in principle, assessed by tests (Klieme et al., 2004: 15).

In computer science, a lot of work has to be done until our domain is ready for the definition of standard in this sense; CS runs far behind traditional subjects like mathematics. The *Principles and Standards of the National Council of Teachers of Mathematics* (National Council of Teachers of

Mathematics (NCTM), 2000), are the best-known and most influential example internationally. They describe framework conditions for instruction on all grade levels, from the beginning of primary education to the end of secondary schooling and provide guidelines for improving mathematics teaching by moving towards comprehension- and problem-based instruction. In particular the NCTM presents a definition of *problem solving* that might be transferred to CSE as well: 'Problem solving means engaging in a task for which the solution method is not known in advance. In order to find a solution, students must draw on their knowledge, and through this process, they will often develop new mathematical understandings. Solving problems is not only a goal of learning mathematics, but also a major means of doing so' (NCTM, 2000: 52).

Some proposals for educational standards in informatics have been published in Austria (Dorninger, 2005) and from the German *Gesellschaft für Informatik* (GI) (Gesellschaft für Informatik e V, 2008).

Recently the CSTA Standards Task Force presented its K-12 Computer Science Standards (Revised 2011) in a draft version (Seehorn et al., 31 March 2011). These standards may be comprised by the subcategory *standards* (of the category *intentions* in the DM). It defines three levels for the learning outcomes, where the highest is divided into three discrete 'courses':

- level 1 (recommended for grades K–6): Computer science and me
- level 2 (recommended for grades 6–9): Computer science and community
- level 3 (recommended for grades 9–12): Applying concepts and creating real-world solutions
- level 3A (recommended for grades 9 or 10): Computer science in the modern world
- level 3B: (recommended for grades 10 or 11): Computer science principles
- level 3C: (recommended for grades 11 or 12): Topics in computer science.

To avoid the perception that CSE should focus exclusively on programming, five complementary and essential strands throughout all three levels are distinguished:

- computational thinking
- collaboration
- computing practice
- computers and communication devices and
- community, global and ethical impacts.

These strands are further illustrated by lists of competencies that represent the proposed standards. Additionally the draft paper also offers a variety of activities, assigned to the levels and strands, respectively that show in detail what classroom teaching might look like.

16.5 Summary

In this chapter we have considered some quite challenging questions relating to how we can be sure we test and measure students' learning accurately and objectively. This is a complex field which needs to be addressed within CSE, although the development of standards and competencies is still in the early stages of development. The change to a competency approach has been driven partly by PISA, an international assessment measure by which the achievements of young people in different countries can be compared. However, even at a local level, it is important to have an understanding of the potential inaccuracies of traditional testing methods and new methods for ameliorating the situation.

Key points

- In the area of summative assessment, there is a move from defining and measuring learning outcomes to being able to specify more broad-ranging competencies.
- Previously, learning outcomes have been categorized through the use of taxonomies such as Bloom's, the revised Bloom's taxonomy by Anderson and Krathwohl and the SOLO taxonomy.
- Competencies describe learning outcomes from the viewpoint of the 'customers' of educational institutions.
- More rigorous methods for measuring test results can give us accurate information. Item Response Theory (IRT) is starting to replace classical test theory as a method by which tests can be evaluated for reliability and validity.
- Educational standards are sets of competencies that explain in detail the minimal or average learning outcomes of educational institutions, regions or countries.

Further reflection

- Consider how students in your country participate in summative assessments, at the national, regional or school level. To what extent are the measurements of student performance in computer science reliable, valid and objective?
- Consider the educational standards in your country for CSE in schools. How are these made explicit to teachers and students?

References

Adams, HF (1936). 'Validity, Reliability and Objectivity' 47(2) *Psychological Monographs* 329–350.

Andersen, EB (1973). 'A Goodness of Fit Test for the Rasch Model' 38(1) *Psychometrika* 123–140.

Anderson, LW and DR Krathwohl (2001) *A Taxonomy for Learning, Teaching, and Assessing: A Revision of Bloom's Taxonomy of Educational Objectives* Abridged edn (New York, Longman). Available at: wwwgbvde/dms/bowker/toc/9780321084057pdf

Bartholomew, DJ, F Steel, I Moustaki and JI Galbrath (2008). *Analysis of Multivariate Social Science Data* (2nd edn) Chapman and Hall/*CRC statistics in the Social and Behavioral Sciences Series* (Boca Raton Fl, CRC Press/Taylor & Francis).

Biggs, JB and KF Collins (1982). *Evaluating the Quality of Learning: The SOLO Taxonomy; Structure of the Observed Learning Outcome Educational Psychology Series* (New York, Academic Press).

Birnbaum, A (1968). 'Some Latent Trait Models and Their Use in Inferring an Examinee's Ability' in FM Lord, MR Novick and A Birnbaum (eds), *Statistical Theories of Mental Test Scores* (Reading, MA, Addison-Wesley) 395–479.

Bloom, BS (1956). *Taxonomy of Educational Objectives: The Classification of Educational Goals* (New York, David Mackay Company Inc). Available at: wwwworldcatorg/oclc/277182491.

Cronbach, LJ (1951). 'Coefficient Alpha and the Internal Structure of Tests' *16*(3) *Psychometrika* 297–334.

Cronbach, LJ and PE Meehl (1955). 'Construct Validity in Psychological Tests' 52 *Psychological Bulletin* 281–302.

Dörge, C (2010). 'Competencies and Skills: Filling Old Skins with New Wine' in *Key Competencies in the Knowledge Society* (Berlin, Springer) 78–89.

Dorninger, C (2005). 'Educational Standards in School Informatics in Austria' in RT Mittermeir (ed), *Lecture Notes in Computer Science: From Computer Literacy to Informatics Fundamentals* (Berlin, Springer) 65–69.

Duffy, TM and DH Jonassen (1992). *Constructivism and the Technology of Instruction: A Conversation* (Hillsdale, NJ: Lawrence Erlbaum Associates) Available at: wwwlocgov/catdir/enhancements/fy0745/92022781-dhtml

Fuller, U, CG Johnson, T Ahoniemi, D Cukierman, I Hernán-Losada, J Jackova, E Lahtinen, TL Lewis, D McGee, CR Thompson, E Thompson (2007). 'Developing a Computer Science-specific Learning Taxonomy' 39(4) *SIGCSE Bulletin* 152–170.

Gesellschaft für Informatik e V (ed), (2008). Grundsätze und Standards für die Informatik in der Schule Bildungsstandards Informatik für die Sekundarstufe I: Empfehlungen der Gesellschaft für Informatik e V, erarbeitet vom Arbeitskreis (Bonn, Bildungsstandards).

Hartig, J (2008). 'Psychometric Models for the Assessment of Competencies' in J Hartig, E Klieme and D Leutner (eds), *Assessment of Competencies in Educational Contexts* (Toronto: Hogrefe & Huber Publishers) 69–90.

Hartig, J, E Klieme and D Leutner (eds), (2008). *Assessment of Competencies in Educational Contexts* (Toronto, Hogrefe & Huber Publishers).

Hawkins, W and JG Hedberg (1986). 'Evaluating LOGO: Use of the SOLO Taxonomy' 2(2) *Australian Journal of Educational Technology* 103–109.

Hubwieser, P (2007). 'A Smooth Way Towards Object-oriented Programming in Secondary Schools' in D Benzie and M Iding (eds), *Informatics, Mathematics and ICT: A Golden Triangle*, Proceedings of the Working Joint IFIP Conference: WG31 Secondary Education, WG35 Primary Education; College of Computer and Information Science, Northeastern University Boston, Massachusetts, USA. 27–29 June 2007.

Hubwieser, P (2008). 'Analysis of Learning Objectives in Object-oriented Programming' in R T Mittermeir and M M Syslo (eds), *Lecture Notes in Computer Science, Informatics Education – Supporting Computational Thinking*, Third International Conference on Informatics in Secondary Schools – Evolution and Perspectives, ISSEP 2008, Torun, Poland, 1–4 July 2008, 142–150.

Hubwieser, P, MN Giannakos, M Berges, T Brinda, I Diethelm, J Magenheim, P Yogendra, J Jackova and E Jasute (2015). 'A Global Snapshot of Computer Science Education in K–12 Schools' in ITICSE-WGR '15, *Proceedings of the 2015 ITiCSE on Working Group Reports* (New York, NY, ACM) (65–83).

Klieme, E (ed), (2004). *The Development of National Educational Standards: An Expertise* (Berlin, Bundesministerium für BildungundForschung).

Kramer, M, P Hubwieser and T Brinda (2016). 'A Competency Structure Model of Object-oriented Programming' in *International Conference on Learning and Teaching in Computing and Engineering (LaTICE)* IEEE Xplore Digital Library, 1–8.

Leutner, D, J Hartig and N Jude (2008). 'Measuring Competencies: Introduction to Concepts and Questions of Assessment in Education' in J Hartig, E Klieme and D Leutner (eds), *Assessment of Competencies in Educational Contexts* (Toronto, Hogrefe & Huber Publishers) 177–192.

Magenheim, J, W Nelles, T Rhode, N Schaper, SE Schubert and P Stechert (2010). 'Competencies for Informatics Systems and Modeling: Results of Qualitative Content Analysis of Expert Interviews' in *Education Engineering (EDUCON), 2010 IEEE*, 513–521.

Mager, RF (1961). *Preparing Objectives for Programmed Instruction* (San Francisco, Fearon Publishers).

Martin-Löf, P (1974). 'Exact Tests, Confidence Regions and Estimates in Memoirs' Vol 1 in *Proceedings of Conference on Foundational Questions in Statistical Inference* (Aarhus, 1973) 121–138.

Meerbaum-Salant, O, M Armonia and M Ben-Ari (2010). 'Learning Computer Science Concepts with Scratch in ACM' (ed), *ICER '10: Proceedings of the Sixth International Workshop on Computing Education Research* (New York, NY ACM) 69–76.

Mullis, IV, MO Martin and T Loveless (2016). '20 Years of TIMSS: International Trends in Mathematics and Science' Lynch School of Education, Boston College and International Association for the Evaluation of Educational Achievement (IEA): Achievement, Curriculum, and Instruction Boston, MA.

National Council of Teachers of Mathematics (2000). *Principles and Standards for School Mathematics* (Reston, VA).

Neugebauer, J, J Magenheim, L Ohrndorf, N Schaper and S Schubert (2015). 'Defining Proficiency Levels of High School Students in Computer Science by an Empirical Task Analysis'. Results of the MoKoM Project: Informatics in Schools Curricula, Competences, and Competitions: Proceedings in *8th International Conference on Informatics in Schools: Situation, Evolution, and Perspectives*, ISSEP 2015, Ljubljana, Slovenia, 28 September–1 October 2015, (New York, NY, Springer International Publishing) 45–56.

Neugebauer, J, P Hubwieser, J Magenheim, L Ohrndorf, N Schaper and S Schubert (2014). 'Measuring Student Competences in German Upper Secondary Computer Science Education' in Y Gülbahar nd E Karatas (eds), *Informatics in Schools Teaching and Learning Perspectives* (Heidelberg, New York, Springer) 100–111.

Organisation for Economic, Co-operation and Development (2013) Pisa 2012 'Results in Focus: What 15-year-olds know and what they can do with what they know' (Paris, OECD). Available at: wwwoecdorg/pisa/keyfindings/pisa–2012-results-overviewpdf

Rasch, G (1960). *Probabilistic Models for Some Intelligence and Attainment Tests Studies in Mathematical Psychology: Vol 1* (Copenhagen: Danmarks pædagogiske Institut).

Robinsohn, SB (1967). *Bildungsreform als Revision des Curriculum Aktuelle* (Pädagogik Neuwied aRh, Luchterhand).

Rost, J and CH Carstensen (2002). 'Multidimensional Rasch Measurement via Item Component Models and Faceted Designs' 26(1) *Applied Psychological Measurement* 42–56.

Rychen, DS (2003). 'Key Competencies for a Successful Life and a Well-functioning Society' (Toronto, Hogrefe & Huber Publishers).

Schubert, SE and P Stechert (2010). 'Competence Model Research on Informatics System Application' in IFIP (ed), *New Developments in ICT and Education Workshop of WG 31*, 28–30 June 2010, Amiens.

Seehorn, D, S Carey, B Fuschetto, I Lee, D Moix, D O'Grady-Cuniff and A Verno (2011). *CSTA K–12 Computer Science Standards: Revised 2011* (New York NY, Standards Task Force).

Seidel, T and M Prenzel (2008). 'Assessment in Large-Scale Studies' in J Hartig, E Klieme and D Leutner (eds), *Assessment of Competencies in Educational Contexts* (Toronto, Hogrefe and Huber Publishers) 279–304.

Smith, PL and TJ Ragan (2005). *Instructional Design* (3rd edn) (Hoboken, NJ, Wiley). Available at: wwwgbvde/dms/bowker/toc/9780471393535pdf

Wald, A (1943). 'Tests of Statistical Hypotheses Concerning Several Parameters When the Number of Observations Is Large' *Transactions of the American Mathematical Society*, 426–482.

Weinert, FE (1999). *Concepts of Competence: Definition and Selection of Competencies* (Elektronische Ressource (Sl), OFS).

Weinert, FE (2001). 'Concept of Competence: A Conceptual Clarification' in DS Rychen and L Salganik (eds), *Defining and Selecting Key Competencies* (Toronto, Hogrefe & Huber Publishers) 45–65.

Glossary

Algorithm A process for solving a problem or achieving an outcome, built from steps that a computational device can execute.

Binary representation Representing information on a computer using just two digits (usually written as 0 and 1).

Coding A loose term for computer programming (and when used more precisely, the part of programming that involves converting an algorithm or plan to a programming language); the word has other common meanings in computer science, including encryption coding, compression coding, channel coding, binary codes, markup language codes and more.

Competency A complex disposal of behaviour that can be applied to solve a certain task or problem that is relevant in 'real' live.

Computational thinking The thought processes involved in formulating a problem and expressing its solution in such a way that a computer could effectively carry it out.

Constructionism A form of constructivism that emphasizes student learning through the creation of concrete projects that are shared with others. Constructionism has inspired the design of toolkits such as Logo, Lego Mindstorms and Scratch.

Constructivism A theory of learning that describes how students start to build their knowledge and understand though questioning, direct experience and reflection.

Culturally responsive teaching The inclusion of students' cultural references as a way to empower students to learn.

Curriculum Characterization of learning in terms of rationale, content, learning outcomes, and instructional strategies. A curriculum can take the form of a formal document ('intended' curriculum), but can also appear as the learning that actually takes place (implemented' or 'attained' curriculum).

Debugging Working out why a program doesn't do what it was intended to, and fixing the problem.

Diversity The representation of different kinds of individuals and different kinds of social or cultural groups.

Duality reconstruction The analysis of digital artefacts in terms of structure ('how does it work') and function ('what does it do') in order to understand the interaction between the artefact and the outside world.

Educational standard A set of competencies depicted in detail that were decided by educational authorities to be the minimal or average learning outcomes of educational institutions.

Equity The creation of opportunities for historically underrepresented populations to have equal access to and participation in computer science education.

Growth Mindset The belief that one's abilities can be developed through hard work.

Hybrid network A network consisting of human and digital actors, with human-human, human-computer and computer-computer connections and interactions.

Inclusion The active and intentional engagement with diversity such that a range of individuals are able to fully participate.

Integrated learning Learning where multiple subjects are used at the same time.

Interaction The interplay between digital artefacts and the world, which can be viewed on three levels: interaction between a human and a computer, interaction within more complex hybrid networks and interaction between computing and society as a whole.

Kinaesthetic activities Activities where physical, tangible objects are used as representatives of abstract concepts and/or where physical activities are used.

Learning objective A description of goals that educators aim to achieve in terms of learning progress of their students.

Meta-design Design of digital artefacts as a (socio-technical) problem-solving framework that allows others to design their solutions, as opposed to design of such artefacts by directly implementing a concrete problem-solving strategy.

Metonymy A figure of speech in which a thing is not mentioned directly but via a closely associated thing (e.g. the name Hollywood can be used to refer to the movie industry associated with that neighbourhood). Extremely common in human language but not in programming languages.

Misconception An underdeveloped or flawed idea about specific content. Different educational theories have different definitions for what a misconception (or 'alternative conception') is; we use the term in a loose sense.

Notional machine The capabilities of a particular programming system (language and environment), which the system draws on as it executes programs. 'What the system can do for the programmer, and what it can't.' Understanding a notional machine is necessary in order to reason reliably about program behaviour and to instruct the system effectively.

Objectivation The identification of (in particular, human) actors and their behaviour with information processing units and processes.

Pair programming Two people work together at one computer to write code, switching frequently between working the keyboard and mouse, and directing the work.

Pedagogical content knowledge (PCK) Knowledge about particular content from the perspective of learning and teaching: What difficulties does the content pose for learners? What methods and tools work for teaching the content?.

Semantic waves An approach to explanation that involves giving technical concepts but then relating them in some way to concrete (or material) situations or contexts that are already understood, before then explicitly linking back to the new concept.

Superbug The beginner mistake of instructing a computer much as one would instruct a human being with interpretive powers.

Turing completeness A distillation of the kinds of structures that digital devices can execute, which helps to understand the limits of computation and the range of structures needed to write programs.

Turtle-based language A programming language based on movement (forward, left, right etc.), either physically or on a screen.

Universal design for learning The development of flexible learning environments that can accommodate learning differences.

Unplugged Teaching computer science concepts without using a computer, or at least without using programming as the vehicle.

Index